Annual Report on International Politics and Security 2012 (English Edition)

Chief Editors: Li Shenming, Zhang Yuyan, Li Shaojun
Translator: Liu Yanni
Proof-reader: Leila Kandret, Rachel Frattarola

Paths International Ltd

社会科学文献出版社
SOCIAL SCIENCES ACADEMIC PRESS (CHINA)

Annual Report on International Politics and Security

(2012)

(English Edition)

CONTENTS

Part I Introduction

Chapter 1

International Politics and Security in 2009/10: Analysis and Outlook

Global Politics and Security Report Research Team

The most distinctive feature of the 2009~2010 global, political and security situation was the relative decline of Western major powers, the rise of new emerging powers, and the pushing forward the visible changes in world structure. To tackle global issues such as the financial crisis, climate change and terrorism, the new emerging countries posed enormous influences and took a leading edge in the global political stage. During this process, the change of China's international status gained particular attention. China's rise and the changes in its foreign policies in order to better defend its national interests led to a series of negative reactions from some other countries. The claim of "China Threat" grew louder and the territorial disputes between China and its neighboring countries intensified. Under these circumstances, China was faced with the opportunity of playing a larger role on the international stage, but was also confronted with new diplomatic challenges to resolve troubles and disputes.

1. Structural Dynamics of the World Pattern and the Rise of Emerging Powers

The world structure underwent apparent changes. One of the main reflections was the declining influences of great Western powers, which became trapped in the financial crisis, while the status of new emerging countries rose sharply. Suffering from two wars and the financial crisis, the United States found it difficult to dominate world affairs with its limited capacities. China, representing the new emerging countries, played crucial roles in solving the global economy and governance issues. In this process, the international institutions changed as well. The voices of new emerging countries were getting louder in various multi-diplomatic occasions. In some international institutions, the new emerging countries obtained an equally important status with Western developed countries.

1.1 The Decline of the U.S. and Its Strategic Adjustment

After the September 11th attacks, the United States found itself trapped in the Afghanistan and Iraqi wars and had difficulty carrying out its foreign policies. The 2008 mortgage crisis further weakened the power of the United States. The Obama administration had to make strategic adjustments in U.S. foreign policies after taking office, emphasizing that the United States did not have the capability to and should not cope with the challenges confronted by the interconnected world and its power grew through the prudent use of it. The government should not set goals that go beyond their responsibility, their means or their interests. They must weigh all of the challenges that the nation faced, renew alliances and forge new partnerships. The United States *National Security Strategy* issued in May 2010 clearly explained their strategy adjustment.

Other countries that were also struggling against the financial crisis had no choice but to make strategy adjustments as well. One of the reflections was the reduction of military expenses. In 2009, the total military expenses of Europe amounted to 386 billion USD, 27 billion USD less than that of 2008. Plenty of European powers, including Great Britain, Germany and Switzerland cut their military expenses. In October 2010, David Cameron, the Prime Minster of the United Kingdom unveiled *The Strategic Defense and Security Review*, declaring that, in the next four years, the U.K. would reduce its defense budget by eight percent and, within the next ten years, the U.K. would not have an active aircraft carrier. As a traditional naval power, the disarmament and the decision to quit their aircraft carrier was viewed as a shift from a seemingly powerful country to aseemingly small country and thus a break-up with the "great power dream." Another example of this trend was the NATO's wish that Russia could share the responsibility of European defense.

1.2 The R3ising Status of G-20

The rising status and influence of new emerging powers was the result of the relative strength changes of different countries. It did not present the form of power politics, but was reflected through the transition of institutions. The year 2010 was the first year that G-20 took the place of G-8 to become the prime institution of global economy steering. This transition indicated that the great power relations had entered into a new era.

After the Cold War, the developed countries, including the United States and European Union, were caught in economic recession. However, the new emerging countries, Brazil, Russian, India and China (BRIC), maintained rapid economic growth, and became the driving force of global economic development. In this context, the world economic affairs could no longer be dominated by several developed countries; G-20, with members of new merging countries, became the premier forum for global cooperation. In the G-20 summit held in June 2010, a series of major issues, such as global economic development, the European sovereignty debt crisis, international financial institution reform and supervision on global trade and finance were discussed. New emerging countries gained the rights of say in the main table of the global economic affairs.

The rising status of G-20 enabled more countries to play in the center of the global stage, which not only reflected the multilateralism in global affairs, but also witnessed a foreseeable development of multi-polarity.

1.3 Active Multilateral Diplomacy of New Emerging Powers

Another example of the rising influences of new emerging powers was the strengthening cooperation institutions among them, including the BRICs and India, Brazil and South Africa (IBSA). In April 2010, the leaders of BRIC held the second summit in Brasilia, discussing the issues of the global economic and financial situation, G-20 affairs, global financial institution reform, climate change and the cooperation among the four countries.

Established in 2003, IBSA was a coordinating mechanism amongst the three emerging countries to unify their common interest and promote cooperation among developing countries. The fourth summit was held in Brasilia in April 2010 to discuss the economic cooperation among the three countries. These cooperation mechanisms enabled the new emerging powers to gain a greater say on the global stage.

In addition to institutionalized cooperation, new emerging powers played a more and more independent role in solving the current global issues, especially Russia, Brazil and Turkey. Russia, though no longer a superpower anymore, still posed crucial influences, particularly on international security issues. Russia furthered nuclear disarmament with the United States. On the one hand, Russia fought with the United States in terms of the U.S. missile defense system in Romania and Bulgaria; on the other hand, Russia cooperated with Germany and France, aiming to be the new three dominating powers in Europe. Since 2009, Brazil not only positively promoted the integration of South America, but was also actively engaged in the resolution of major international issues. Turkey supported the autonomy of Palestine, claimed an ally in Iran and served as the mediator between the United States and Syria. Through unique foreign behaviors, Turkey declared to the international society that Turkey was no longer a pawn of the United States and the western world, but was to be a major power in the Great Middle East.

2. Conventional Security of Politics and Military

Though in today's international relations, the status of global issues increased, political and military interactions among countries in order to safeguard sovereignty still played a vital role. Examples included the world armed conflicts, especially the major armed conflicts, arms races and disarmament negotiations, military deployment and drills, etc.

2.1 The Major Global Armed Conflict

In 2010, there was no distinct change in the overall situation in terms of the major global armed conflicts. The major changes laid mainly upon the Iraqi and Afghanistan wars. On August 31, 2010, the U.S. Army began to pull out of Iraq. The United States did gain something out of the war. The pro-U.S. Iraqi government guaranteed the strategic interests of the United States in the Middle East. During the Iraqi political reconstruction, different parties fought against each other for domestic political power and constant violent events were expected to occur. However, the Afghanistan situation continued to deteriorate. In December 2009, a new general strategic plan was approved by the Obama administration, which said that more troops would be sent to Afghanistan. Though the western countries wished to better Afghanistan as soon as possible, it remained a question whether the Afghanistan government would able to shoulder the responsibility of a democratic government afterward the United States fully withdraws. However, if the allied forces withdraw too quickly, Taliban might regain control of Afghanistan.

In Africa, peace progressed in Darfur and the Sudan greatly advanced. However, within Darfur, there are still several armed organizations fighting with each other. It is still uncertain whether permanent peace can be realized.

2.2 Arms Races and Disarmament

In terms of the global military situation, arms races and the reduction of military expenses go hand by hand. On the one hand, though the world was hit by the global financial crisis and economic recession, the global military expenses rose to a historic record high. Arms races could be found in some countries and regions in Southeast Asia and South America. On the other hand, the major European countries were stricken by the sovereignty debt crisis, thus conducted tight fiscal policies. As a result, defense expenses were largely reduced, and the strengths of some traditional military powers were declining.

According to the latest statistics provided by the Stockholm International Peace Research Institute (SIPRI), the total global military expenses in 2009 amounted to 1531 billion USD, increasing by 5.9% than that of 2008. In 2009, 65% of the countries in the world increased their military expenses, including 16 countries of the G-20. The United States remained the country with the largest military expenses, mainly due to the huge expenditure in Iraq and Afghanistan. In Southeast Asia, South Asia, Middle East, South and North America, some countries began arms expansion, among which the arms races in Southeast Asia and South America were the most serious.

Two trends deserve our attention in the arms control and disarmament area. The first one was in April 2010, when the United States and Russia signed a new nuclear disarmament treaty agreeing to reduce their deployed nuclear warheads by 30%. This disarmament treaty was the one with the largest reduction scope ever between Russia and the U.S. in the past several decades. Secondly, the U.S.-Russia dispute on the missile defense system in Eastern Europe ended with the compromise of the United States. In September 2009, President Obama made an astonishing decision to cancel the Bush administration's move to put land-based missile defense systems in Poland and the Czech Republic; Instead, a sea-based midcourse missile defense system would be deployed in Northern Europe and Southern Europe waters.

2.3 Military Exercises and Military Deployments

In recent years, the United States concentrated its military actions and deployments in Asia-Pacific region. According to the new *National Security Strategy*, in the premise of maintaining the global leadership, the U.S. shall realize the appropriate use of military forces and the balance of resource allocation by forging strong security alliances and establishing diversified cooperative partnerships. The most distinctive adjustment in the U.S. military strategy was that while the U.S. was to remove troops from Iraq, more forces were to be sent to Afghanistan. The emphasis of military activities moved to the Asia-Pacific region. From the frequent U.S. military exercises in the Asia-Pacific region in 2010, it could be concluded that the U.S. still deployed military forces as the main strategic measures.

The reasons why the United States shifted its military strategic focus eastward and returned back to Asia-Pacific are because of the following: first of all, since the Asia-Pacific region gradually became the global political and economic center, the United States wished to reassure its influence and leading role in Asia; secondly, the U.S. was deeply concerned with China's rise in power and aimed to contain China; moreover, the

U.S. desires to benefit from the abundant resources in Asia, which is also why the U.S. remains in a neutral relationship with Vietnam and involved in the South China Sea dispute.

3. New Security Problems and the Challenges of Global Governance

In the non-traditional security area, countries all over the world are faced with a growing number of global issues challenges. The major issues include terrorism, the financial crisis, climate change, energy, refugees and immigrants and so on. The governments of different countries, international organizations and non-governmental organizations conducted multi-level governance to tackle these problems. These interactions have been one of the most important parts of international politics.

3.1 Terrorism

From 2009 to 2010, the intensity and quantity of global terrorism were similar with the year before. According to the *Country Reports on Terrorism 2009* released in August 2010, in 2009, there were 10,999 terrorism incidents in 83 countries, 234 of which had caused a casualty of more than 10 people. In the first half of 2010, there were a total of 5,305 terrorist attacks with as many as 6,180 casualties.

By observing the development of global terrorism, it could be noticed that terrorism, as a violent means, has become the major strategy for some organizations and it has an increasingly close link with war-like behaviors. In terms of regional distribution, Pakistan, Yemen and Somalia have become the main heavily stricken areas of terrorism.

Faced with rampant terrorism activities, the international society has taken some new measures concerning the deepening international cooperation, perfecting domestic anti-terrorism legislations and improving anti-terrorism crisis managements, though the actual effects were not satisfactory. The differences and conflicts of some countries have severely undermined the positive outcomes of international anti-terrorism cooperation.

3.2 Energy Politics Issues

Although conflicts exist in modern world energy politics, cooperation remains to be the main stream. Some nations exert efforts to reinforce its territory existence in order to compete for oil and gas resources. Central governments conflict with local governments or anti-government forces over prospective and developing petroleum resources. Russia,

Ukraine and Turkmenistan disputed over the issue of international petroleum transportation. The concept of "complementary advantage and mutual benefit" become the theme of the petroleum industry. Since 2009, China, Russia and Saudi Arabia have signed a large number of treaties concerning political and economic cooperation. "Oil for loan" has become one of China's strategies in international energy cooperation.

Looking ahead, territory disputes triggered by energy resources will prevail or even worsen but the possibility of violence is low. In oil-rich Mid-East, Africa, South America and Central Asia, energy investment disputes will prevail for some countries that try to maintain their advantages, while followers will attempt to enlarge their investments. Tensions will occur in energy transport lines, whether in land or waters. However, the conflicts are not likely to escalate. As a result of the rising status of new emerging powers in the global political economy, they will play a more important role in energy politics.

3.3 Climate Change Negotiations

During the Copenhagen Climate Conference in December 2009, tough negotiations and heated discussions erupted on how to cope with the future climate change, as the Tokyo Protocol would expire by the end of 2012. The developing and developed countries differed from each other in many aspects, including, but not limited to, the division of responsibility, emission reduction targets, technology and fund aids. During this political meeting, it seemed impossible to make breakthroughs, especially since the United States was both unwilling to accept the binding protocol and did it want to lose their leading role in climate change issues.

As a non-traditional security issue, climate change currently plays an increasingly important role in bilateral and multilateral diplomacy of global politics. In 2010, climate change was listed as a main issue in various global and regional meetings, such as the Global Economic Forum, the European Union Leader Summit, the G-8 Summit, the G-20 Summit, the Asia-Europe Summit and APEC Conferences. Countries all around the world attach great importance to this issue and it has become the main driving force pushing multilateral negotiations forward.

3.4 International Organizations and Global Governance

Global issues require global governance. In 2010, the United Nations, regional and international organizations passed a series of reforms to improve their abilities to cope with new situations and challenges of global politics. There are three points concerning the reform the United Nations that call for attention: firstly, the reform of the Security Council moved to the governmental negotiation over "draft text" phase; secondly, the establishment of UN Women marked the UN's progress in terms of realizing gender equality and improving women's status; and thirdly, peace-keeping reforms continued to move forward. In the regional level, ASEAN, EU and integration in Latin America made significant progress. As for the trans-regional international groups, the Group of 77 and Non-Aligned Movement adjusted their objectives and missions according to the new global situation, with an expansion of focuses to more global issues, including climate change, sustainable development, world peace, security and so forth.

From the overall trend of global governance development, it could be seen that with the continuing development and adjustment of multi-level regional organizations and groups, the influences and contributions of international organizations in coping with global issues are increasing. At the same time, the cooperation among the UN, regional and sub-regional organizations, and trans-regional groups is enlarging. Coordination and cooperation will become the most important features of the future global governance.

4. China's Emergence and its Security and Foreign Affair Challenges

Since the world structure is changing, the rising of China has become one of the most important factors to influence the global situation. With the expansion of China's diplomatic activities and global influences, other countries have changed their policies to that of China and therefore their relationships with China are different from that before. The rising of China now not only faces new opportunities but challenges as well.

4.1 The Fluctuations in the China-U.S. Relationship and New Break-in Period

The 2009~2010 China-U.S. relationship still worked within the framework of intertwined conflicts and cooperation, but with greater fluctuations. The military interactions between the two countries called for attention, showing that power politics, which may result in conflict, does exist in the bilateral relationship. Meanwhile, it should be seen that mutual interdependence also influenced the behaviors of both countries. The huge fluctuations in the China-U.S. relationship since 2010 indicates that the general structure remains unchanged, but the impacts of conflict and cooperation grow.

The future China-U.S. relationship will still co-exist in conflict and cooperation. The rising of China requires an expansion of national interests and strength, while the United States desires to maintain its strength and sphere of influence. During this break-in period, the two countries could fall into confrontations. For both sides, it could be a either long or short time. The key is to find a balance and establish mutual understandings. Since China aspires for peaceful development and has no intention to become an authoritative power, or for global dominance against the U.S., there is little room for misjudgments. Hence, the tensions could be eased and the two sides can co-exist as strategic partners in global governance issues.

4.2 Surrounding Security Environment of China

As for the surrounding security environment of China, there were a series of unexpected incidents and intense issues calling for attention in the past year. In Northeast Asia, the situation of Korean peninsula experienced many changes. Tensions have risen since March 2010 when the South Korean warship *Cheonan* sunk near North Korean waters. The situation continued to worsen when, a month later, the two sides underwent artillery fire around Yeonpyeong Island. With a new leader, Kim Jong-il, whether or not changes would be seen in North Korean foreign policies remained unknown. The China-Japan relationship endured a difficult time owing to the boat collision incident in disputed waters near Diaoyu Islands. In September 2010, a Chinese fishing trawler collided with two Japanese Coast Guard patrol boats in the disputed waters near the islands, which led to strong reactions in both countries. In Southeast Asia, the territorial disputes over South China Sea waters were escalating and the interference of forces outside the region complicated the disputes. In the Middle East, the Afghanistan War remained in a deadlock, the anti-terrorism efforts in Pakistan deteriorated and turmoil stroke The Kyrgyz Republic. All these are unstable factors that could threat the surrounding security of China. These security issues not only include traditional security problems such as territorial disputes and arms races, but also non-traditional security threats like terrorism and nuclear proliferation. The situation is extremely complicated since there are both national interest disputes between China and its neighboring countries, and the strategic involvements of major powers such as the United States.

4.3 The Soaring "China Threat Theory"

Between 2009 and 2010, the rise of Chinese power and status not only influenced its interaction with the United States, but also had negative impacts on its relationships with neighboring countries. Some countries were concerned, even nervous, with China's rise in power, and thus made negative responses towards China's justified demands to defend its national interests. Due to the "China Threat Theory" and the strong responses from neighboring countries, it became more and more difficult to solve territorial disputes between China and its neighboring countries.

Influenced by the "China Threat Theory," the neighboring countries had taken a series of diplomatic measures to defend themselves against China. From the diplomatic interactions of the several major surrounding countries of China, their intention of diplomatic checks and balances was apparent. Strategically, the United States and its allies were weaving a defense net, from the Japan Sea to South China Sea, and then to the Indian Ocean. The United States re-established its leadership in Asia through this opportunity.

Of course, it should be noticed that the development of this kind of prevention and containment would not lead to all-round confrontations between China and its neighboring countries. Just as the China-U.S. relationship, other surrounding countries will not become China's enemy. The mutual interdependence and common interests between China and those countries exist as well. Therefore, if they find the relationship with China too intense, they will make efforts to normalize the relationship. In 2010, this phenomenon occurred in the China-Japan, China-India and China-Vietnam relationships.

Generally speaking, though a tense atmosphere exists in China's relationship with the outside world, it is unlikely that it will result in confrontations among nations. Since China aims for peaceful development, it is unlikely that an imbalance of power or an eruption of non-resolvable interests disputes will occur. Under the current structure, neighboring countries' cautions against China can be dismissed. Thanks to mutual interdependence and common interests, after a period of clashes and reconciliation, the tense relationships between China and its neighbors would be normalized gradually. From this point of view, China could maintain a cooperative relationship with the United States, Japan, India and ASEAN through diplomatic endeavors.

Since the relative power change is the fundamental factor that shapes inter-national relationships, the troubles and problems China currently faces will not be solved within a short period of time. In the coming years, a tense atmosphere would exist in China's relationship with its neighbors. China should diplomatically cope with these new challenges.

Part II 'China's Relations with the Great Powers in the World and Its Neighboring Countries'

Chapter 2

Dynamics of the International Relations of the Powerful States and the Global Pattern

Li Shaojun

"World structure" refers to the overall structure of great power relations. Though current international politics cannot be simply defined as "great power politics," great power relations still play a vital role. Based on the review of the global situation of 2010, it could be concluded that apparent changes have taken place in world structure and there are some new features and trends that deserve attention.

1. Structural Dynamics of the International Relations of Powerful States

It usually takes a long time for great power relations to take on structural change. Two important facts should be considered when judging the situation of 2010. The first was the release of the new United States *National Security Strategy*, which showed that the United States had realized the difficulty in attempting to control world affairs by its unilateral power, the need to re-evaluate its power and the means to use its power. The other was the replacement of the G-8 with the G-20 as the main dialogue mechanism of global economics. This key transition indicated that new emerging powers and great western powers were engaged in zero-sum competitions in their influences on the global stage.

From the perspective of power politics, though the United States retained its status as the only super-power since the end of the Cold War, its capability to dominate world affairs is declining. After the September 11th attacks, the United States was trapped in the Afghanistan and Iraq War, which hindered its capability to carry out foreign policies. The 2008 financial crisis further undermined the status of the United States. Under these circumstances, the United States had no choice but to adjust its foreign strategy.

In 2009, President Obama emphasized in his inauguration speech that "our power grows through its prudent use." In his remarks at West Point in December of the same year, he stressed that the government should not set goals that went beyond their responsibility, their means or their interests. They must weigh all of the challenges that the nation faced and realize the connection between national security and economy. The cost of the wars in Iraq and Afghanistan approached a trillion USD. The United States must use diplomacy to renew alliances and forge new partnerships. No one nation could meet the challenges of an interconnected world acting alone, including the United States.[1] The declaration reflected that the United States had to re-evaluate its power and the means to use its power.

The *National Security Strategy* issued in 2010 highlighted that diplomacy would be the strategic focus, and they would enhance diplomatic and development capabilities with the faculty to both prevent conflict and to work alongside military. War would be the last resort. This adjustment showed the contraction of the United States strategic force. In August 2010, the United States officially began to pull out of Iraq. The number of American soldiers in Iraq reduced from 144,000 to 50,000 by 2009. Meanwhile, the strategic focus moved eastward, with the U.S. armed forces in Afghanistan amounting to 100,000. Through this adjustment, the U.S. aimed to fulfill the commitment of completely pulling out from Iraq and partially withdrawing from Afghanistan by 2011.

Based on the analysis of the U.S. foreign behaviors, it could be concluded that even though the United States did not give up the fight, the military expenses kept rising sharply, and its military activities around the world remained rather active. As long as it could not manage to end the two disturbing wars and the financial crisis, figure out feasible solutions to the Iran and North Korea nuclear issue, achieve concrete progress in anti-terrorism, or play a leading role in solving global issues such as the climate change, it cannot reverse their difficulty in dominating world affairs. The predicament faced by the United States was exemplified by its hesitation to participate in military interference to Libya in 2011. This is the basic change in the great power relations in the past year.

In terms of the evolution of international institutions, G-20 officially replaced G-8 and gained remarkable status in 2010, which constituted another key fact to the structural dynamics of great powers. Since the 1970s, G-7, and later the G-8, had served as the world economic and political forum, but they were both diplomatic clubs of great powers. In the new century, with the change in the state of world affairs, especially the rising of new emerging powers and the deterioration of various global problems, meetings among the western powers cannot solve the current global issues. The 2008 financial crisis marked the

---

1 See *President Obama on the Way Forward in Afghanistan and Pakistan*, translated by IIP, http://www.botong.com.au/news/world/2009-12-03/56626.html.

end of a global economy era dominated by a single "rich club." When the United States and Europe were trapped in the financial crisis, the new emerging economies represented, by the "BRIC countries," became the driving force and took the leading edge of the world economic development. In this context, the original international order and great power institutions were damaged, and the G-8 faced the danger of being marginalized. To keep its status and catch up with the current trend and to strengthen dialogues with newly emerging countries, the G-8 once planned to establish an institutionalized dialogue mechanism. During the G-8 summit in May 2009, the host country, Italy, attempted to immobilize the G8+5 (G8 plus the five main developing countries including China, India, Brazil, South

Major Index Ranking of G20 Members

Area	Member	Territory	Population	GDP	Oil Production	Oil Consumption	Military Expenses
Africa	South Africa	25	24	32	42	29	42
North America	Canada	2	36	10	6	10	13
	Mexico	15	11	14	7	11	31
	The United States	3	3	1	3	1	1
South America	Argentina	8	31	30	25	26	52
	Brazil	5	5	8	9	6	12
East Asia	China	4	1	3	5	2	2
	Japan	61	10	2	48	3	7
	Republic of Korea	108	25	15	65	9	11
South Asia	India	7	2	11	23	4	10
Southeast Asia	Indonesia	16	4	18	21	17	32
West Asia	Saudi Arabia	14	41	26	2	8	8
Eurasia	Russia	1	9	12	1	5	5
	Turkey	37	17	17	61	28	16
Europe	EU						
	France	42	21	5	56	12	4
	Germany	62	15	4	43	7	6
	Italy	71	23	7	46	15	9
	UK	79	22	6	19	14	3
Oceania	Australia	6	55	13	29	18	14

note: territory, population(Estimated number of July, 2009), Oil Production and Consumption(Estimated amount of 2009), rankings are quoted from CIA World Factbook. GDP ranking is based on IMF 2009 data; military expenses ranking is based on SIPRI Military Expenditure Database 2009 data.

Africa and Mexico) mechanism. However, during the G-20 Pittsburgh Summit four months later, this mechanism was "terminated." A leaders' statement was released by the countries at the end of the summit, declaring that G-20 would replace G-8 and become the premier forum of international economic cooperation. In 2010, such framework transition was achieved through G-8 and G-20 summits, which indicated that new economies obtained a bigger say at the "main table" and reflected the transitions of international relations and power structure.

The growing status of G-20 and the strengthening influence of new emerging powers portrayed a new power politics landscape. G-20 is a more representative group in terms of the number and nature of its member countries. The power and national strength of these countries determine that this institutionalized platform has the form and nature of traditionally defined power politics. According to statistics, the population of G-20 countries accounts for 61% of the world total,[2] the GDP total (estimated number from 2010) takes up 77%[3] and export accounts for 61%[4] as well. Though there is a huge strength gap among the member countries of G-20, compared with the other more than 170 countries all over the world, they are still the leading economies and pose unmatched regional influences.

According to the ranking, the first eight countries in terms of territory, the first 14 in military expenses, and the first 12 in oil consumption are all G-20 members. Based on the data provided by he International Monetary Fund (IMF), the nominal GDP of G-20 member countries are all among the first 32 in the world.[5] Counted by Purchasing Power Parity (PPP), they were within the top 24.[6] China, India, the United States, Indonesia and Brazil are the first five countries in population[7]; the largest four exporters are China, Germany, the United States and Japan.[8] Saudi Arabia and Canada are the world's first two largest oil reserves. Saudi Arabia, Russia and the United States are the top three oil producers in the world. G-8, plus China, India, Brazil and Mexico, are among the top 20 in terms of the voting power in IMF. Judged from the statistics, G-20 could be seen as a "rich club." Though some countries cannot be defined as "great power" literally, there is no

---

2 See http://en.wikipedia.org.

3 See CIA World Factbook.

4 See CIA World Factbook.

5 World Economic Outlook Database, October 2009, International Monetary Fund.

6 World Economic Outlook Database, April 2009, International Monetary Fund.

7 Estimated number in 2010, see http://en.wikipedia.org/wiki/List_of_countries_by_population.

8 The World Trade Organization, accessed 26 March 2010, INTERNATIONAL TRADE STATISTICS.

question that G-20 is an interactive platform for great power politics. The small countries, who often hold a critical view, know better in this situation.

For example, Norway is one of the critics of G-20. Norway, as the largest donator to World Bank and United Nations Development Programme, has no rights of say in G-20, like the other 170 countries. Jonas Gahr Store, the Foreign Minister of Norway argued that, "G-20 is a self-appointed group. It may be more representative than the G-7 or the G-8, in which only the richest countries are represented, but it is still arbitrary. We no longer live in the 19th century, a time when the major powers met and redrew the map of the world. No one needs a new Congress of Vienna."[9]

If we compare today's G-20 with the Congress of Vienna in the 19th century, it should be noticed that though they both present the form of great power politics, their natures remain different. The Congress of Vienna was a diplomatic tool for European powers to perform power struggles and thus was the product of power politics, while G-20 is a global governance structure, a forum for western developed and new emerging countries to discuss world affairs together, and thus the product of international cooperation. This structure shows that the great power relation is entering a new era, different than ever before. Only from the perspective of global governance can we provide an appropriate explanation of today's great power relations.

2. The Sino-American Relations

With the structural change of great power relations, the relationship between the main powers is changing as well. While the world closely watches the decline of the United States, the rise of China has also attracted the world's attention. As a result, the significance and sensibility of the China-U.S. relationship is increasingly apparent. During 2010, the interaction between China and the U.S., to a large extent, determined the trend of the global situation. Generally speaking, the two sides have achieved great progress in strategic dialogues and cooperation, while the power politics confrontations intensified at the same time. A conflict-cooperation structure with a larger scope was displayed.

2009 was the first year of the Obama administration, and the China-U.S. relationship witnessed a positive development. Mutual visits paid by political leaders and government high officials enhanced the political, economic and military cooperation and communication.

---

9 "Norway Takes Aim at G-20:'One of the Greatest Setbacks Since World War II'," *Der Spiegel*. 22 June 2010. http://www.spiegel.de/international/europe/0,1518,702104,00.html.

The leaders of the two countries agreed to establish a positive and cooperative China-U.S. relationship in the 21st century and take real measures to a build partnership to meet common challenges.

However, in early 2010, the China-U.S. relationship went through many changes. Plenty of events, such as the Google case, arms sales to Taiwan, Obama's meeting with the Dalai Lama, and the pressure of depreciation of RMB, intensified bilateral relations. In addition, the military exchange was suspended. However, the meetings of leaders from both sides, especially the Second China-U.S. Strategic and Economic Dialogue, showed a strong willingness to cooperate. In the dialogue, Hillary Clinton stressed that the U.S.-China relationship should be built on the basis of cooperation rather than conflict and the two sides saw the opportunity for mutually beneficial solutions. During the meetings, Hillary quoted that, "There is a Chinese proverb that speaks of treading different paths that lead to the same destination." Timothy Geithner, United States Secretary of the Treasury, also said that "There's a Chinese saying that eloquently reflects this same wisdom: 'Share fortunes together, meet challenges together.'" These statements meant that the U.S. was fully aware of the mutual interdependence between China and the United States.[10] However, even though concrete achievements had been made through the economic dialogue, the strategic dialogue failed to enhance the mutual trust in security.

In the summer of 2010, the mutual distrust in security worsened. In addition to the confrontation in military diplomacy, both sides were engaged in military exercises, which were considered as the most attractive landscape of the 2010 China-U.S. relationship. During this period, with South Korea, Japan and other Asia-Pacific nations, the United States conducted a series of large-scale military exercises. Three large nuclear-powered submarines appeared near China. The media reported that this meant as many as 462 tomahawk missiles were laid out around China. Meanwhile, China also conducted some military drills. Among the interactions between nations, military maneuvers were a definite expression of firm stands. The frequent military actions of the United States were aimed at deterring China. China's response also sent a message: China would take decisive actions to defend its own national interests.

Reviewing the China-U.S. relationship in the past year, it is clear that both conflict and cooperation exist. Though this has been the phenomenon for the past several decades, the situation does intensify. The willingness to cooperate displayed in the Second Economic and Strategic Dialogue was unprecedented. Frequent military maneuvers are also rarely

10 Xiong Zhengyan, *A Refreshed China-U.S. Dialogue in Beijing*, *Cankao NEWS*, May. 27th, 2010.

seen. To analyze from a structural perspective, this is the result of the enhanced dual driven force behind the China-U.S. relationship.

First of all, the mutual interdependence between China and the U.S. continues to deepen, and the financial crisis further bands the interests of both sides together. In the fourth quarter of 2009, the United States exports to China for the first time exceeded 20 billion USD and increased by 32% in 2010 compared to the previous year. This indicates that the economic relationship with China is crucial to the American economy.[11] The financial ties between China and the U.S., especially the large dollar bonds held by the Chinese government, contributed to the so-called "Financial Balance of Terror." Besides their economic relationship, the two sides are mutually dependent in many other global issues, including climate change, nuclear non-proliferation and anti-terrorism. China is the permanent member of the Security Council of the United Nations and a nuclear power, has enormous geopolitical significance in East Asia, enjoys particular diplomatic influence as the largest developing country, and is one of the largest emitter of green house gases. All these facts determined that the U.S and China must cooperate to solve these urgent global issues. Mutual dependence also serves as the structural basis for the China-U.S. relationship.

Of course, the strengthening Chinese power leads to another structural problem, namely, the intensifying of China-U.S. power politics relations. In 2010, the GDP of China surpassed Japan, and became the world's second largest economy, suggesting that China's power had risen to a higher level. With China's development, Chinese interests were bound to expand. With the global expansion of Chinese economic activities, China also has more needs to protect its security interests. In recent years, since China's military power is strengthening, China gradually showed its determination to further enhance its interests, especially the marine interests, which may inevitably result in confrontations with the United States.

The United States attaches critical importance to naval supremacy, because freedom of navigation, as ensured by the Navy, is critical to America's ability to influence power by moving men and equipment over 70 percent of the earth's surface and to maintaining world trade and commerce. In recent years, the United States believed that the rising of China had challenged its supremacy. "There's no question that the Chinese have a sense that they've been putting up with things for decades that have rankled them," says Denny Roy, a senior fellow at the East-West Center in Honolulu. "Now, they are starting to push back."[12] Since

---

11 See The US-China Business Council, http://www.uschina.org/.

12 Ishaan Tharoor, "On North Korea and More, China Flexes Its Muscles." *Time*, Thursday, Jul. 22, 2010. http://www.time.com/time/world/article/0,8599,2006001,00.html.

2009, foreign media reported that China issued a new strategy of "far sea defense" and is building a long-range blue water capability for its navy. An element of China's new strategy is to extend its operational reach beyond the South China Sea and the Philippines to the "second island chain" of the Pacific, where America has traditionally exercised naval supremacy.[13] To the United States, this new strategy is unacceptable. Faced with China's new military strategy, what the United States can do is exercise caution. In 2010, the mutual distrust between China and the United States deepened and the military drills were the reflection of this kind of confrontation. This is the result of the structural conflict between the United States and China.

Corresponding to the development of this conflict, the relationship between China and the U.S. over the South China Sea issue also intensified. In March 2010, during the visit of the deputy Secretary of State of the United States, James Steinberg, and Jeffrey A. Bader, Senior Director for East Asian Affairs on the National Security Council of the White House, Chinese high officials expressed that, "South China Sea is the core interests of China" and informed the United States clearly, that "China would brook no American interference there." According to them, the United States, now tries to internationalize the South China Sea dispute and therefore, makes the issue more complicated. In the ASEAN Regional Forum (ARF) held in July, U.S. Secretary of State, Hillary Clinton claimed that the territory disputes among countries around the South China Sea have become the major security and diplomacy issue in this region, and the U.S. had a "national interest" in seeing a peaceful international mediation. To stop Chinese power and influence from moving southward, the United States conducted a series of diplomatic activities tried to ally with the surrounding countries, especially Vietnam. Due to the high potential of risk between China and Vietnam as a result of territorial conflict, supporting Vietnam's territory claims is one of the important methods for the United States to offset China's great strategic weight. In addition to diplomatic actions, the United States and Vietnam have started unprecedented military cooperation as well. For example, American *USS George Washington* aircraft carrier visited Vietnam and a joint military exercise was held. Some analysers believed that the Obama Administration was beginning to harden its position on China by playing to the parallel anxieties of Beijing's Asian neighbours.[14]

The rising conflicts between China and the United States indicates that power politics

13 Robert C. O'Brien, "America Must Immediately Reverse the Downsizing of its Navy as China Grows on the High Seas," *Huffington Post,* May 4, 2010.

14 Alan Dupont, "U.S. enlists China's worried neighbours," *The Australian,* August 03, 2010.

plays an important role in the interaction of the two sides. However, thanks to their mutual dependence, tensions could be reasonably eased and the main structure of international relations kept as it is. By observing the China-U.S. relationship during 2010, we can see that both conflict and cooperation are shaping the bilateral relations. As strategic partners, the two sides need and can cooperate on plenty of major issues within the framework of mutual interdependence. On the other hand, however, with the relative decline and rising of power, the conflicts, in the sense of power politics, will intensify. Under this structure, the China-U.S. relationship is like a pendulum, swaying between cooperation and conflict, sometimes within a small scope, sometimes with large fluctuations. Whatever it is, with the restraints of mutual interdependence, the conflict is within control. The dynamics of the China-U.S. relationship in the past year reveal that both sides are moving towards a new breaking-in period. The rising China needs to further accommodate to its new role. The United States also has to be more familiar with China's new role.

3. The Emerging Influences of the Emerging Great Powers

During the structural change of great power relations, another distinctive trend was the rising influence and status of new emerging powers. On the one hand, the new emerging powers were enlarging their rights to voice their opinion by cooperating in multilateral platforms. On the other hand, they were conducting positive diplomatic activities to pose unique influences on solving hot global issues.

From the perspective of multilateral cooperation, new emerging powers cooperate with western developed countries within the platform of G-20 to discuss the important global issues. In addition, they enhance mutual cooperation mechanisms and establish their own "clubs," which add new elements to the structure of great power relations. The typical examples of these cooperation mechanisms are the "BRICs" and IBSA. In the 2009 Copenhagen Conference, China, India, Brazil and South Africa cooperated with each other. Since then, the terms G-4 and BASIC were coined by some scholars to describe this union.

The acronym "BRICs" was first coined by Jim O'Neill, the chairman of Goldman Sachs Asset Management, in his 2001 paper entitled "*The World Needs Better Economic BRICs.*" In 2003, in another report, "*Dreaming with BRICs: The Path to 2050,*" Goldman Sachs predicted that by 2050, the new six major global economies would be China, the United States, India, Japan, Brazil and Russia. Since then, the four countries of China, India, Russia and Brazil received the world's attention as emerging economies and the term "BRICs" became popular.

Whether "BRICs" would develop as Goldman Sachs predicted remains unknown. However, in recent years, the economic growth of these new emerging marketing countries has gained momentum. According to the statistics of IMF, from 2006 to 2008, the average economic growth rate of these four economies was 10.7%. According to the estimated number of CIA World Factbook, the total GDP of the four countries accounts for 16.7% of the global total.[15] With the economic development, the trade among the four countries achieved huge progress as well. According to the 2009 data, China has become the largest trade partner to Brazil and India, and the third largest trade partner to Russia.

Since the BRIC countries are new emerging economies different from western powers, they have many common views in international relations. Therefore, with their rising power and status, they gradually realize the necessity to exchange views over some major global and regional issues and make a common sound in the international stage. In June 2009, the leaders of the BRIC countries held the first summit in Yekaterinburg, Russia and made their first show in the international stage. During the conference, they exchanged views over issues such as coping with the international financial crisis, G-20 summits, international financial institution reform, food safety, climate change, and the prospect of future dialogues and cooperation with BRIC countries. Urged by the four countries, breakthrough progress was achieved at the G-20 Summit in September 2009, which urged the IMF and World Bank to re-allocate and transfer respectively 3% and 5% of voting share to new emerging and developing economies. This is an enormous victory for the latter.

In April 2010, the second BRIC Summit was held in Brasília, Brazil. The Communiqué later released highlights that, the four countries have a strong commitment to multilateral diplomacy with the United Nations, playing the central role in dealing with global challenges and threats, and welcomed the fact that the G-20 was confirmed as the premier forum for international economic coordination and cooperation of all its member states. The summit also expressed their ambitious to reform the Bretton Woods institutions. Reforming these institutions' power structures first and foremost required a substantial shift in voting power in favor of emerging market economies and developing countries to bring their participation in decision making in line with their relative weight in the world economy.

BRICs as a cooperation regime, has shown its effect, namely, elevating the influences of new emerging economies in the global stage. Some media commented that the BRIC

15 *"Creator of BRICs: Four Countries Standing in the Center of Global Policy-making"*, Guangzhou Daily, April.12th 2010.

summit may not only be the temporary tool to emit strong signals to the United States. The four countries not only focused on the strategy to overcome the financial crisis, but also scheme on the new world order in the post-crisis era. "BRICs" is not a vague literal phrase any more, but has become a political reality.[16] In April 2010, Jim O'Neill, creator of the "BRIC" acronym, stated that the BRICs are binding together to voice their opinions and stand in the center of global policy-making process, in terms of trying to reform IMF, G-20 and G-8.[17]

Other than BRICs, another new important club for emerging economies is India-Brazil-South Africa Forum (IBSA). Established in 2003, IBSA is a coordinating mechanism amongst three emerging countries to unify their common interest and promote cooperation among developing countries. Since India, South Africa and Brazil are major powers in Asia, Africa and Latin America respectively and all have huge regional influences. They possess certain representative and symbolic meanings. Therefore, the common views over some major global issues that come through dialogue and cooperation are quite powerful.

Since establishment of IBSA, four summits have been held and three countries hosted in turn. The fourth summit was held in Brasilia, Brazil in April 2010. Judging from the current situation, the cooperation amongst the three nations focuses more on domestic issues. Altogether there are 17 trilateral workshops within IBSA, covering transportation, science and technology, energy, health care, tourism and so on. However, due to the regional significance and G-20 membership of the three countries, there is no doubt that their future cooperation would pose enormous impact on the structure of great power relations.

In addition to conducting institutionalized international cooperation, some new emerging powers, particularly Brazil and Turkey, which are both G-20 members, have played vital roles in world affairs though their unique diplomatic activities.

In recent years, it has become a common saying on the media that "Brazil emerges as a rising power." As a South American power, the rapid economic growth and active diplomacy enabled Brazil to stand under the spotlight of the global stage. The size of the country, the territory and population of Brazil both rank the fifth in the world. According to the 2009 data, the GDP of Brazil rose to the 8th globally. It is the second largest economy

16 *Brazil President Lula: BRICs as a Political Entity*, report by New Century Weekly, April. 13th, 2010.

17 "*Creator of BRICs: Four Countries Standing in the Center of Global Policy-making*", Guangzhou Daily, April.12th, 2010.

following the United States in the Western Hemisphere and the second behind China among the developing countries. Brazil is one of the world's major food exporters. Petrobras, Vale of Brazil, and Embraer are the representatives of Brazil's world-class enterprises. Since 2003, the economy of Brazil has maintained rapid growth. According to the statistics provided by Brazil Finance Ministry, Brazil's GDP grew by an average of 3.6% each year during the 2003~2009 period, and is expected to grow 6.5% in 2010 and by an average of 5.7% annually from 2011~2014.[18]

With their economic growth, Brazil also developed its military strength. In Latin America, Brazil had the largest military expenses. In 2010, military expenses totaled 28.096 billion USD, increasing by 9.3% compared with that of 2009. In September 2009, Brazil signed a contract with France, planning to import advanced weapons, such as a nuclear-powered submarine, from France. If this plan was fulfilled, Brazil would be the first country in Latin America and the seventh in the world to own a nuclear-powered submarine.

To further elevate their international status, Brazil won the bid for hosting the 2014 World Cup and 2016 Olympic Games. These confirmed Brazil's powerful image. With the increase of its international influence, Brazil realized that it has become a newly emerging country that enjoys high status and can play a vital role as a leader of developing countries in the global economic and political interaction.

Since 2009, Brazil has taken the advantage of the evolving international pattern to carry out a positive diplomatic strategy and expand its influence in world affairs. On the regional level, Brazil took the leading role and promoted the integration of South America. On the global level, Brazil's president Lula criticized Germany for its unwillingness to shore up Greece which was severely trapped in the European sovereign debt crisis, acted as mediator for the Israeli-Palestinian conflict and Iran nuclear issue with Turkey, and supported Argentina, rather than Great Britain, in the Islas Malvinas territorial and oil disputes. Their full participation in global affairs indicates that Brazil has been decisively moving to the center of global political stage.

As another new G-20 member, Turkey is following the same path as Brazil. Though in terms of territory area, population and GDP, the ranking of Turkey is quite low, its unique geopolitical location and relationship with eastern and western countries gains Turkey an important position in the international relationship. The frustration endured in its attempt to

---

18 "Brazil to Enjoy 5.7% Annual Growth Through 2014, Government Says," *Latin American Herald Tribune*, Aug. 10, 2010, http://laht.com/article.asp?ArticleId=362566&CategoryId=14090.

join the EU has stimulated Turkey to seek diplomatic breakthroughs eastward. Turkey began to keep a distance with Israel, establish strategic relations with the Arabian and Islamic world, and support the autonomy of Palestine. The adjustment of befriending Iran and mediating between the United States and Israel implies that Turkey intends to establish its new important role in the western and eastern world. Turkey's foreign policies have attracted wide attention.

Turkey is currently adjusting its foreign policy. A typical example of this is its conflict with Israel on the Gaza issue. On May 31, 2010, a Turkish-flagged international passenger ship, the MV Mavi Marmara, headed to the Gaza Strip was seized by Israel navy, which caused the deaths of eight Turkish citizens and a Turkish-American. Turkey had a fierce response, recalling its ambassador to Israel, urging the Security Council of the United Nations to organize an emergency meeting, and cancelling three planned military exercises with Israel. It was commented that Turkey had taken advantage of the Israel-Turkey crisis over the ship to re-define its strategic position. Turkey wishes to play a leading role in the Arabian world, possibly overtaking the United States and the Western world. Turkey no longer views itself as a puppet of the United States. This comment revealed the concerns of western countries: Is Turkey turning away from the west?[19]

Based on the analysis of the great power relationship in 2010, at both the global and regional level, the status and influences of new emerging powers are rising. This phenomenon is a reflection of certain international structure dynamics. In the discourse of power politics, this structure cannot be called "multi-polarity" yet. However, in the new global politics stage, it could be understood as a trend towards multi-polarity. There are many explanations accounting for this change, one of which is that the major western powers were trapped in crisis and another is that the new emerging powers manage to seize the opportunity and realize their strategic demands. There is strong uncertainly about whether the future pattern would continue to evolve accordingly. However, it is definite that new emerging powers represented by China will play greater roles in the future.

---

19 Mary Beth Sheridan, "Turkey's foreign policy moves raise concern in West and at home," *The Washington Post*, Monday, June 7, 2010.

Chapter 3

Evaluating China's Relations with its Neighboring Countries

Wang Lei

In the past year, two factors have led to an intensified trend of the security situation in China's periphery: one is the outstanding rising of China; the other is the excessive reaction that the peripheral countries had to China's development. The problem is mainly highlighted in the dispute on territorial rights between China and peripheral countries, the emergence of military confrontation in China's periphery, and the clearance of the periphery's foreign containment to China. Though those adjustments will not change the overall cooperation framework between China and peripheral countries, China is now facing the severe challenge to stabilize the security of the periphery.

1. The New Dynamics on the Relations Between Emerging China and its Neighboring Countries

During 2010r, there were two new changes on the international pattern: the first was the uprising of China becoming more prevalent, even though it had also suffered from the international financial crisis's severe influence. In the second quarter of 2010, China's Gross National Product (GNP) surpassed Japan, which maked China the second-largest economy only after the United States. [20]The second change was, because of the shock and distress of the financial crisis, it was very difficult for the western traditional powers to gain economic recovery, and the international status decreased, too. The fluctuations of the international power structure caused the strength and status of China to improve, and put China in a remarkable and sensitive position.

Under these changes, a new situation has appeared in the relationship between China and its peripheral countries. With the improvement of China's strength, the enlargement of

20 David Teather, "China overtakes Japan as world's second-largest economy," *Guardian*, August 16, 2010.

the national profit, and especially the enhanced efforts that China puts to maintain China's rights and interests, there are more and more discussion from the outside about China's turn in diplomatic policies. China is thought to become increasingly harsh and arrogant, and is giving up the original principles of 'keeping a low profile' and 'smiles diplomacy.'"[21] China's reactions to events like climate change, RMB's exchange rates problem, Google's withdraw from mainland China, the South China Sea problem, and ship-collision at Diaoyu Islands, etc, have all been spotlighted by the international society. Various evidence has shown that the rapid uprising of China has drawn forth the so-called "External Response Syndrome," namely the western world's worry and sense of loss in power due to China's rapid uprising.[22] In fact, there are increasing worries, questioning, jealousies and even containment from not only the western countries, but also the peripheral countries and areas. The main concern is where the rapid rising China will go in the future, and how will the country use its influence. In corresponding with the "External Response Syndrome," China faced more friction and conflict in peripheral areas in 2010. Furthermore, the peripheral countries' territory disputes, their nervous military relationship with China, as well as diplomatic containment to China have all been clarified.

In the southeastern area, since October of 2009, China's fishery boats have suffered constant blame, protest and disturbances from neighbors of the Association of Southeast Asian Nations (ASEAN) while doing fishing protection and cruises in the South China Sea. The related countries in the ASEAN are eroding China's rights and interests in the South Sea, meanwhile, those countries are further promoting the South China Sea problem to become multilateral and international issue. Now, some countries in the area are trying to contain China by consulting international organizations and inviting external forces.

The Sino-US relation has gone through a series of conflicts in 2010. As the strategic focus tilted to the Asia-Pacific region, the United States strengthened its military and strategic arrangement to China's periphery. In 2010, the United States again made arms sales with Taiwan, and underwent an intense reconnaissance of China. In addition, the two countries had open disputes on problems such as China's military transparency, the exchange rate of RMB, and South China Sea conflict, etc. After the deterioration of the situation in the Korean Peninsula, the United States took the opportunity to enhance their alliance with Republic of Korea and Japan, and actively organized a large-scale, high-intensity

---

21 John Bolton, "Confronting China's Snarl," *Wall Street Journal*, Aug 10, 2010.

22 WEI Xuan: *Trouble for an Emerging China*, United Morning Post, April 28th 2010, http://www.zaobao.com/special/forum/pages8/forum_zp100428.shtml.

military maneuver in the sensitive seas of China's periphery, which forced China into a series of military maneuvers. Among the newly shifted Asia-Pacific strategies, the United States enhanced their relation with the ASEAN again, and increased military cooperation with countries like Thailand, the Philippines, Indonesia, Vietnam, India, and Australia, etc. These actions show the United States may have increasing doubts and worries about China's rise in power, and the purpose of building a surrounded, contained and balanced alliance against China is more clarified.

The Sino-Japanese relations also underwent many fluctuations in 2010 and even regressed because of the ship-collision event. Since 2009, the routine military maneuvers of the Chinese naval fleet in the waters of Okinawa, the East China Sea and so on have sparked Japan's attention, question and constant accusations. In September of 2010, the new edition of Defense White Paper of Japan gave a high profile tor the military trend of China, and held that China lacked transparency in defense policies and military power, and called to enhance the military alliance of U.S.-Japan and alert Chinese military expansion. [23] With regards to the Sino-Japanese ship collision, the harsh attitude and series of actions of Japan, demonstrated that with the growing strength of China, the tones of "Japan-US alliance against China" and "Constraining an emerging China" were carried out as political actions.

In the South Asia area, India is purchasing a large quantity of military equipment, and trying to enhance the country's dominant position in South Asia.[24] In 2010, the military cooperation between the United States and India was obviously enhanced. India bought a large quantity of military equipment from the United States, and the joint military maneuvers of the two countries have already enlarged from the Indian Ocean to Pacific Ocean, as well as the striking cooperation in the nuclear area. [25]The public holds that, though the direction of strategic cooperation of India and the United States still needs some further observation, the tendency of the United States getting close to India to constrain China has already been clear to see.

Generally, in 2010, China, as a rising power, has entered a new phase in its relationships with the peripheral countries. In this phase, though most of the bilateral

---

23 *Defense of Japan 2010*, Ministry of Defense, Japan, http://www.mod.go.jp/e/publ/w_paper/2010.html.

24 Actually, India has become the second purchasing power of weapons in the world, only after the Saudi Arabia, "India becomes world's 2nd largest arms buyer," *Pakistan Observer*, http://pakobserver.net/detailnews.asp?id=21047.

25 India started the first nuclear experiment in 1974, and it refused to participate in Nuclear Non-proliferation Agreement, not sign the Comprehensive Nuclear Test Ban, The United States continuously agreed with the nuclear cooperation with India demonstrated that the U.S has two standards on nuclear issue.

relations are normal, the rapid rising of China's strength has aroused a general doubt and fear from the peripheral countries. Small peripheral countries, like the ASEAN countries, want to rely on the United States to contain China, but are unwilling to fight against China. The United States, Japan, and India are both cooperative and harsh with China. Of course, what we should have noticed is that, though a lot of conflicts appeared in the relation between China and the peripheral countries as a result of the change in international structure, the situation is still under control. In fact, though a lot of conflicts appeared in China's relations with the United States, Japan, India and ASEAN, all parties will make their relation return to the normal state soon after conflicts come to a resolution. This shows that all the parties are making efforts to adjust to the new structure, and conflicts did not replace cooperation to become the main trend.

2. The Increasing Land Tensions between China and its Neighboring Countries

With the change of the international structure, there is a tendency for the territorial sovereignty between China and the peripheral countries. The ship-collision event between China and Japan, the South Sea dispute between China and the related ASEAN countries and the territorial boundary problem between China and India were direct representations to this tendency.

2.1 The Sino-Japanese Ship-Collision Event and the Influence to Sino-Japanese Relations

On September 7, 2010, the patrol boats of Japan Coast Guard collided with fishing boats from Fujian in waters near the Diaoyu Islands. That the Japanese boats tracking, clashing, and intercepting the Chinese fishing boats followed the accident mentioned above and the so-called "Judicial Procedure" was started, and China's fishermen and fishing boats were illegally detained. What Japan did seriously violated the Chinese territorial sovereignty and the human rights of the Chinese citizens. China was forced to suspend the bilateral contacts above provincial and ministerial level, suspend the increase in flights and the expansion of Sino-Japanese contacts on aviation rights, and delay the coal comprehensive conference with Japan. [26]Though Japan released the people and boats by

26 Jeremy Page, "China Suspends Talks With Japan," *Wall Street Journal*, Sept 19, 2010, http://online.wsj.com/article/SB10001424052748703556604575501483896375018.html.

the pressure from the international community, the ship-collision event has caused a serious shock to the Sino-Japanese relations and the security situation of the North-East Asian region.

Firstly, Japan refused to recognize existence of the territorial dispute in the East China Sea during time, detained Chinese citizens and fishing boats according to its domestic law, and arrested and sued the Chinese captain. Those acts showed that Japan had started to maliciously destroy the Sino-Japanese precedent of a continuous dialogue and mutual understanding on the problem in the Diaoyu Islands for more than three decades. The event shows that Japan presents a harder line on Sino-Japanese dispute of territory.

Secondly, the event shows that some forces within Japan, mainly the right-wing conservative and the Young Strategic Turks, tried to take the opportunity to make a breakthrough on the diplomatic security policy, and to finally realize the adjustment in Japan's defense strategy and military arrangement, especially to enhance the strategic purpose against China's defense on the islands of the southeast.[27]

Lastly, those acts of Japan's right-wing conservative force have greatly stirred up the nationalist sentiment against China and Japan, deteriorated the popular will and public atmosphere of China and Japan, and destroyed the improving process to the Sino-Japanese relations. [28]In fact, the ship-collision event did not only lead to a shift backward in the Sino-Japanese political relations, but was also a strike in the economic relations, people-to-people contacts and tourist activity of the two countries.[29]

2.2 The Multilateral and International Trend of the South Sea Dispute

In 2009, China faced five severe challenges in dealing with the dispute of the South Sea sovereignty:

Firstly, the related ASEAN countries further enhanced real control to their possession of the islands and reefs, and the resources development intensity by domestic legislation and administrative appointment. For example, in March of 2009, Abdullah Ahmad Badawi, Prime Minister of Malaysia at the time, went to Swallow Reef ("Layang Layang Island" by its Malaysian name) in the Spratly Islands for the first time, and announced Malaysia's

---

27 WU Huaizhong: *Lessons Should Be Learnt*, September 27th 2010, People's Daily Edition 2.

28 Harumi Ozawa, "Japan nationalists rally against PM, China," Yahoo News, Oct 2, 2010; James T. Areddy, "Chinese Protest Against Japan," *Wall Street Journal*, Oct 16, 2010.

29 "11,000 cancelled Japan-China flights amid row: airlines," *Independent*, Oct 19, 2010; "China issues Japan travel warning after tourists attacked," *People Daily Online*, October 01, 2010.

"possessing" sovereignty to this reef. [30]In addition, on April 1, 2010, with the escort of two Vietnamese naval vessels, Vietnamese President Nguyen Minh Triet visited the Bech LongVi, the disputed area between Vietnam and South China Sea.[31]

Secondly, countries like Vietnam, the Philippines, and Malaysia took the opportunity when the United Nations Demarcation Committee asked the signatory nations to hand in the scheme for exclusive economic zone and the delimitation of the continental shelf, handed in the individual scheme, and tried to provide "legal" basis for possessing the islands and reefs of South China Sea. Among them, on May 6, 2009, together with Malaysia, Vietnam handed in their scheme of the delimitation of the continental shelf 200 sea miles south to the South China Sea. Again on May 7, Vietnam alone handed in a scheme of the delimitation of the continental shelf at partial regions in the middle of South China Sea.[32]

Thirdly, with pressure from the domestic political fight and financial crisis, some countries in the ASEAN recently took constant actions on the South Sea issue. In fact, those acts were to both gain the military and the public political support, and to ease the dissatisfaction to the economic situation from the public, while hoping to transform the domestic people's attention by external disputes.

Fourthly, with the rapid promotion of China's strength, and the enhancement in protecting rights, related countries in the ASEAN worried that partial power in South Sea area will gradually lean to China. Therefore, some countries tried to enhance their initiative on South Sea issue by "taking initiative," and force China to accept the accomplished fact.

Fifthly, related countries actively introduced external forces into the South Sea dispute, turning the issue into a multilateral and international one, so as to put more pressure on China. In fact, this purpose received active responses from some countries. In 2010, the United States signed the *Treaty of Amity and Cooperation in Southeast Asia*, strengthened the military cooperation with some countries, and launched open attacks to China on the South Sea issue. In addition, countries like Japan and India also gradually enhanced their political, economic and military presence in the South-East Asia region.

2.3 Sino-Indian Boundary Dispute and the Potential Danger of Sino-Indian Relations

In the past year, Sino-Indian relations have shown a clear dual character. On one hand,

---

30 SHAO Jianping, LI Chenyang: *Ways of ASEAN Countries Dealing with Seawater Conflicts and the Relevation of Their Resolution on South China Sea Sovereignty*, Modern Pacific-Asia Issue 4, 2010, P148.

31 LI Jinming: Trend of South China Sea, World Knowledge, Issue 11, 2010, P15.

32 LI Jinming: Trend of South China Sea, World Knowledge, Issue 11, 2010, P16.

mutual visits from high-level personnel were constant, and both sides of China and India increased their coordination and cooperation in international and regional affairs. However, on the other hand, lacking mutual trust was a big obstacle that troubled the development of Sino-Indian relations.

On October 3, 2010, Indian Prime Minister Manmohan Singh again visited the so-called "Arunachal Pradesh" (the "southern Tibet of China"). At the same time, India constantly strengthened its military existence near the Chinese border area. After arranging an advanced fighter plane made in Russia and two mountain divisions, India would have more than one hundred thousand people in that area.

Within India, government officials and scholars were preaching the "China threat theory," and appealing that India should keep intimate relations with the United States and western countries,[33] and emphasized that "Indian troops should further strengthen their ability so as to face the double challenge of China and Pakistan." [34]In fact, India's many reports about China have already led to an increasing anti-Chinese sentiment from the Indian public.[35]

Various evidences have shown that, with the rapid promotion of China's strength, India has a complex mentality toward China. Among that, there is a sense of loss and jealousy that India falls behind of China, together with India's fear of China's strength advantage, and also India's expectation to cooperate with China. This mentality makes Indian elites, strategists and the public be highly sensitive to any action taken to China. This sensitivity causes India to be prejudiced when judging the policies and acts of China.

3. The Increasing Military Conflicts in China's Neighboring Countries

The intensified military relations of China's periphery are mainly shown as: the nervous situation of the North-East Asian region led by Cheonan incident and Yeonpyeong shelling incident; the frequent high-intensity military maneuvers at China's periphery; and arms purchasing and arrangement in a large scale.

3.1 A Sharp Deterioration of the Korean Peninsula Security Situation

On March 26, 2010, the guard ship Chenoa of Republic of Korea (ROK) was bombed

33 "India air force chief says wary of China's military," *Reuters News*, May 24, 2009.

34 "Indian deception against China," *Pakistan Daily*, Jan 23, 2010, http://www.daily.pk/indian-deception-against-China-15184/.

35 "Hostility runs high against China in India: state media," *India Express*, May 23, 2010, http://www.indianexpress.com/news/hostility-runs-high-against-china-in-india-state-media/622593/0.

and sank in the western sea of ROK, and 46 of the 104 officers and soldiers on board died. After the incident, led by ROB, an international group called "The Joint Civilian-Military Investigation Group" was formed with investigators from the United States, Great Britain, Australia and Sweden. On May 20, the mission published the investigation results, saying that Cheonan sank because of the torpedo attacks from Democratic People's Republic of Korea (DPRK)'s mini-submarine. DPRK refused to take ROK's accusation. Afterwards, ROB implemented a severe economic sanction against DPRK, and also launched large-scale military maneuvers with the United States aimed at DPRK, and relations between the two Koreas have fallen into a nervous high-tensioned state.

On November 23, 2010, because ROK launched dozens of bombs into the disputed waters of the Koreas at the annual routine military maneuver, DPRK then bombarded the Yeonpyeong artillery position of ROK, and ROK returned with over 80 bombs. DPRK all-together launched over 170 bombs, causing casualities in Yeonpyeong Island, and cut power and caused a fire hazard in many places. ROK's bombardment also caused some loss of the Democratic People's Republic of Korea (DPRK).

After the crisis situation, in order not to make the situation worse, China repeatedly urged the concerned parties to exercise restraint, performed diplomatic efforts, and advocated to solve problems through dialogue and negotiation. However, the United States took the opportunity to enhance their alliance with ROB and Japan, led the aircraft carrier entered the western waters of DPRK (Democratic People's Republic of Korea) Peninsula, and got substantial concessions from ROB in the negotiations of the free trade agreement with ROB. ROB sought to enhance the defense ability of "Five Islands in Western Sea," map out more radars and precision-guided weapons, and adjust the combat guidelines at the same time. With the further enhancement of the military and political alliance of US-Japan-ROB, under the loss of balance in the general safety structure situation, DPRK, which has no insured safety, can hardly give up possession of nuclear weapons. DPRK's nuclear issue is getting more complex.

The deterioration of the Peninsula situation greatly burdens China on the issues of politics, military and strategies. A "united front" by the United States, Japan and ROB has been urging China to join in the action alliance to punish DPRK. When China did not take the same position, some countries even put pressure on China by undertaking military maneuvers at the sensitive waters around China and interfering in China's internal affairs. According to the current situation, the nervous state of the Korean Peninsula has already caused severe shock to Sino-ROB, and Sino-US relations.

3.2 Frequent Military Maneuvers of China's Peripheral Countries

In the past year, the united military maneuvers of China's peripheral countries have greatly surpassed that of before, both in the aspects of frequency to density, and from scale to intensity. As a result, China suffered an obvious military security burden.

In the North-East Asian region, especially after the Cheonan incident and Yeonpyeong shelling incident, the united military maneuvers of the United States, ROB and Japan were getting more frequent. For example, the RIMPAC (Rim of Pacific United Military maneuver) in 2010 included not only allied countries of the United States like Australia and Japan, but also some South-East Asian countries like Singapore and Malaysia. Reasoned by facing the military provocation of DPRK, the United States and ROK have jointly undergone large-scale military maneuvers in succession in areas like the Sea of Japan and the West Sea (near China's Huanghai Sea). In addition, after the Sino-Japanese ship-collision event, together with United States Forces stationed in Japan, Japan's self-defense forces performed united military drills at the end of 2010. The theme was set as "In case the possessed islands away from mainland Japan suffer from force violation, how would Japan and the United States take joint action to gain their right to control the island again."

In the South-East Asian direction, "Cobra Gold" 2010 and "Karat" 2010 series of united military exercises dominated by the United States, the scales set new record large. On August 11, 2010, the United States, with Vietnam, held a united marine military drill that lasted for a week, among which the attentive *USS George Washington* nuclear–powered aircraft carrier appeared in the South China Sea. Though American authority declared that the united military drills held by the United States with related ASEAN countries belonged to normal military communication, it was concerning to some ASEAN countries' that attempt to contain China with external forces, so the real strategic purpose of the United States still needs close observation.

In the South Asian region, the US-Indian military cooperation is warming rapidly. On April 23, 2010, US-Indian navy held an untied military drill called "Malabar 2010" at the Arabian Sea. Up until now, the drill sphere has enlarged from surrounding waters of Malabar, India to Mumbai waters, and also from North-West Waters of Arabian Sea to waters east of Okinawa, Japan. In addition, from October 12, 2009 to October 29, 2009, India and the United States held the largest army allied maneuver so far.

All in all, with the promotion of China's strength and position, in 2009, compared with previous years the united military maneuvers held in China's peripheral regions represented the four characters of high-density, large-scale, high-intensity, and combat-emphasized. Though most of the maneuvers were routine ones, and also "not directed against the third countries" is emphasized, there are elements that threaten and protest China.

3.3 Enhancement of Armament of Some Peripheral Countries of China

Apart from united military maneuvers, the factors that make the military relations more nervous around China also include the large-scale military purchases and the constant enhancement of the military arrangement of the peripheral countries.

In the North-East region of Asia, with the sudden anxiety over the situation of the Korean Peninsula, the United States, Japan and ROB strengthened their military arrangement and strategic cooperation to face the regional potential threat. The new edition of *Defense White Paper* and *Mid-term Defense Force Development Plan* of 2010 openly expressed a desire to enhance the U.S.-Japanese alliance, and to counter the military expansion of China. Japan's defense ministry had already decided to further increase the defense budgets of the 2011 fiscal year, and to enhance military purchase. The Japanese Maritime Self Defense Force (JMSDF) also decided to increase the number of submarines from 16 to 22, and also to enlarge the duration of service. Evidence showed that the defense focus of Japan was transforming to the South-Western waters. This measure apparently took the strategic purpose of enlarging their guard of the East Sea waters, and contending against China's regional influence. Meanwhile, the ROB was also actively trying to buy high-altitude unmanned reconnaissance aircraft and stealth fighters.

In the South-East region of Asia, ASEAN countries were constantly enhancing armaments, and countries like Vietnam, Malaysia, Indonesia and the Philippines were expanding their strength in navy and air force. Among them, Vietnam had already reached a contract worth 2.4 billion USD to buy six "kilo-class" diesel-electric Russian-made submarines and 12 Su-30MK2 multi-purpose fighters. Malaysia spent more one billion USD in buying two diesel-powered submarines from France, and one of the two has gone for formal service since September of 2009.

In the South Asian area, India was constantly seeking regional military and strategic advantages by purchasing military equipments in a large quantity. Now, India has already become the second-largest arms buyer only after Saudi Arabia.

4. The Political Unrest in China's Neighboring Countries

In 2009, some countries around China remained in a continuous political unrest, and even engaging in sanguinary conflict. For example, conflicts in 2010 included the Thai Red Shirts protests, the Myanmar Kokang conflict, the Manila hostage incident, the confusing political situation in Pakistan, Afghanistan and anti-terrorism state, and the constant outbreak of unrest in Kyrgyzstan, etc. All those events indicate that the unrest caused by some countries' political transition has shocked and influenced China's rights and interests and bilateral relations.

4.1 The Unsteady Political Situation of Myanmar

In 2010, the central government of Myanmar and the minority special zone kept wrestling with the problem of adaptation, by needs of domestic politics, the military government tried to thoroughly extinguish the minority's arms that were "self-supporting with arms, self-management with lands," and also forced the minority to go for general election after transition. In August, the Myanmar government forces took action against the comparatively weak Kokang allied forces that were, which led to a direct Kokang armed conflicts.

Though the military actions that government forces took have formed great shock to arms of all nationalities, and forced them to make some concessions in the negotiation with the government, arms of all nationalities did not fully give in. Some comparatively big national arms are still circling around with the government, and are watching for chances to enhance military strength.

On November 7, 2010, Myanmar held the first national general election of multi-party system in two decades. This election was generally regarded as an important election to promote Myanmar to transit from a military regime to an elected government. The Federal Parliament elected from general election will elect the president and vice president within 90 days after general election, and also form a new government.

What's worth mentioning is that, in 2010, there were once some shaky relations between the United States and Myanmar. Firstly, there was U.S. Senator Webb's visit to Myanmar, and Hillary Clinton said publicly that the United States would review and adjust policies on Myanmar. With the further promotion of Myanmar's general election, the United States was gradually enhancing its influence in Myanmar's political situation in various ways. Meanwhile, India was also actively strengthening the impact of Myanmar. As an important constitute of India's "Eastward" policy, India regards Myanmar as its springboard to its expansion in South-East Asian region.

Myanmar is an important neighbor of China, and its domestic situation will directly influence China. The military actions the government arms took in Kokang did not only lead to one Chinese civilian dead and two injured, but also a large number of refugees fled to China, and severely affected the safety and stability of China's South-West border area. In order to prevent incidents of this kind from happening again, China further enhanced the communication and cooperation with Myanmar's government after the Kokang conflict.

4.2 Kyrgyzstan's Continued Unrest

On April 7, 2010, a large-scale political unrest occurred in Talas in northern Kyrgyzstan, and quickly spread into the cities, including Bishkek. Kurmanbek Bakiyev, President of Kyrgyzstan at the time, ordered the country into a state of emergency and announced a curfew, resulting in further loss of the situation. The opposition quickly formed a "provisional government" led by Roza Otunbayeva, and gradually took control of the situation. On April 15, Bakiyev was forced to resign as president. With this, the political situation of Kyrgyzstan finished their radical change within days.

However, the stability only kept for two months. In Osh, a city in southern Kyrgyzstan, another large-scale conflict broke out, and spread to the peripheral regions of Osh with large-scale riots, which at least 191 casualties, nearly 2,000 people injured, and 300 thousand refugees fleeing to peripheral countries. Unrest in Osh was not simply a national conflict. The incident reflected many problems that Kyrgyzstan was unable to solve for a long time, including political factions, the North-South divide, economic imbalances, livelihood issues, and ethnic conflicts, etc. Though the situation in south Kyrgyzstan had already been stabilized, those problems will hinder future development of the countries in that region.

5. Tendency and Outlook of China's Relations with its Neighboring Countries

Facts have shown that the relations between China and the peripheral countries are undertaking new changes. With the background of financial crisis and in the process of global management, the prominence of China's position and influence, the expansion of the national interests, and peripheral countries' doubts, have increased the contradictions, frictions and conflicts. This situation has caused a change in structure. In order to adjust to this new structure, all sides are facing new challenges. According to the current situation, more and more people believe in the "China Threat Theory" by some peripheral countries, so there are more diplomatic measures and military actions taken to counter China's rising. The intimate interactions of U.S.-Japan-ROB, U.S.-ASEAN, U.S.-India, and India-Japan-

Vietnam all create diplomatic and military pressure toward China. This situation may exist for some time. China is faced with the challenge of adjusting relations with peripheral countries and eliminating diplomatic and military containment.

From the aspect of national interests, though China's contradictions, frictions and even conflicts with peripheral countries have the possibility of further intensify, they are still under control, for all parties will not allow the basic relational framework of cooperation to be destroyed. In fact, the Sino-U.S., Sino-Japan, Sino-India and Sino-ASEAN relations have an essential interdependence and common interests in all areas. All parties know that the problems have to be faced individually, regional or international, should be solved by cooperation. All parties will pay an unperceivable price if the conflicts were to get out of hand.

The current relations between China and the peripheral countries clearly show the feature of "Safety Dilemma." The mistrust between the two parties leads to increased tension. China is building a prosperous society in an multifaceted way, which calls for peaceful development. Enhancement in power and expansion of interests is necessary for this process. The containment from peripheral countries by this situation will inevitably lead to corresponding responses from China. Allowance of the upgrading of this situation will lead to confrontation, which does not meet the common interests of all parties.

In the future, the relations between China and peripheral countries will return to a normal state after some fluctuations. This phase is a continuous process for all parties. During this process, all parties should judge again the self and the counter party, and adjust the way of interaction through constant dialogues, and form some proper norms. China's peaceful development should fit in her superpower status, and the peripheral countries also need to adapt China's development as a superpower. If proper action norms can be built up by interactions of all parties as quickly as possible, this running process will be shortened. This caters to the interests of all parties.

Part III International Security

Chapter 4

Significant International Armed Conflicts: 2009~2010

Xu Jin

1. The General Situation of International Armed Conflicts

Fluctuation was very small in the number of major armed conflicts in 2009 compared to that of the previous year, and significant changes did not appear in the international security situation. The Stockholm International Peace Research Institute's 2010 annual report shows that, in 2009, 17 major armed conflicts occurred in 16 locations worldwide, one more in quantity than that in 2008. The Heidelberg Institute for International Conflict's annual report (*Conflict Barometer 2009*) demonstrates that, in 2009, there were a total of 31 serious global crisis wars, which included 24 serious crises and 7 wars. Compared with 2008, the total amount of serious crisis and war fell was nine, of which the number of serious crisis fell to seven and war fell to two. The Center for Systemic Peace Director Monty G. Marshall wrote in *Major Episodes of Political Violence 1946~2009 that 18 violent conflicts continued to 2010. In 2009, 11 were significantly weakened or even ceased, and 12 were at the risk of resurgence.* A comprehensive view shows that the 2009~2010 world's major conflicting countries or regions included: Afghanistan, India, Pakistan, the Philippines in Asia; Iraq, Israel, Palestine, Turkey in the Middle East; Colombia in South America; Democratic Republic of Congo, Somalia, Sudan, Chad in Africa. Details can be seen in the following table.

Table 1 Major Global Violence 2009~2010

Asia	Middle East	America	Africa
Afghanistan India(terrorist organizations) Pakistan (Taliban) Philippines(Abu Sayyaf)	Iraq Israel-Palestine Turkey(Kurdistan Workers Party)	Columbia	Somalia Sudan Democratic Republic of Congo

2. Armed Conflicts Across National Borders

As in the previous year, there are no major armed conflicts between two state governments, but there were cross-border armed conflicts involving several nations.

2.1 Violent Conflict between Israelis and Palestinians

On May 31, 2010, the Israeli navy intercepted a delivery fleet of humanitarian supplies and the pro-Palestinian civilians to Gaza. The Israeli army boarded and had a fierce conflict with the crew, leading to about 15 deaths. The fleet was led by pro-Palestinian organizations and the Turkish Human Rights Association, with some ships flying the Turkish flag. The Israeli army claimed that they had commanded the fleet to retrace to Cyprus or head for Israel port of Ashdod to remove supplies so that they could transfer to the Palestinians in Gaza before the start of interception. On June 2, the UN Security Council issued a presidential statement condemning Israel's action. The outbreak of global protests against Israel caught it in a passive diplomatic situation. It had to take soft and hard policies, on the one hand rejecting the request of international intervention, and continuing to intercept humanitarian vessels shipping to Gaza, while on the other hand, limitedly releasing the blockade on Gaza, and allowing some civilian supplies to enter. On September 2, peace talks between the two parties resumed after a 20-month break under the pressure and mediation of the U.S. In fact, the two sides did not have much confidence in the peace talks; instead, they accused each other before the talks. Historical experience shows that peace process between Palestinians and Israelis is very fragile, filled with many uncertainties. Any negative factor can halt the peace process. It is difficult for both parties to break the circle of "hold peace talks- break talks -conflict- resume talks."

2.2 Iraq War

On August 31, 2010, U.S. troops withdrew from Iraq, symbolizing the end to the Iraq War, which lasted seven years and five months. Americans did not claim victory in this war because the war was a complex and tangled legacy to the United States, Iraq and the international community. United States paid a high cost for the war — a total of 4,430 soldiers killed (4,748 soldiers of coalition forces killed, as seen in Table 2), about 32,000 people injured, 742.3 billion USD spent (more than the cost sum of both the Vietnam War and the Korean War), and posed a heavy burden to U.S. economy. In February 2008, "Foreign Policy" magazine conducted a public opinion survey among the retired and active duty U.S. military officers. Nearly 90% thought the U.S. military force has been significantly reduced, while 80% thought the U.S. could not currently afford to launch another large-scale war. To some extent, American society was torn down by the Iraq War. Since the war, the antagonistic relations between conservatives and liberals continue to exist. Some scholars even assert that liberal internationalism as one of the foundations of U.S. foreign policies since the Cold War ended. George W. Bush grounded the war by reason of the Iraqi government secretly developing weapons of mass destruction, which was later found out to be misinformation. Coupled with the subsequent event of the torturing Iraqi prisoners and so on, it resulted in a serious damage to America's national image. However, the U.S. succeeded in defeating Saddam Hussein in the Middle East region to help shape a more favorable geo-strategic setup. The United States has practically controlled the oil resources of Iraq, and provided business-leading opportunities to its domestic enterprises. The full stop to the war in Iraq also means that the United States started a strategic adjustment and reflected on its past. In 2010, it will turn to the rising nations likely to pose a threat to its hegemony status. The U.S. is apparently more experienced in containment of these countries than exporting democracy and terrorism to the Arab world.

Table 2 Death Toll of the Coalition Force during Iraq War Unit: Person

Year	U.S.	U.K.	Others	Total
2003	486	53	41	580
2004	849	22	35	906
2005	846	23	28	897
2006	822	29	21	872
2007	904	47	10	961
2008	314	4	4	322
2009	149	1	0	150
2010	60	0	0	60
Total	4430	179	139	4748

Resources: http://www.icasualties.org

For Iraq, the U.S. succeeded in overthrowing despotism and tyranny, but failed to bring about freedom and democracy, and, on the contrary, led to separatism and terrorism. According to statistics, from January 2005 to August 2010, 8,376 Iraqi policemen were killed, and up to 48,657 civilians lost their lives in all kinds of violence. After the withdrawal of U.S. troops, the Iraqi government's ability to lead their people out of the chaos and despair remains to be seen. Since the summer of 2009, the security situation in Iraq presented the following characteristics: First of all, the Iraqi security forces and civilians are still targets in most terrorist violence. As shown in Table 3, 2,802 Iraqis died in 2001, less than the number of 3,119 people in 2009. Since April 2010, U.S. and Iraqi forces began breaking down al-Qaeda, having arrested or killed 34 senior leaders. However, al-Qaeda still held strong counterattack capability. On May 11, the terrorist organization launched attacks in several cities, causing the death of 102 people and the injury of 350 people. In addition, the Shiite-Sunni sectarian conflict was never called off.

Secondly, even though political reconstruction made some progress, competitions among different parties remained fierce. In March 2010, "Iraqi List" led by Allawi won 91 seats in the Iraqi parliamentary elections, while "Coalition Rule of Law" led by Maliki won 89 seats and "Iraqi National Union" led by the Shiite won 70 seats. Allawi narrowly won the election. However, the Iraqi Constitution does not clearly define on how the largest party's leader is to play the role of the prime minister. Allawi and Maliki were busy with associating with political forces, competing for prime minister. At the end of 2010, the political deadlock lasted for eight months was broken up after a separation of powers agreement. Maliki was re-elected as the prime minister. Third, the reconstruction process was still difficult. In recent years, the Iraqi economy obtained a certain degree of growth, with GDP increasing from 58 billion USD in 2003 to 100 billion USD in 2008. On July 6, 2010, the Iraqi government announced the National Development Plan (2010~2014), which covered more than 2,700 projects, involving total funds of up to 186 billion USD, expected to create three million to four million new jobs. Iraqi Prime Minister Nouri al-Maliki remarked with confidence: "Iraq is right along a path of national economic reconstruction."

Table 3 Iraqi Death Toll in 2011 **Unit: Person**

Month	Security Force	Civilian	Total
January	17	118	135
February	32	204	236
March	31	152	183
April	21	240	261
May	48	231	279
June	49	127	176
July	37	497	534
August	90	273	363
September	37	111	148
October	44	141	185
November	28	146	174
December	25	103	128
Total	459	2343	2802

Resource: http://icasualties.org/Iraq/IraqiDeaths.aspx

2.3 Afghanistan War

Since 2008, the counterattack momentum of the Taliban in Afghanistan became extremely strong. The United States was forced to shift the focus of the war on terror to Afghanistan, and launched several rounds of siege actions, which have achieved some results, but also led to a great increase in casualty. As shown in Table 4, the death toll of coalition forces reached 52, 1.77 times than that in 2008 of 295. The casualty rate in 2010 (711 persons) increased by approximately 36% than in 2009.

Table 4 Coalition Force Death Toll in Afghanistan War Unit: Person

Year	Jan.	Feb.	March	April	May	June	July	Aug.	Sept.	Oct.	Nov.	Dec.	Total
2001	0	0	0	0	0	0	0	0	0	3	5	5	12
2002	10	12	14	10	1	3	0	3	1	6	1	8	69
2003	4	7	12	2	2	7	2	4	2	6	8	1	57
2004	11	2	3	3	9	5	2	4	4	8	7	2	60
2005	2	3	6	19	4	29	2	33	12	10	7	4	131
2006	1	17	13	5	17	22	19	29	38	17	9	4	191
2007	2	18	10	20	25	24	29	34	24	15	22	9	232
2008	14	7	20	14	23	46	30	46	37	19	12	27	295
2009	25	25	28	14	27	38	76	77	70	74	32	35	521
2010	43	53	39	34	51	103	88	79	57	65	58	41	711

Resource: http://icasualties.org/OEF/ByMonth.aspx

On December 3, 2009, the U.S. government approved a strategic plan for the next 12~18 months against the Taliban. It recognized the initiative that the Taliban took in the country, but pointed out that the vast majority of Afghans do not support the Taliban. If there is no local people's support, the Taliban terrorists are easily recognizable by U.S. troops. Therefore, coalition forces and the Afghan government have to provide security to local residents, so as to deprive the Taliban of the survival basis. To this end, the United States sent 30,000 more troops to Afghanistan in 2010. NATO allies sent an additional 16,000 troops, the coalition forces sent additional 150,000, and the Afghanistan army expanded to 305,000 in October, 2011. U.S. military admitted that it could not control Afghanistan in such a short term, in order to turn focus on major regions and population centers. To this end, coalition forces and the Afghanistan troops initiated military action in February 2010 in Helmand Province to attack the logistical hub of the Taliban and the hub for opium smuggling. On February 27, coalition forces successfully captured the region and the Afghan government officials stationed in more than 1,900 officials for rebuilding local government administration. On June 28, U.S. and Afghan troops killed more than 150 Taliban militants in Kunar Province. The action aimed to defeat the Taliban's attempt to open up new front in the province. However, the plan of capturing Kandahar province encountered a temporary setback in early June, mainly due to the failure in obtaining the support of local tribal elders. On September 1, the U.S. re-launched a military action code-named "Kandahar Cooperation," with a total of 25,000 U.S. troops and Afghan National Army members joining the war. The action aimed to cut off the route Taliban entering Kandahar and to capture Taliban supreme leader Mullah Omar's home - Singh Saar village.

On July 21, the International Conference passed the resolution on Afghanistan to accomplish the transfer of security and budgetary responsibilities to the Afghan government before 2014. The era of "Afghan people running Afghanistan on their own" was not an unreachable dream, but the Kabul Government's ability to realize it remains unknown.

3. Important Domestic Armed Conflicts in Different Regions of the World

South Asia, Southeast Asia and Africa are the regions where the internal armed conflicts, civil wars and terrorist incidents frequently occur. Causes leading to continued conflicts are complex, including separatism, ideological divergences, religious and ethnic conflicts, struggles for power, competition for resources and government incompetence. Most of these conflicts are so "stubborn" that it is difficult to find effective solutions.

3.1 Major Domestic Violence in South Asia and Southeast Asia

India has been labeled as a country where terrorist and anti-government organizations are very active. As shown in Table 5, in 2010 government forces killed 772 terrorists at the cost of 371 of its men sacrificed and 759 civilians killed. This indicates that the security situation in 2010 continued to improve compared with the previous year. Table 6 shows India's leading anti-government forces concentrated in three states of Kashmir, Assam, and Manipur, but the extreme leftist Nasar, also known as India Communist (Maoist) armed force, is an exception. It conducts armed struggles in 233 counties of 20 states, the influence covering 40% of the territory and 35% of the population. It has established its own governmental system in the 92,000 square kilometers. India's Interior Ministry said that in the past three years, 91% of the country's armed violence was caused by Nasar, causing at least 2,700 deaths. Indian Prime Minister Manmohan Singh regarded the armed faction as "the biggest security threat." Nasar is an armed guerrilla equipped with modern arms, and has established a mature and organized internal system at the three levels of Party, politics and military. They also adopted policies such as gender equality, land reform and other reform measures to intimate with the lower class. Kashmir is another region where India's armed factions are very active. India has accused militants in the region have received support from Pakistan and thus became cross-border terrorists. Table 7 shows that these armed factions in 2010 killed a total of 105 civilians and policemen, while 270 of their own were killed.

Table 5 India Domestic Conflicts Death Toll Unit: Person

Year	Civilian	Government troop	Terrorist	Total
2005	913	287	1319	2519
2006	1104	388	1273	2765
2007	1009	404	1185	2598
2008	1019	372	1220	2611
2009	720	431	1080	2231
2010	759	371	772	1902

Resource: http://www.satp.org/satporgtp/countries/india/database/indiafatalities.htm

Table 6 Classification of India Domestic Conflicts Death Toll Unit: Person

	Civilian	Governmenttroop	Terrorist	Total
AndhraPradesh	0	1	0	1
ArunāchalPradesh	0	0	0	0
Assam	48	12	98	158
JammuandKashmir	36	69	270	375
Maharashtra	18	0	0	18
Manipur	26	8	104	138
Mizoram	0	0	0	0
Meghalaya	3	0	17	20
Nagaland	0	0	3	3
Punjab	0	2	2	4
Tripura	0	2	1	3
UttarPradesh	2	0	0	2
Nasar	492	231	189	912
Total	759	371	772	1902

Resource: http://www.satp.org/satporgtp/countries/india/database/indiafatalities.htm

Pakistan's security situation in 2009 was the worst since 2005. As can be seen from Table 7, in 2009, a total of 3,319 people died in the terrorist attack, 510 more than in 2008; in addition, 8,389 terrorists have been killed, 2.15 times of that in 2008. Security situation in Pakistan has improved for the better in 2010. 5,170 terrorists were killed in 2010, while government forces lost 469 people, and 1,796 civilian died in the conflicts.

Table 7 Death Toll in Terrorist Violence in Pakistan

Year	Civilian	Governmenttroop	Terrorist	Total
2005	430	81	137	648
2006	608	325	538	1471
2007	1523	597	1479	3599
2008	2155	654	3906	6715
2009	2324	991	8389	11704
2010	1796	469	5170	7435

Resource: http://www.satp.org/satporgtp/countries/pakistan/database/casualties.htm

The Taliban is now the number one terrorist target in Pakistan. The organization expanded rapidly since its inception in 2007 and had the confidence to attack Pakistani army and navy headquarters, the High Court and other government institutions. Pakistani Taliban are mainly entrenched in three areas of Swat, Pakistan and South Waziristan Joule that are easily defendable, but difficult for attack. In the first half of 2009, tens of thousands of Pakistani government troops made a deep trust into the Swat valley to wipe out the Taliban, and achieved some results. However, it is very difficult to eradicate the Taliban. Since the second half of 2009, the Taliban began its resurgence, creating several terrorist bombings in Islamabad and other cities. On July 9, 2010, suicide attacks initiated by Taliban killed 105 people and caused more than 100 injuries in northwest regions. The Taliban claimed the attack was targeted at pro-government tribal elders.[36] On July 19, 2010, U.S. and Pakistan held the second round of ministerial-level strategic dialogue. United States announced a 500 million USD assistance to Pakistan, which was part of the 75 billion USD aid program approved by U.S. Congress in 2009. The new aid program mainly aimed in energy and medical fields, to help develop the economy of Pakistan, and therefore to ease domestic anti-American sentiment. U.S. Secretary of State Hillary Clinton urged Pakistan to list the Haqqani organization as a terrorist organization. It is reported that the organization is supported by Pakistani intelligence, which is the main reason Pakistan is reluctant to take action against Haqqani.

36 http://www.chinanews.com.cn/gj/2010/07-11/2394596.shtml

3.2 Major Domestic Conflicts in Africa

Earlier in 2010, major changes took place in Sudan. From January 9~15, referendum was held in the southern region. The results showed that more than 98% of voters in the southern region supported separating from Sudan. On February 7, Sudanese President Omar al-Bashir accepted the referendum results. Southern Sudan will soon announce its formal establishment as Southern Sudan Republic in July 2010.

Darfur's political process has made significant progress. On February 23, 2010, the special session of the Darfur peace talks held in Doha, the Sudanese government and the opposition "Justice and Equality Movement" signed a ceasefire agreement at the meeting. On July 21, the United Nations and Darfur region's major rebel "Justice and Equality Movement" signed the Memorandum of Understanding, the latter committed to the protection of children's safety and rights of international conventions. However, several Darfur armed forces are still fighting each other, even killing and attacking AU and UN peacekeepers. On May 7, the African Union - United Nations Hybrid Operation in Darfur was ambushed in South Darfur, where two peacekeepers and military personnel killed and three seriously injured.

In Somalia, the situation remains volatile. The transitional government managed to fight against the biggest anti-government organization, the Youth Party, in support of foreign powers. On July 19, 2010, the combat between the Young Party militants and government forces killed five people and injuring another 23 civilians, including 10 children. The organization said the attack occupied the new site, while the government said they defeated the offense by the Youth Party. Youth Party has extended terrorists activities into neighboring Uganda. On July 11, 2010, they made two explosions in the Ugandan capital Kampala suburb, killing 64 people and injuring 65. The organization's spokesman, Ali Mahmoud, said, this was in retaliation for Uganda sending peacekeepers to Somalia. International organizations in Africa attached great concern on Somalia's security situation. On July 27, 2010, the AU Summit decided to deploy an additional 4,000 peacekeeping soldiers to Somali. On September 3, Wamunini, AU deputy representative on Somalia, said an offense launched by Somali rebels in Mogadishu has been under control. If there are sufficient personnel and equipment, the African Union peacekeeping force has the ability to control northern Mogadishu.

4. Conclusion

In the strict sense, major international armed conflict was no longer in existence since

2009, and there is only the existence of cross-border armed conflicts since 2009. This phenomenon can be extended into 2010. With the withdrawal of U.S. troops, the war in Iraq is increasingly changing into a domestic armed conflict. If the coalition forces can realize the withdrawal in July 2011, the war in Afghanistan will shift to the domestic armed conflict as well. Of course, there may occur new cross-border armed conflicts, for example, if the Somali Youth Party continues terrorist attacks on neighboring countries, then, Kenya, Uganda and other countries may send troops to Somalia to help the transitional government to fight against the Youth Party.

In most of the current cross-border armed conflict, troops sent by foreign countries can only win in the combats, but lose in the war. As in the case of Israel to Hamas, the U.S. military in Iraq and Afghanistan can beat the rebels on the battlefield and entitled to absolute military superiority, but they are difficult to achieve completely success in destroying opponents or to maintain long-term stability of the local security situation. Most of their opponents have a more solid mass base, and are skilled in adopting guerrilla strategies, such as using low-tech weapons to fight against the high-tech, to hit and run, hiding among the mass, etc. U.S. troops in Iraq and Afghanistan emphasized the intimacy to the local people, economic development, social reconstruction, in the aim to make the rebels lost people's support. However, foreign occupation can never directly accomplish this task, but only be the role of an assist to the local government. Therefore, the local government's ability to govern is the key factor to realize the end of the war and a decent withdrawal from the country.

Chapter 5

International Military Situation: 2009~2010

Gao Hua

1. The Adjustment of the USA's Military Strategies

In the first of 2010, the United States government successively issued *Quadrennial Defense Review, Nuclear Posture Review Report* and *National Security Strategy Report*. With this series of important strategic reports, the adjustment on the safety strategy of the United States, diplomatic and military strategies had been shown.

The basic points for the new safety strategy of the United States are "diplomatic contact" and "international alliance," calling for sharing international safety compulsory by nations. The obvious change of the report is that they gave up the "pre-emptive" strategy carried out by President George W. Bush after the September 11th attacks. The Obama government moderates the concept of anti-terrorist war and emphasizes to keep military advantages and pay more attention to diplomatic and other non-military forces to face the challenges of national security and clarifies that military forces will be the last measure, while diplomatic efforts will not take effect.

The national security strategy of President Obama can be concluded as "one goal, two general situations, four general benefits, two approaches and three stresses."[37] The "one goal" is to "recover the leading position of the United States" who will "never and ever be the second." "Two general situations" are "to work on construction at home" and "to play an important role abroad," which demonstrates the two general situations of the strategic idea of the United States to emphasize the recovery of its own power and the international influence. "Four general benefits" refer to the national security benefit of the United States, including security, prosperity, value and international order. "Two approaches" are: 1) maintaining powerful alliances—NATO, Asia and North American allies as a basic supporting strength and; 2) establishing cooperation relations with other influencing powers

---

37 Yi YANG: How Does China Face With The Strategic Adjustments Of The US, Global Knowledge Weekly, July 12th to 18th 2010, Edition 24.

in the 21st Century— such as China, India, Russia and others. "Three stresses" are paying attention to maintaining the absolute advantage of the military forces of the United States, to reasonable usage of its military forces and to the balance of the military resources configuration. This report stated that challenges, which the U.S. faced, were: 1) recovery and strengthening of its domestic security; 2) destroy, fight against and beat Al Qaeda and its extreme violent followers in Afghanistan, Pakistan and all around the world; 3) prevent the spread of nuclear and bio-chemical weapons and nuclear materials; 4) promote the peace, the security, and the development of the "Greater Middle East"; 5) invest to increase the power and capability of the friend nations; and 6) guarantee the safety of the internet (electromagnetic space). Among these, the most important two tasks are to fight against Al Qaeda in Afghanistan and Pakistan and to avoid the spread of weapons of mass destruction around the world.

In 2010, the most important adjustment of the United States' military strategy was to withdraw troops from Iraq. On August 31, 2010, President Obama delivered a speech at the White House, proclaiming the end of the seven-year war in Iraq and planned to withdraw troops before the end of 2011. This was a measure that he had to take in order to get rid of the war problem. He tried to gain a "bargaining chip" in the mid-term vote of the senate by withdrawing troops from Iraq on the due date.

After withdrawing troops from Iraq, the United States' strategic focal point moved to the military focus on Afghanistan. On December 1, 2009, in West Point, Obama announced to increase 30,000 soldiers to Afghanistan and highlight the future victory of the war. The more important meaning of Afghanistan War towards the U.S. is that it not only is concerned with the result of the anti-terrorist war of America, but also decides the future of the Middle Asia geographic strategy of America, which was based on Afghanistan and having impact on the Eurasian area.

In addition, when the United States withdrew itself from Iraq, it immediately showed signs of using forces towards Iran and, at the same time, the United States showed off its military forces in Eastern Asia and Northeastern Asia Sea, weaving a big military net around China. From the point of view of its national security strategic goal, in the near future, the United States will focus its strategic power on the resolution of nuclear issues.

Within one year, the United States held a series of military exercises around the Pacific Rim, Northeastern Asia and Southeastern Asia. The show of military forces was still one of the important links of its strategic measures, which aroused people's focus on the situation of this area.

Since June 23, 2010, the biennial, multi-national Pacific Rim Exercises were held in

Hawaiian territorial waters, including navies from 14 countries—the United States, Canada, Chili, Columbia, France, Australia, Indonesia, Japan, Malaysia, the Netherlands, Peru, South Korea, Singapore and Thailand with more than 20,000 people and brand new equipment of sea, land and air forces. The nuclear power flight carrier *Regan* turned up and F-22A participated in the exercises for the first time. This exercise clarified its goal for preventing China and other new military powers in the Pacific-Asia area.

From July 25 to 28, 2010, the United States and South Korea held joint military exercise named "Indomitable Will" on the Japanese Sea. The aircraft carrier "George Washington," (the biggest landing ship in Asia, also called "Lonely Island") and more than other 20 ships, more than 200 planes including F-22 fighters turned up for the exercise, with more than 8,000 soldiers. This was the largest military exercise between the U.S. and South Korea since 1976. Japan, for the first time, dispatched four MSDF officers as investigators participating in the exercise. From August 16th to 26th, the United States and South Korea re-held a second joint military exercise on the east Korean Sea (Japanese Sea) and west Korean Sea (Huanghai Sea). From September 27th to 31st, they, again, held one anti-submarine military exercise on the Huanghai Sea. The contribution of the aircraft carrier *George Washington* brought a new challenge to the Northeastern Asia, which actually was a test on the sensitive area of China for its strategic idea.

On August 11, 2010, after the normalization of the diplomatic relationship between the United States and Vietnam, they firstly held a joint military exercise at the South China Sea. The U.S. dispatched guided missile destroyer USS *John S. McCain* and nuclear power aircraft carrier *George Washington* to the exercise. The U.S military said that this exercise was for protecting common interests of the U.S. and Vietnam. The potential threatening towards China of U.S.-Vietnam joint military exercise was more serious than the U.S.—South Korea exercises. Vietnam is on the south border of China and if the U.S. continues to keep a foothold in Vietnam, it means that the U.S. occupies the bridgehead to mainland China. On November 23, 2010, after the Yeonpyeong shelling between South and North Korea, the United States, together with South Korea and Japan, fueled on the intense situation by holding large scale joint military exercises around the neighboring sea. The U.S. not only dispatched aircraft carrier *George Washington* to the Huanghai Sea, but also launched the third flight carrier to East Asia. The spate of military exercises kept the Korean peninsula and the whole Northeastern Asia situation intense.

In addition, the United States announced to involve itself into South China Sea issue. In the second half period of July 2010, Secretary of the United States Hillary Clinton claimed that the resolution of the sovereignty over the South China Sea concerning with "the national interest of the United States" at the Foreign Ministries Conference of the 17th ASEAN Forum held in Hanoi, Vietnam. On August 18th, Robert Willard, Pacific Commander of the United States, said that the United States will keep its military presence in the South China Sea and hoped that neighboring nations should actively develop their forces to protect "their own territorial waters." The intent of the U.S. was to seemingly return to Southeast Asia by military exercises and contain China by Huanghai Sea and South China Sea, bringing an unprecedented presence.

The meaning of the series of military exercises in Pacific-Asian district led by the United States is as follows:

1) The United States of America was afraid of being excluded from Asia, therefore it gradually moved military strategic focus to the East. In the past decade, because of the anti-terrorist war, the U.S. over-stretched itself and suffered from subsequent failures and frustration. Wars of Iraq and Afghanistan occupied most of strategic resources of the U.S., which made it have no time to tend to the East and the Northeast Asian affairs and its influence in this area gradually decreased. Therefore, after Obama took office in the White House, he claimed the return to Asia and Southeast Asia, becoming the "Pacific President" deeply involved in Asian affairs.

2) The United States was suffering from "Asia Anxiety," or strategic panic. It regards China as its new focus for the global geographic strategy. The Four-Year Defense Estimate Report of the United States clarified that the development of Chinese military forces would be a "threat" towards the U.S. in the future and claimed that the U.S. must upgrade its military forces based in the Pacific Asian area to face with the coming Sino-U.S. conflicts.[38] The basic military strategy of the United States towards China is: strategic threat, front constrain, induce together with pressure as mainstream, avoid large scale wars, limited strikes, all-round preparation and win by fast attacks.[39]

3) In order to cope with China, whose international influence continuously increases, the United States, again, made full use of "offshore balance strategy," maintaining the conflict and laying wagers on both sides. It tried to unite as many countries as possible to arouse conflicts between China and its neighbors, by which the U.S. had no need to constrain China by war. It can be seen that China has been trapped in a C-shaped strategic encirclement, which starts from Japan to neighboring countries along South China Sea,

---

38 *Quadrennial Defense Review: Enhance Modernization of Equipment and Expand the Size of the Army*, [US] Defense News, web, July 27th 2010.

39 Yinan JIN, *On the Military Strategy of the U.S against China*, Global Knowledge Weekly, May 31st to June 6th 2010, Edition 23.

then to India and Afghanistan. From the sea to the land, both are surrounded by the United States and leave only a small part in the Northeast Asia next to Russia. The United States established a C-shape strategic military distribution that was called the "NATO of Asia."

2. Analyzing the Current Situation of Military Expenses

Military expense is one of the important quantitative indicators for researching on military. It measures the investment on military forces of the nation.

2.1 General Introduction of the Global Military Expenses in 2009

Under the background of the global financial crisis and economic depression, governments had to reduce public expenses to balance deficit. However, in 2009, the proportion of global military expense was not reduced, but reached a historical height.

Table 1 Military Expense Estimate for the World and Regions by Stockholm International Peace Research Institute of Sweden (SIPRI)
(The unit is billion USD. Statistic by constant price and exchange rate of USD in 2008.)

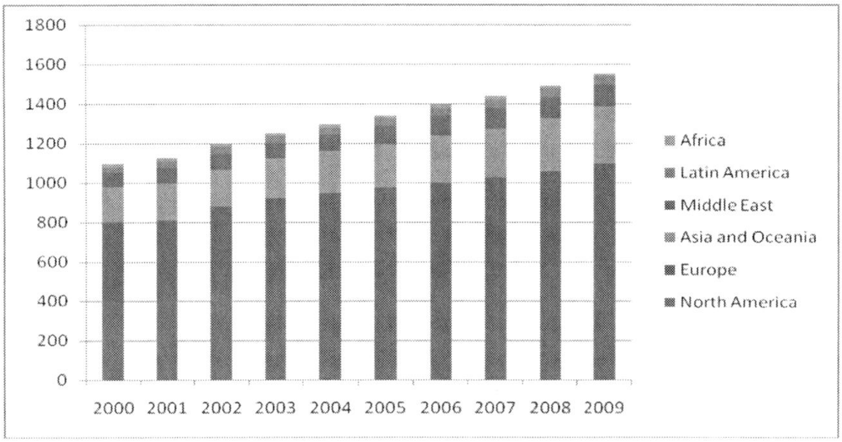

Resource: *SIPRI Yearbook 2010*, Oxford, Oxford University Press, 2010. p.178

The latest index published by Stockholm International Peace Research Institute of Sweden (SIPRI) showed that in 2009, the total volume of the global military expense reached 1521 billion USD, 5.9% more than 2008 and 49% more than 2000. The global military expense of 2009 accounted for 2.7% of the global GDP with 224 USD per capita in the whole world.[40] In 2009, 65% of the nations all over the world increased their military

40 Stockholm International Peace Research Institute, *Armaments, Disarmament and International Security, SIPRI Yearbook 2010*, Oxford University Press, 2010. P.177.

expenses, with 16 members of the Group of Twenty. Military expense of Africa was 27.4 billion USD,[41] 6.5% more than 2008. Central America spent 5.6 billion USD, with 9.7% increasing from 2008 and South America spent 51.8 billion USD, increasing 7.6%.[42] The military expense of the Middle East reached 103 billion USD.[43] Asia and Oceania spent 276 billion USD on military with an 8.9% increase. The report pointed out that in 2009, the highest military expense of the United States still ranked the first in the world, which spent 661 million USD, with a real increase of 7.7%,[44] which accounted for 43% of the total amount of the military expense of the world. China ranked the second with 100 million USD as military expense in 2009. France was the third one with 63.9 million USD. Number five was UK with 58.3 billion USD. Russia followed UK with 533 billion USD. Japan ranked the sixth, spending 51.8 billion USD.

2.2 The Military Expense of the U.S. Still Ranked the First in the World

As the nation with the highest military expense, the increasing part of the military expense of the U.S. can be concluded as war expense, especially the expense of the Afghanistan War, which reached a historical level. In 2009, the United States tripled its troops in Afghanistan with a real expense higher than that of Iraq. Based on the national defense budget of the United States for 2010, the military activity in Afghanistan spent 65 billion USD and that of Iraq is 61 billion USD.

During the period of economic depression, the United States' finances could hardly bear the burden. At present, the national debt of the U.S. is 12.7 trillion USD.[45] Over-budgeted military expense has dragged down its economic development. Therefore, defense departments from the Pentagon to the intelligence bank were seeking for ways of reducing military expense. President Obama promises that the military expense would increase only 1% year by year. Robert Gates, Minister of the Defense Department, thought that the United States' army is currently over expanded. The United States must decrease its expense. He asked for the "military industry and enterprises to start adjustment," getting ready to reduce civilians and changing "dinosaur-like clumsy bureaucratic organization." He also illustrated the plan to reduce 100 billion USD for defense. Even if the United States reduced half of its defense expense, the amount it spent is still higher than its present or

41 *SIPRI Yearbook 2010*, p.178.

42 *SIPRI Yearbook 21010*, pp182~183.

43 *SIPRI Yearbook 2010*, p.186

44 *SIPRI Yearbook 2010*, p.197.

45 *SIPRI Yearbook 2010*, p.189.

potential competitors.

2.3 Reducing Military Expense is the Key Tone of European Nations

The total military expense of the whole of Europe was 386 billion USD in 2009,[46] which was 27 billion USD less than 2008.[47] The defense budget of Europe was about half of the amount of the defense expenditure of the U.S.. Economic and financial crisis shook nearly all defense bases of the European countries, which forced them to reduce duplicate expenditures. Russia plans to increase military expense to renew the equipment, but it is difficult to carry out such plans. Although some of the more prosperous countries from Central Europe increased military expenses, Great Britain, Germany, Bulgaria, Croatia, Estonia, Lithuania, Romania, Serbia, Slovakia, Ukraine and Switzerland all reduced their military expenses.

At present, Great Britain, Germany and Switzerland are brewing substantial disarmament. The British Royal Air Force will be reduced to the smallest scale since the First World War.[48] On October 19, 2010, British Prime Minister David Cameron published the first *Strategic Defense and Security Report*,[49] in which it was said that in the following four years, the military expense would be reduced by 8%. The amount would reach the portion figured by NATO, which equaled to 2% of its GDP. 42,000 positions in the Department of Defense and army will be reduced, including 5,000 people of Royal Army and Air Force, 7,000 people of ground forces and 25,000 civilians of the Department of Defense.

The Minister of Defense of Germany hopes that the exiting 250,000 officers and soldiers can be reduced by one third, or to 163,500, and the civil compulsory service system can be discarded.[50] The draft of Swiss *Military Report of 2010* issued that the regular troops of Switzerland would be reduced from 120,000 to 95,000. For NATO, it means a transfer of the module: "the troop we need" (decided by the tasks) should be changed into "the troop we can afford" and "intelligent" reduce of the defense expenditure.[51]

---

46 *SIPRI Yearbook 2010*, p.192.

47 The total military expense of Europe was 413 billion USD. (*SIPRI Yearbook 2009*, p.219.)

48 *British Air Force Will Be Reduced to the Scale of World War One*, [Britain] *The Daily Telegraph* Web, August 6th 2010, Thomas Hardin.

49 www.chinanews.com, October 20th 2010.

50 Reuter [Berlin] August 13th 2010.

51 Wolfgang Ischinger, (Pre German Ambassador for UK and USA, Chairman of Munich Security Conference): *We Can Still Protect Luxembourg*, June 17th 2010, [Germany] *Times Weekly*.

2.4 Southeastern Asian Countries Involved in Arms Race

It is worth noting that it has been said that, "developing countries are walking on a dangerous way of arms race."[52] Annual Report of SIPRI pointed out that the fiercest competition is happening in Southeast Asia and South America. Asia occupied half of the top five arms race areas.

First, the military expenses of Southeast Asian countries significantly increased and most of their governments tried to defend themselves in front of their people. They regarded China or other neighbors as "imaginary" enemies and tried to explain the legitimacy of the arms growth. The defense expenditure of Indonesia in 2010 increased 20% than in 2009, which reached about 40 trillion Rupiah. The military expense of Singapore accounted for more than 5% of its GDP.[53] Malaysia and Vietnam, both of whom have territorial disputes with China around Spratly and Paracel Islands, became "leading figures" of Southeast Asia.

Secondly, from 2005 to 2009, the Pacific-Asia area bought most of the weapons in the world, with its purchases accounting for 41% of the world. Compared with the imported weapons of Southeast Asia in 2005, the quantity nearly doubled.[54] The growth of imported weapons reached a staggering three-digit increase. Singapore became the first ASEAN country that was listed in top ten nations for imported weapons after the end of the Vietnam War.

The first incentive for the arms race among Southeast Asian countries came from the interior. The arms race was firstly against the potential enemy at the same level within Southeast Asian area and then against the emerging China that was their Asian neighbor. The core issue was that Southeast Asian countries did not have the institute to break the military expand.

As military purchases are concerned, the United States, Russia, Germany, France and UK are the top five weapons sellers in the world. Their regular sales for exporting weapons accounted for 75% of the total amount of the world. The sales of the United States and Russia take up 30% and 24% respectively.[55] The United States plays a very powerful role in stimulating global arms and it regards wars as strategic investment and wants to upgrade the national strength by wars.

---

52 Agence France-Presse Stockholm March 14th 2010.

53 Xinhua News Agency, Tokyo, August 13th 2010.

54 Afence France-Presse, Stockholm, March 14th 2010.

55 *SIPRI Yearbook 2010.*

2.5 Reasons for Arms Race in South America

South America is one of the other focus areas for the arms race in the world. In 2009, the military expenditure of South America rose to 51.8 billion USD, increasing 7.6% than in 2008. Brazil and Columbia were the two countries with the highest military expenses in this region, accounting for 16% and 11% of the total amount respectively.[56] The present Latin America is faced with a serious threat: on the one hand, the militarization of the United States has reached a peak, but on the other hand, Latin American countries started an arms race that has never been seen during the past decades. The risk for conflicts was based on the reasons listed below:

The first is the control and interference of the United States. One quarter of the natural resources and energy that the United States needs are from the Latin America region. In order to maintain its supremacy, the United States placed its control over Latin America as the first position in its strategy and carried out a duplicate military strategy by both establishment of its own military base and making use of local troops. A half of a century after the Forth Fleet of the United States was dismissed, it was rebuilt in the Latin American region. In addition, four military bases for the United States were set up in Panama. On June 29, 2010, Costa Rica Parliament adopted a resolution, agreeing on the entrance of the United States troops and warships in its harbor and the privilege of immunity while "undertaking tasks" and "participating in humanitarian actions."

Second, South America was faced with threats from both the United States and the speaker of the United States, —Columbia. 15% of the budget of Columbia was used as military expenses, which was the highest in the world for the proportion.[57] October 30, 2009, Columbia and the United States signed the agreement allowing the United States army to use at least seven of the military bases in Columbia with 5 billion USD as economic help. Foreign ministries of South American countries forecasted that the United States army's entrance to Columbia would arouse military tension and the arms race in Latin American region at the same time.

Third, the internal reason for speeding up the arms race in South America was rooted in the lack of trust among the participating countries. Regional threat and conflict or the pressure for the neighbors' purchase of arms was felt. Within five years, the expenditure for

---

56 *SIPRI Yearbook 2010*,P183

57 The present military expenditure is approaching 5% of the GDP, reference to Doug Bandow–Specialist assistant for the pre-president Regan: *Kingdom Under Bankruptcy*, [American] *National Interests* Bimonthly Magazine Web, April 19th 2010.

purchasing new weapons, update and maintenance of existing ones reached 176 billion USD.[58] Although the governments exclaimed that it was "not for wars, but for drug smuggling and terrorism," they knew the reality in the heart.

3. Cooperation and Conflicts in the International Arms Control

In 2010, new aggressive affairs turned up in the international arms control, which were of significant meaning for the change of the international structure and the security for everyone. On the one hand, the international community made great efforts to promote the procedure of nuclear disarmament and non-proliferation and gained achievements. On the other hand, the global nuclear security was still faced with serious challenges.

3.1 New U.S.-Russia Agreements for Nuclear Disarmament

On April 8, 2010, U.S. President Obama and Russian President Medvedev signed the new *Strategic Arms Reduction Treaty,* or the so-called STRAT II, in Prague, the capital of the Czech Republic. It replaced the START I signed between U.S. and Russia for the first phase. The new START reduced about one third of the strategic and long-range missiles that could be deployed by both sides, limited the maximum number of strategic nuclear warheads and bombs below 1,550, which, compared with the number of 2200 agreed in *Strategic Offensive Arms Reduction Treaty* (SORT) in the year of 2002, was 30% less. Deployment and non-deployment types of launch equipment (silo base for intercontinental ballistic missiles, submarine launcher for submarine-launched ballistic missiles and heavy bombers for nuclear tasks) matching for these nuclear warheads or bombs were limited within 800 sets. The so-called non-deployment launchers referred to trident submarine, which was under repair, etc. The upper limit for deployment launchers was 700 sets, which was 50% less than the number agreed by the first START (which was 1600). The reduction goal under the new START should be carried out within seven years since it took effect. Its valid period is ten years and it can also be prolonged to another five years.

This new treaty is the nuclear reduction treaty with the widest extent in the past few decades, which defined the goal for the U.S. and Russia, who together own 95% of the nuclear weapons in the world, to reduce one third of their strategic nuclear warheads within seven years. Its positive meaning and great importance lie in the following: 1) the new

58 Xinhua News Agency, Mexican City, November 30th 2009.

treaty went back to the mainstay of super powers implementing arms control since U.S. President Kennedy, gave up unilateralism established by George W. Bush and set up international cooperation over nuclear nonproliferation; 2) the signature and implement of this treaty, to some extent, reduced the over-kill nuclear capacity of the U.S. and Russia whose strategic nuclear capacity would be more transparent and foreseeable; 3) the new treaty improved the relationship between Russia and the U.S. and became the first diplomatic achievement after President Obama took office, who called for the establishment of a non-nuclear world. President Obama wanted to obtain diplomatic initiative by this treaty; 4) the new treaty could be used to put pressure on Israel, Iran and North Korea and asked them to give up nuclear weapons; and 5) releasing the capital pressure for maintain nuclear warheads was a win-win result for both the United States and Russia.

On this nuclear disarmament treaty, the following doubts existed in the international community: 1) how to deal with the reduced nuclear warheads was not clarified by mandatory regulations in the treaty; 2) it was unclear whether the western world would continue the support Russia for the destruction of nuclear warheads; 3) a big gap on nuclear warheads check still lies between the two sides; 4) during the recent thirty years, the United States committed itself to research and deploy missiles defense system. Russia kept cautious because of its lack of current anti-missiles system. For the stand issued by NATO for establishing European guided missiles defense system together with Russia, Russia insisted that it must be based on equality in both sides, define the responsible districts and list the threats together.

3.2 The First Nuclear Security Summit in the World

From April 12 to 13, 2010, the remarkable First Nuclear Security Summit was held in Washington, D.C., the United States capital. Including President Hu Jintao of P.R.C, leaders and representatives from 47 nations and the heads of the United Nations, the International Atomic Energy Agency, European Union and other international or regional organizations participated in the summit. Attendees signed *Washington Nuclear Security Summit Announcement* and *Washington Nuclear Security Summit Work Plan,* not only reached a broad consensus, but also expressed the will of each nation to maintain and strengthen the international nuclear non-proliferation institute.

During the summit, President Hu Jintao gave a speech entitled *Hand In Hand to Face with Security Challenge, Promote Peace and Development Together* that issued five viewpoints on how the international community could deal with nuclear security challenge.

This was the first time that a Chinese leader expressed viewpoints specializing nuclear security issues on a multilateral stage. As a power of nuclear energy development, China always attached great importance to nuclear security issues and has been opposed to nuclear proliferation and terrorism. President Hu Jintao's participation in the summit was of significant meaning for guaranteeing the conference. His speech demonstrated that China plays a positive role on the international stage and showed the image of a reliable power to the world.

It should be mentioned that not long after the First Nuclear Security Summit, from April 17th to 18th, the two-day Iran Nuclear Disarmament Conference was held in Tehran with the topic of "*Nuclear Energy For All, Prohibit Nuclear Weapons.*" 56 nations' governments, including Russia, France, China and Pakistan, and delegates of international organizations and non-governmental organizations, took part in the conference. President Ahmadinejad of Iran participated and gave a speech. Although the attendees were ministers or vice-ministers, it was still of great importance. The difference was that this meeting was not reported by the media, as the First Nuclear Security Summit was. The United States fell into fury on this conference.

3.3 U.S. Adjusted Anti-Missiles Defense Plan in Eastern Europe

The anti-guided missiles system was the biggest point of dispute between the United States and Russia. In the early 1990s, the United States started its planned development of anti-guided missiles system and regarded it as a specialized task and long term project for constraining Russia. On January 22, 2007, the United States officially proposed to the Czech Republic and Poland to deploy one anti-guided missiles radar station and 10 interceptor missiles, i.e. anti guided missiles, respectively, in these two countries. This would be the first anti-guided missile equipment of the United States deployed in Europe, which cost 10 billion USD each year. The U.S. believed that the use of anti guided missiles system would upgrade the security level of its nation and the technology progress could develop unprecedented. The United States emphasized that it was defense against the threat from Iran, not aimed at Russia. However, it was strongly opposed by Russia. Except for the temporarily halt from *Treaty on Conventional Arms Forces in Europe*, Russia claimed to quit from Short-Range Missiles Treaty and regarded the anti missiles system as the goal for the guided missiles of Russia. On September 17, 2009, President Obama announced to cancel the plan to deploy anti missiles system in Czech Republic and Poland. Instead of this plan, the U.S. would deploy sea-based midcourse defense system in North and South European seas. In the past, the United States never compromised to the major competitor on strategic issues. The cancellation of anti guided missiles system from Eastern Europe caused a global uproar.

Obama dismissing the Eastern European anti missiles plan was based on various considerations. First, the judgment on threat changed. At the beginning, the United States thought to deal with the long-range and event continental guided missiles of Iran, but then it realized that the threat from short-range missiles of Iran was more serious. Therefore, the United States must set up new anti missiles system. Second, to the request of matured technology and low risk, sea-based defense system is more efficient than land-based. Third, it should smooth the relationship between U.S. and Russia and could create a good atmosphere for further discussion on the reduction of offensive arms. In addition, being close to Russia could constrain the ambition of Iran. Forth, the United States wanted to reduce national defense budget. Fifth, inside the Czech Republic, opinion differed on the deployment of anti missiles system and some political forces strongly opposed this.

At the beginning of 2010, reports for the deployment of anti missiles system in Romania and Bulgaria by the United States aroused the fierce action in Russia who thought that U.S.' deployment of anti missiles system in Romania and Bulgaria destroyed the organic relationship between strategic offensive and defensive weapons. It could be used to devalue the constrain capability of Russia and threatened the national security of Russia. Therefore, Russia must take measures on technology and diplomacy to perfect its own strategic offensive weapons and modernize and enlarge the deployment of its own anti missiles weapons. In addition, Russia suggested that all nations with potential anti guided missiles capability to carry out one treaty to limit, from both quality and quantity, the anti guided missiles system deployment to keep a general strategic balance.

It was proved that the so-called adjustment of the U.S. was only to move the deployment place from Poland and Czech Republic to Romania and Bulgaria. This is the old approach for the new government that uses a new plan to take place of the old one. The United States does not hope to cancel the deployment plan of guided missiles in Eastern Europe, but plans to establish a flexible and large defense system over the whole Europe and Middle East area. It was reported that the United States would deploy sea-based guided missiles defense system of lower cost, better flexibility and better intercept capability by four phases around the Atlantic Ocean and Mediterranean. It could be seen that the mistrusting relationship between the United States and Russia was difficult to change and their conflict on guided missiles defense issues would be lasting for a long time.

4. Tendency and Outlook of the International Military Situation

The development of the recent two years' global military situation showed obvious characteristics and prominent trends.

First, the global anti-terrorism wars approached the end; the United States would gradually move the military strategic focus to traditional competitors. All combats units withdrew from Iraq by August 31, 2010 and the withdrawing from Afghanistan planned to start in July 2011. This shows the end of the 10-year anti-terrorism war is approaching. President Obama and the following governments of the United States would focus the strategy on the political powers. The Pacific-Asia area, where the balance of power is changing fast, would catch most of its attention. In reality, the strategic deployment of the United States started to move towards the east since the end of the last century. Anti-terrorism war obstructed and postponed its procedure. Since 2010, the United States announced its return to Southeast Asia and enhances the U.S.-Korean alliance by Cheonan Accident and Yeonpyeong shelling. From the second period of 2011, the United States would likely accelerate the eastward movement of its strategic deployment and prepare for the possible future military confrontation in Pacific-Asia area.

Second, international financial crisis has an impact on the military expenses of the great powers and the comparative military strength; the United States kept its absolute advantage in military area. Military strength is one of the important pillars for great powers and supremacy to maintain their international position. Military expense, among items in financial expenditure, has an obvious compulsory feature. Therefore, although faced with the international financial crisis, major powers would not significantly reduce their military expenses to impact the military construction and strength. The rise of proportion of military expenses around the world was powerful evidence. As the unique super power in the world, the United States would continue its absolute advantage in military expense and the military area. Its position as a super military power cannot be shaken.

Third, the regular force of the United States owns great advantage over any other country in the world. Under this background, the position of nuclear weapons continuously declined in the military strategy of the United States. Actually, the phrase "non-nuclear world" issued by Obama was only a moral slogan. The only focus for U.S. was the establishment of anti-nuclear proliferation and anti-guided missiles system. On the anti-nuclear proliferation issues, the stands of the five nuclear powers are the same. The differences lie in details. On the anti-guided missiles issue, the stand of the United States differs greatly from that of Russia. The Obama government gave up the plan of anti missiles system in Eastern Europe temporarily, but it won't let Eastern Europe be the empty area in the net of its anti guided missiles system. Whether the European Guided Missiles Defense System over the whole Europe, which was led by NATO while Russia was invited, can be realized is still a major problem between the United States and Russia.

Part IV Hot International Issues

Chapter 6

Global Terrorism and Counter-Terrorism: 2009~2010

Shao Feng

1. The General Evaluation of the Global Terrorist Actions

Currently, the most professional and systematic statistics and strategic assessments of global terrorism development are provided by the U.S. government. *The Country Reports on Terrorism 2009* (the media used to term it "*Global Terrorism Report*") issued by the U.S. Department of State on August 6, 2010, offered a systematic account and analysis on the global terrorism development in 2009. According to the report, in 2009, al-Qaeda core in Pakistan remained the most formidable terrorist organization targeting the U.S. homeland. Al-Qaeda and its branches, especially the branch in the Arabian Peninsula, were actively engaged in operational plotting against the United States. The expansion of this organization was dangerous because it continued to recruit, train and deploy operatives to join them. - However, in 2009, al-Qaeda had experienced several significant setbacks. Their military strongholds were eliminated due to the Pakistani military operations and the group continued to suffer leadership losses. As a result, al-Qaeda found it increasingly difficult to raise money, train recruits, and plan attacks outside of the region.

This report assessed the global terrorism development in six regions in the world. In Africa, the major terrorist groups that threatened U.S. security were the local Somalia al-Shabaab and foreign al-Qaeda branches. Their alignment constituted the most serious terrorist threat to the United States and its alliances in the Horn of Africa. In the East Asia-Pacific region, huge progress against terrorism had been made owing to the multinational cooperation, capability construction, public support and anti-terrorism political willingness. Necessary mechanisms were developed in order to reduce factors that could be taken advantage of by terrorists. In Europe, no large-scale terrorist attack occurred in West Europe. To a large extent, this was because of the anti-terrorism efforts made by European countries. Many Middle East and North Africa countries, including Iraq, Israel, Lebanon, Algeria and

Saudi Arabia, have cooperated with the United States in anti-terrorism. In South and Central Asia, since the terrorists groups had expanded their scope of activities and networks, more violent attacks were witnessed in 2009. For most countries in the Western Hemisphere, the terrorist threats posed by transnational groups were comparatively lower; instead, these regions mainly suffered from the harassments from the Columbia Revolutionary Armed Forces, Columbia National Liberation Army, and some other radical leftist Andean groups.

The statistical data in the report were provided by the U.S. National Counterterrorism Center. In 2009, there were 10,999 terrorist attacks in a total of 83 countries and caused 14,971 casualties. In 2008, 11,725 attacks occurred and 15,727 people were dead or injured. Comparatively speaking, the quantities of both the attacks and deaths had reduced slightly and this had been a continuing decrease for the second year. Still in 2009, there were 234 high-casualty attacks, each of which killed more than 10 people, almost the same as the previous year. -However, the number of people who were killed, injured or kidnapped during the terrorist attacks in 2009 reached 58,142, a little higher than the 2008 data, which was 54,653.

In 2009, the region which was most heavily stricken by terrorist attacks was South Asia, taking up 44% of the total. South Asia was also the region with the largest causalities for the second year in a row, accounting for 42% of the total. The Middle East suffered 30% of the total attacks. Also in 2009, the terrorist attacks taking place in South Asia and the Middle East took up 2/3 of the total 234 high-casualty attacks.

In 2009, both in terms of terrorist attacks and causalities, Iraq, Afghanistan and Pakistan were listed as the top three.

According to the latest data, in 2010, globally, there were 11,595 terrorist attacks, resulting in 13,183 casualties. The situation in 2010 was generally the same with that of 2009 and the general situation did not change much.

In September 2010, one of the reports released by the U.S. Bipartisan Policy Center listed the nine Terrorists Threats that the Obama administration was faced with, including: 1) al-Qaeda Central; 2) al-Qaeda in the Arabian Peninsula; 3) Somalia al-Shabab; 4) al-Qaeda in Iraq; 5) al-Qaeda in Maghrib; 7) Taliban in Pakistan; 8) Lashkar-e-Taiba in Kashmir; 9) Uzbek militant groups in Uzbekistan.

Though statistics are compiled from the U.S. perspective and subjective elements could not be avoided, currently there exists no other nation, state or international organization that obtains a stronger capability to shoulder this strenuous and arduous task. Therefore, the contents and data in the U.S. terrorist reports are quoted in this text as the main evidence to judge the global anti-terrorism situation.

Terrorist Attacks and Deaths in Major Countries

Country	2009		2010	
	Terrorism Attacks	Casualty	Terrorism Attacks	Casualty
Iraq	2458	3654	2688	3364
Afghanistan	2126	2778	3306	3202
Pakistan	1916	2671	1331	2150
India	698	663	860	809
Somalia	501	1441	589	1353
Israel	488	8	150	2
Thailand	483	401	418	265
Russia	429	337	396	314
Columbia	354	323	269	230
Philippines	283	241	260	176
D.R. Congo	197	1685	98	348
Algeria	76	128	46	67
Yemen	56	73	196	178

Data Source: National Counterterrorism Center, Worldwide Incidents Tracking System(WITS)

Certainly, other regional organizations and countries have gathered some regional statistics and data, which could serve as a complement. For example, one Indian assessment report claimed that, nowadays, the situation in South Asia was "more killing, more peace and a greater fragility." According to the statistics provided by the website The South Asia Terrorism Portal of The Institute for Conflict Management, in 2009, the number of deaths directly resulting from terrorism amounted to 29,638 in South Asia, a sharp increase compared with 20,733 in 2008. However, by October 10, 2010, the number of casualties was reported to be as few as 7,881, an apparent decrease. The main reason for the huge fluctuations of the statistical data was that in May 2009, the government army eliminated the Sri Lanka anti-government armed force, Liberation Tigers of Tamil Eelam, and the domestic peace in Sri Lanka was restored.

Generally speaking, compared with the previous year, the 2009~2010 global terrorism remained in a similarly serious level, both in terms of quantity and intensity. The main terrorist threat came from the religious extremist terrorism represented by al-Qaeda, nationalist-separatism terrorism and other extreme anti-government armed forces. To see from the geographical distribution of terrorist activities, South Asia and the Middle East were still the most heavily stricken areas. The situation in Yemen and Somalia were worsening as well.

2. The New Characteristics of Global Terrorism

The 2009~2010 global terrorism development not only obtained the traditional features, but also presented some new characteristics.

i. Global Terrorist Attacks Occurred with High-Intensity and in a Large Scale

In recent years, the global terrorist attacks continued to take place with high intensity and in a large scale. It has been common to witness large-scale terrorist attacks with a casualty of over a hundred people. From 2009 to 2010, this trend continued. In order to create a terrifying atmosphere within the society through mass destruction, the terrorist groups in various countries seemed to be engaged in a killing competition, to see which attack would result in the most deaths. The bloody scenes of the attacks were expected to pose greater influence through the exaggeration of the media, so that the group responsible for it could gain a higher "reputation" and influence. They aimed to produce greater impacts to the social stability and exerted stronger pressure to the government.

ii. Transnational Terrorist Groups Consciously Deployed Terrorist Attacks as a Strategic Counter Method

In terms of the forms of terrorism, current terrorism in some countries presented a very distinct characteristic, namely, terrorism was closely related to political confrontation and war and terrorism constituted an important component of political struggles and wars, and therefore took on a strategic significance.

Theoretically speaking, terrorism is the last strategic resort for the disadvantageous side in the domestic or international politics. Their strategic choice order is supposed to be political resolution-military confrontation-terrorism.

There is no doubt that political resolution should be the best strategic choice. However, the incompatible nature of political goals in issues such as ethnical separatism and hegemony politics in the real politics determines the impossibility to solve disputes by political resolution. Military confrontation becomes the next choice after political resolution. There are two forms of military confrontation: formal military wars and guerrilla wars. Military wars require absolute strengths, while guerilla wars depend on comprehensive support from the public. Normally, it is difficult for the disadvantageous sides to achieve their goals by military means. Under hopeless circumstances, it is impossible to use political resolution or military confrontation and they are still unwilling to give up their political goals, so it is likely that the disadvantageous side deploy terrorism as the complementary, or even the main, means to fight. Therefore, it could be concluded that terrorism is a kind of desperate strategic choice. From the perspective of rational choice, terrorism can not only gain the highest benefits with low cost, but also poses the greatest influences. The behavioral logic of terrorism is: initiating terrorist attacks; causing media attention-creating social panic; exerting political pressure to the other side; elevating self-status and bargaining chip; force the other side to concede; achieving political goals.

The September 11th terrorist attacks were indeed a turning point of world history. Various terrorist groups around the world seemed to "wake up" overnight. They did everything they wanted, without any limitations and concerns, broke any civilization principle, rules and behavioral taboos that were handed down and accumulated through thousands years of human history. Terrorist attacks evolved from small-scale murders, aimed at representative and symbolic figures of the other side that obtained absolute political strength, to large-scale and fearless mass murders in the societies governed by their opponents. The latter shocked the public and caused huge political impact through the wide broadcast of the modern advanced news media. Their strategic goals were to force the counterparts to concede, change their policies, or even admit failure.

Before the September 11th attacks, terrorism was a desperate strategic choice by the disadvantageous side while, after that, it became an initiative and conscious strategic choice. As a matter of fact, the logic of terrorism behaviors did not change much. The only change occurred in the first section of the chain: the unlimited scope of targets in the terrorist attacks, the diversified choices of methods and the large-scale casualties. This would cause a change in nature, leading to a chain reaction in the sections after, finally resulting in a stronger will of the terrorist groups. On the contrary, the governments and international societies were gradually losing confidence in winning an overwhelming victory in anti-terrorism wars.

The Iraq and Afghanistan wars were the two typical examples. The United States could easily overthrow Saddam Hussein and the Taliban with its absolute military advantage. However, after years of anti-terrorism wars, the U.S. still failed to stabilize the political and security situation in the two countries; instead, it was severely trapped in the quagmire of terrorism and just could not get rid of it. In 2010, the Obama administration finally decided to pull out of Iraq and planned strategic steps to withdraw troops from Afghanistan. However, the al-Qaeda, Taliban and other terrorist groups refused to let the U.S. go. The constant terrorist attacks plotted by them made the U.S. "decent withdraw" a dream. If the U.S. failed to draw out of Iraq and Afghanistan with dignity, to some extent, it meant that the U.S. admitted its failure and the "reputation" and confidence of the global terrorist groups would largely increase, bringing negative impacts to the future anti-terrorism struggles of the international society.

iii. Pakistan has Become the Third "Holy War Battlefield" of Global Terrorism

Recently, the security situation in Pakistan continued to deteriorate. With constant major terrorist attacks, Pakistan gradually became the third "holy war battlefield" of global terrorism after Afghanistan and Iraq. Russell Travers, the U.S. National Counterterrorism Center's Deputy Director for Information Sharing and Knowledge Development, said, "In terms of the large-scale attacks, each of which caused more than 10 deaths, Pakistan has slightly surpassed Iraq for the first time. As for the suicide bombing cases, Pakistan also overtook Iraq. In 2009, in the northeastern frontier provinces of Pakistan, altogether, 940 attacks took place while the there were only 16 cases in 2005."[59]

Comparatively speaking, some new characteristics and trends were displayed in the terrorist attacks and counterterrorism efforts in Pakistan. These new features showed that the localization process of terrorism in Pakistan continued to speed up and expand. Pakistan is no longer the manufactory of the global terrorism industrial chain, but more like a self-sufficient market of terrorist activities. In the foreseeable future, the worsening security situation in Pakistan is unlikely to be reversed. The international society feared that Pakistan might follow the road of Balkan Peninsular and Taliban and become a failed state, which surely would pose huge challenges to the global and regional security. The Western countries, especially the United States, were deeply concerned that the terrorists might acquire the nuclear weapons and materials in Pakistan and there was a great chance that these would cause serious nuclear disasters.

In August 2010, a high official from the Pakistan Inter Services Intelligence Directorate said, "Domestic terrorist has replaced the Indian army and became the largest threat to its national security." According to the national security assessment report of this organization, currently 2/3 of the great threats that Pakistan was exposed to came from terrorism, not India or any other country. This was the first time since Pakistan's independence in 1947 that India was not listed as its top threat. However, many experts believed that if the Kashmir issue was not solved, India remained to be Pakistan's fundamental strategic opponent.

---

59 See *The Counterterrorism Report of the U.S. Department of State: Al-Qaeda Remained as the Largest Threat*, Singapore Zaobao, August 7th, 2010.

iv. Al-Qaeda Shadow Over Yemen and Somalia: An Approaching Nightmare

Currently, Iraq, Afghanistan and Pakistan have become the main battlefields of global terrorism and counterterrorism efforts. However, the world and leaders of countries should notice that as the continuing integration of global terrorist groups and local radical forces, Yemen and Somalia, which are the two countries that controlled the access to the Red Sea, are gradually becoming the new global terrorist basement and anti-terrorism battlefields. If their goals are achieved, it would mean that they would control the economic lifeline of the global economy. It would be an approaching nightmare to the counterterrorism groups, which have already run short of ways to tackle terrorism.

In July 2004, Abu Hafs al-Masri, a Yemen terrorist organization, openly declared that they would turn Yemen into the "third terror swamp" after Afghanistan and Iraq. To judge from the current situation, Pakistan has become the third. So the international society is concerned about whether Yemen would become the fourth.

On December 25, 2009, Christmas Day, a man tried to ignite an explosive device on the Northwest Airlines flight 253, which flew from Amsterdam in the Netherlands to Detroit, Michigan, in the United States. The device failed to fully detonate and only a few people, including the suspect himself, were slightly injured. The suspect named Umar Farouk Abdulmutallab, a 23-year-old Nigerian man, claimed that he was assigned by the al-Qaeda to hide the device in the crotch of his trousers and take it onto the plane. He told the investigators that about another 20 extremists were trained in Yemen to launch terrorist attacks, such as bombing planes. After this event, al-Qaeda in the Arabian Peninsula hidden in Yemen claimed responsibility for the attack and the counterterrorism situation in Yemen, attracting more attention in the international society.

Yemen now is under great anti-terrorism pressure. Recently in South Yemen, a number of attacks initiated by the armed forces against the information headquarter and security services. Frequent attacks were launched by al-Qaeda in the Southern provinces, where the voice of separation prevailed, such as Abyan, Lahij, Shabwah and Ad-Dali and so on. For example, on June 19, 2010, al-Qaeda issued a statement, accusing the Yemen government, led by President Ali Adbullah Saleh, of killing innocent people, as well as women and children, deciding to set fire on the Yemeni territory and overthrow the current Yemeni regime. In addition, around 200 terrorist suspects were arrested in the Guantanamo Bay detention camp, of about 90 were Yemen citizens. In terms of the numbers of suspects, Yemen has more than any other single country. After al-Qaeda's setbacks and transfer out of Iraq and Afghanistan, the activists managed to re-gather in the mountains in the eastern and southern areas of Sana'a, the capital of Yemen, and merged with al-Qaeda elements in Saudi Arabia. In January 2009, al-Qaeda in Yemen announced the merger and the creation of al-Qaeda in the Arabian Peninsula, and decided to make Yemen its operation base.

Somalia anti-government force, "The Islam Youth Movement," is gradually engaged in a growing number of terrorist attacks, which causes the political instability of Somalia. On December 3, 2009, a suicide bombing occurred in Mogadishu, the capital of Somalia, killing at least 57 people and injuring another 200. Three people who died in this accident were ministers serving in the Somalia transitional government. The bombing took place in a hotel, where a college graduation ceremony was being held, near the government building in Somalia.

In addition, the problem that "Somali pirates are behaving like terrorists" have drawn many people's attention. In recent years, the Somali pirate issue has been constantly disrupting the world economy and relevant countries. The possibility that Somali pirates might turn into terrorists is becoming a core regional security issue. It would severely threaten the stability of the international maritime transportation order and maritime security interests of many countries, and intensify the instability of the Middle Eastern region. It should be noticed that pirating behavior, as a kind of terrorist activity, has shown a tendency to ally with overseas international terrorist groups and speed up its pace to become terrorism. The intervention of al-Qaeda has made the situation more complicated. There is a chance that al-Qaeda may take advantage of the pirate issue and spread terrorism to Somalia. The pirating activities in Somalia provide a foundation for terrorism. As a matter of fact, al-Qaeda has established a relationship with some Islamist armed groups in Somalia.

If this trend continues, the Horn of Africa might become the shelter for terrorist activities. Besides, if Somalia is finally controlled by terrorist groups, since Yemen, the other side of Gulf of Aden, has been swept by terrorism, the Gulf of Aden would become a sea channel surrounded by terrorists. The world is already severely disturbed by terrorism groups, and no one wishes for an even bleaker future.

v. Other Types of Terrorism Other Than Religious Extremists and Nationalist-Separatism Call for More Attention

In recent years, with the rapid development of religious extremist terrorism represented by al-Qaeda and nationalist-separatist terrorism, they have become the two main targets of terrorism research and attacks. Other kinds of terrorism have largely been ignored, no matter in academic research or policy-making areas. However, other traditional types of terrorism, such as left-wing terrorism, right-wing terrorism, single-issue terrorism and criminal terrorism, have not disappeared but displayed a tendency to thrive with the constantly changing international and domestic situation.

The attempt to assassinate President Obama once provoked a great sensation in the United States at the end of 2008. On March 29, 2010, breakthrough progress was made concerning this case. The police accused Daniel Cowart and his co-conspirator, Paul Schlesselman, of plotting to assassinate President Obama. According to the police, these two men were racial extremists and once plotted to rob a gun shop, and use the robbed gun and bullets to shoot in a high school in Tennessee, which mainly consisted of African American students, to show "the power of the white." Later, they planned to murder the then-presidential candidate of the Democratic Party, Barack Obama, because, from their side, a newly elected black president would be an insult to the white people of the United States. In 2008, these two men also planned to shoot 88 black people and decapitate another 14. But they were finally caught and punished. Schlesselman said that their actions were for the purpose of paying homage to Hitler.

Violent terrorist attacks caused by drug trafficking and smuggling are quite common in some Latin American countries. On September 8, 2010, the mayor of the city of El Naranjo, Mexico was shot to death and became the third mayor who died within one month in Mexico. According to the latest statistical data released by the Mexican information agency, the drug war started in 2006 had caused at least 28,000 deaths. Mexican media named it the "Mexican Drug War." According to the U.S. *Washington Post* report on March 3, 2009, the two largest drug trafficking groups now owned armed forces of more than 100,000 people, approaching the 130,000 of the governmental forces. Their weapons are becoming more and more advanced, the capacity of which even exceeds those of the governmental forces. The Mexican drug war is not an ordinary war. The struggles within the drug trafficking groups and those between the drug trafficking groups and the government are taking numerous lives every day. *The Joint Operating Environment 2008*, issued by the U.S. Joint Forces Command, pointed out that Mexico was one of the two countries that bear consideration for a rapid and sudden collapse. The other country was Pakistan. In the coming years, the domestic conflicts in Mexico would cause negative impacts to the national stability; therefore, the United States should make preparations, for this was closely related to U.S. national security. Besides, the regime stability of some Latin American countries would constant suffered from the threat posed by the Revolutionary Armed Force of Columbia, National Liberation Army (Colombia) and other left-wing extremist groups.

Philippines caused the world's attention due to the hostage crisis in August 2010. Actually, the terrorism threat in Philippines was also very serious. On November 23, 2009, 57 people died of the hostage massacre in Mindanao Island in the Southern Philippines. It was estimated that over one million guns were illegally held and shootings frequently occurred in every election season. The most serious violence was identified in the elections of the Southern Philippines, where different armed forces existed, including the Muslim army desiring for independence and personal troops owned by political oligarchs.

vi. An Increasing Number of Terrorist Attacks Aimed at Civilian Infrastructures

Normally, the major terrorist attacks tend to choose civilian targets. It has been estimated that since the 1980s, unofficial targets, such as business and civilian, are always exceeding official targets (including governmental, diplomatic and military targets), and become the first or second targets of terrorist crimes. After the September 11th attacks, this trend became more apparent. It could be foreseen that since countries are putting more emphasis on safeguarding the official targets, such as the governmental, diplomatic and military, while the international terrorist groups are expecting to create more severe terrifying atmosphere, the business and civilian targets would continue to become the main targets of the global terrorist attacks and the attacks against these unofficial targets are bound to increase. The unofficial targets, which possess symbolic meaning or the damage of which may lead to more serious losses and harm, would be more likely to become the target of the global terrorist crime. It would be easy for the terrorists to target civilian infrastructures, such as water and electricity supply, communication and transportation system, or create some man-made catastrophes, such as burning forests, because it is almost impossible to make high-level protections over these targets and the government cannot take care of everything at the same time.

3. The New Strategies, Achievements and Problems of the Global Counter-Terrorist Actions

From 2009 to 2010, to address the rampant terrorist threats, the major countries in the world continued to make efforts in areas such as improving domestic counterterrorism legislation, strengthening anti-terrorism crisis administration mechanism and anti-terrorist forces construction, exploring new technical means to enhance security, deepening and expanding global anti-terrorism cooperation and so on. Globally speaking, the following new measures might be beneficial to enhance the counterterrorism results of the global society.

i. Wide Consensus Reached at Washington Nuclear Security Summit

The Nuclear Security Summit was held in Washington, D.C. from April 12 to 13, 2010, the main topics of which were centered on the nuclear terrorism threat and the countermeasures that the countries around the world and the international society should have. This was a significant multinational conference and drew the attention of various sides. According to the statement of the U.S. Department of State, the only theme of this nuclear security summit, initiated by President Obama, was to tackle the nuclear terrorism threat through international cooperation. The U.S. government hoped that countries could achieve common understandings upon fighting against nuclear threat posed by terrorists and seek effective measures to guarantee nuclear fuel security, and prevent the smuggling of nuclear fuels. Leaders and representatives from 47 countries, including President Hu Jintao of China, and those of the international or regional organizations such as the United Nations, the International Atomic Energy Agency (IAEA) and the European Union attended the conference. Representatives of the participating countries signed the *Communique of the Washington Nuclear Security Summit* and the *Work Plan of Washington Nuclear Security Summit*. They not only reached a wide consensus on globally strengthening nuclear safety and tackling nuclear terrorism threat, but also expressed strong wishes to take common actions to maintain and enhance the international nuclear non-proliferation system.

ii. The U.S. Continued Obama's New Counter-Terrorism Strategy and Officially Withdrew from Iraq

In the "post 9/11 era," with the dissolving panic within the U.S. public, the slogan of "anti-terrorism wars" during the Bush Administration lost its attraction. After Obama took office, he began to readjust the U.S. counterterrorism strategy. Right after his inauguration, Obama declared to reform the U.S. policy concerning the treatment of terrorist suspects comprehensively, including closing the Guantanamo Bay detention camp and forbidding imposing excruciation to the suspects. At the same time, he reiterated the need to stick to the deadline of pulling out of Iraq and shift the strategic focus of overseas anti-terrorism operations from Iraq to Afghanistan and tried to turn the "violent counterterrorism" strategy from Bush's administration to a "comprehensive counterterrorism" model which encompassed various means including military, diplomatic, political and economic ones.

Though faced with the unstable political situation and the difficulty to reverse the intense security situation, the United States still managed to pull its troops out of Iraq. On August 18, 2010, the last U.S. combat brigade withdrew from Iraq and crossed the border between Iraq and Kuwait. About 50,000 U.S. troops would remain in the country, responsible for training Iraqi army and providing relevant assistance.

Meanwhile, the Obama administration was considering how to withdraw from Afghanistan elegantly. Some experts believed that Obama was confronted with a dilemma: if continuing to increase troops in Afghanistan, more investments were needed, which may cause the antipathy of the public and discrepancy within the Democratic Party; however, if they followed the public opinion and pulled troops out of Afghanistan, this may incur the resurgence of al-Qaeda and the United States might again face the danger of suffering terrorist attacks. Not only the U.S. government, but also many other relevant countries, considered it as a huge challenge whether the U.S. could withdraw from Afghanistan elegantly as expected. For example, according to the assessment report issued by the Indian Institute for Conflict Management, the ally led by the United States was seeking an "exit strategy" from Afghanistan. However, an early withdraw of the western forces from Afghanistan would have a devastating influence over not only the South Asian but also the global security and stability.

iii. The Obama Administration Continued to Enlarge Information Agency and Conduct Secret War Operations

Stepping into the 21st century, the major countries in the world, especially the United States, expected to enlarge and strengthen the information system connected to anti-terrorism in a large scale. However, the actual result failed to satisfy the public. Taking the United States as an example, after the September 11th terrorist attacks in 2001, to avoid similar events, the U.S. government constantly reformed and enlarged the information agency comprehensively. According to the *Washington Post* report on July 19, 2010, in the past nine years, the United States had established or reformed at least 263 information agencies. Among the departments of U.S. governments responsible for tackling terrorist attacks, at least 20% were newly established or reformed after the September 11th attacks. At present, about 1,271 government agencies and 1,931 private-owned enterprises were engaged in activities related to information, anti-terrorism and homeland security, in around 10,000 spots in the United States. About 854,000 people were delegated with the most confidential level. The quantity of the information gathered by the U.S. information network rapidly increased. However, with a lack of experienced staff and low information processing efficiency, sometimes due to the limitation of legal authority, the Director of

National Intelligence could not exercise its power over any single department, and some officials of the information departments even questioned why the department existed.

On June 4, 2010, the U.S. *Washington Post* reported that, according to the U.S. military and government high officials, the Obama administration promised to conduct soft diplomatic operations. However, except for Afghanistan and Iraq war area, the Obama administration had largely expanded secret wars against al-Qaeda and other extremist groups across the world. The quantity and budget of special operation forces had both increased and they were deployed in 75 countries. However in early 2009, they were only present in 60 countries. Besides Philippines and Columbia where they had conducted special operations for years, the U.S. special operation force groups now started new operations in Yemen, Middle East and Central Asia. The capacity of special operations required by the While House included not only simple attacks, but also training the local anti-terrorism forces and take coalition actions with them.

iv. Afghan Government Officially Started to Seek Possibility of Political Peace Talks with Taliban

On September 28, 2010, the Afghanistan government established the High Peace Council, an official organization responsible for seeking peace talks with the Taliban. There were altogether 70 members in this council. Waheed Omar, Afghan President Hamid Karzai's spokesman, denied that the establishment of the High Peace Council was related to the U.S. withdraw. He said, "Afghan people need peace; no matter what, we want to seek peace." Karzai had repeatedly appealed the Taliban to give up violence and work with the government, to realize a peaceful and stable Afghanistan. However, the Taliban insisted that, unless the foreign troops withdrew from Afghanistan, they would not participate in the peace talks. Some British and U.S. officials warned that, though some leaders of Taliban seemed to be willing to reconcile with the government, the current contacts between the two sides still remained in the primary stage and peace talks were a long way away.

v. Pakistan Intensified Counter-Terrorism Operations

With the rampant terrorist attacks, the Pakistan government began to intensify the counterterrorism operations. Military circles were initiated in the major areas where the terrorists were entrenched. In 2009, the Pakistani army launched two large-scale operations, "Black Thunderstorm" and "Path to Deliverance," on April 26th and October 17th against Taliban in Swart and the South Waziristan region. To see the result, though serious loss was inflicted to the Taliban in Pakistan, their anti-government/society moods were further aggravated as well. This could be seen from the number, frequency and intensity of the terrorist attacks happened after.

4. Tendency and Outlook of International Counter-Terrorist Actions and its Influence on China

In conclusion, with the current serious terrorist threats, to guarantee national security, countries in the world continued to increase investment, adjust strategy, take various measures to prevent attacks and, at the same time, seek effective international cooperation. However, nearly all the strategic readjustments and new measures fail to address the roots of why terrorism emerges and develops. It is important to counter terrorism, but it requires more wisdom of politicians and experts to design a feasible plan to eliminate the root of terrorism.

Looking into the future, it could be expected that the international society would still face serious terrorist threats and counterterrorism operations would last for a long time. There are four points calling for attention: 1) How will the situation in Iraq evolve as the United States withdrew its troops? 2) Could the U.S. strategy of increasing troops to Afghanistan within a short period be paid back right away and can the withdraw plan from Afghanistan be implemented as expected in July 2011? 3) Under the great pressure from the United States, Pakistan encircled the al-Qaeda and Taliban forces in a large scale. Can these operations continue? Can the anti-terrorism situation in Pakistan change for the better? 4) Will the terrorist groups in Yemen and Somalia further enlarge and can the Red Sea, one of the main arteries of global economy, survive? Compared with Iraq, Afghanistan and Pakistan, the stability of the Gulf of Aden are more important to a larger scale of countries. Once the situation deteriorates, more countries will suffer from terrorism.

China is not a outsider, but a victim of terrorism as well. The main terrorist threats that China is faced with include: 1) The violent terrorist attacks launched by Eastern Turkistan and Tibeten Independence groups would have direct negative impacts over the social stability and national security in western ares of China; 2) China's overseas interests is increasing with the expansion of national strength. International terrorist attacks have posed real threat to the safety of Chinse citizens and property and energy transportation safety; 3) Terrorists groups frequently take actions in China's neighboring countries and regions, including the Central and Southern Asia and they are inclined to infiltrate into China. For example, the religious extremists group, Hizbut-Tahrir started to infiltrate into Xinjiang, China, at the end of the 1990s. Now they have around 20,000 members in Xinjiang and has become the unstable factors to threaten the regional security of Xinjiang, undermining national unity and fueling nation splits. They haveconstituted real threat to China's security and it is believed that the organization was part of the reason for theXinjiang riots on July 5, 2009; 4) The severe terrorism situation in some neighboring countries, such as Pakistan and the Philippines, has jeopardised the stability of China's peripheral security environment and normal personnel exchanges. It can be learned from the Hong Kong hostage crisis in Philippines that, –China not only need to ensure domestic stability and security, but also should take steps to prevent, reduce and tackle the harm brought by terrorism to our overseas interests.

Chapter 7

Climate Change Negotiations: From Copenhagen to Cancun

Wang Dong

From 2009 to 2010, in order to enhance measures to face the climate change and seek for a balance point for the economy and politics, state parties of *United Nations Climate Change Frame Convention* (hereinafter referred to as *Convention*) and *Kyoto Protocol* (hereinafter referred to as *Protocol*) began rounds of hard negotiations with the hope of a following agreement signed before January of 2013. During the Copenhagen Conference, different groups undertook fierce contests. Because of differentiating interests and viewpoints on key issues, the Copenhagen Conference closed fruitlessly, which made the conference held in Cancun, Mexican at the end of 2010 covered with negativity. The 2009~2010 Climate Change Negotiations have become the global hot spot and turned into all-round contest on politics and economic interests among the state parties.

1. The Climate Change Negotiations and Deadlocks Before the Copenhagen Conference

Before the Copenhagen Conference, climate change negotiations had gone through a tortuous process under the frame of the United Nations. In June 1992, on the United Nations Environment and Development Conference held in Rio de Janeiro, Brazil, more than 150 countries adopted the *Convention*, which took effect beginning in March of 1994. It was the first authoritative, universal and comprehensive international frame on climate change, which laid the foundation for international cooperation on climate change. The Convention respectively arranged the rights and compulsories for developed and developing countries and the procedures for carrying out rights and compulsories.

i. Copenhagen Appoints of “Bali Roadmap”

In December 1997, the third States Parties Conference was held in Kyoto and the

Protocol was adopted, which made specific provisions for the major developed countries on the types of reduced greenhouse gas emissions, the schedule and the amount. Based on this *Protocol*, from 2008 to 2012, the amount of the greenhouse gas emission of major developed countries should be reduced by 5.2% than in 1990. Only the United States, among the major industrialized countries, did not sign the *Protocol*; therefore the reduction promise of the U.S could not be carried out. The *Protocol* would expire by 2012. After its expiration, how to continue the reduction of the greenhouse gas emission becomes the "Pre-Kyoto" issue confronted by all nations.

In accordance with the appointments of "Bali Roadmap," state parties should obey the principle of "common but differentiated responsibilities and respective capabilities," comprehensively consider social, economic conditions and other relevant factors and define the goal of greenhouse gas emission reduction. The major developed countries should reduce greenhouse gas emission by 25% to 40% than in 1990. The significant meaning of "Bali Roadmap" lies in the promotion of the *Protocol* that the involved developed countries keep their promise for the first period (2008~2012). "Bali Roadmap" and the second promotion period of the *Protocol* finished the negotiations at the same time, realizing a unified goal and decided to finish the negotiations on the 15th Conference of the Parties of the *Convention* and the 5th Conference of the Parties of the Protocol, which were held in Copenhagen, Denmark in December of 2009. The conferences should enhance the international cooperation on climate change and promote the implementation of the Convention and the Protocol. That is why Copenhagen attracted worldwide attention on where its importance lies.

ii. Five Rounds of Negotiations and Confrontation Before the Copenhagen Conference

For preparing the Copenhagen Conference, state parties held five rounds of negotiations in 2009. In the negotiations, state parties with similar stands formed different groups and drafts for different interests were listed in the plan, including "Danish Draft" for developed countries and "Beijing Draft" (or "Sino-India Draft") for China, India, Brazil and South Africa.

After the five rounds of pre-Copenhagen negotiations, the differences and attitudes of the state parties came to the surface and were clarified. Interests groups or powers association were formed. This was called "two camps, three forces and multi bodies" by the media. "Two camps" referred to developing countries and developed countries; "three forces" were the European Union, Umbrella Group and developing countries; "multi bodies'" combination was divided into "Basic Four" (including China, India,

Brazil and South Africa), Island Nations and the Group of 77. There were both confrontations and conflicts for the stands and attitudes of these "two camps, three forces and multi bodies," which demonstrated the complications of the multi-lateral negotiations on climate changes.

In the process of climate change negotiations, China, India, Brazil and South Africa walked together because of the similar stand and the first letters of each nation formed the word "BASIC"; therefore they were named "Basic Four." Before the Copenhagen Conference, the stand for "Basic Four" was to insist on the climate change negotiations under the frame of the Convention, the Protocol and "Bali Roadmap." The stands and attitudes on climate change issues of "Basic Four" and the Group of 77 were generally the same. Before the Copenhagen Conference, their negotiation viewpoints and attitudes were clarified: the fruit of the Copenhagen Conference should cover the long term cooperative actions, promises of the developed countries, the appropriate palliation for the developing countries on the reduction of greenhouse gas emissions, and the establishment of integrated institutes, capital and technology transfer. At the same time, it should cover the special requests for the least developed countries and developing islands countries and African countries. These countries believed that the capital and technological supports from developed countries to developing ones was a key issue in the negotiations.

The European Union regarded itself as the leader against climate change and supported the *Convention* and the *Protocol*. It once issued a goal to reduce 50% of the greenhouse gas emission by 2050 (including developing countries) in order to limit the global temperature rising within 2 centigrades; therefore, the developed countries would reduce 80% of the greenhouse gas emissions by 2050. The European Union insisted that the United States should carry its responsibility for emissions reduction, but both sides differed from each other on this issue for a long time.

The Umbrella Group included the United States, Japan, Canada, Australia, New Zealand and other countries. They insisted on the mid-term reduction goal and regarded the participant of the developing countries as the pre-condition. These countries composed one group by similar stand. After President Obama took office, the attitude of the United States shifted, but refused the *Protocol*, too. On November 25, 2011, with the Copenhagen Conference approaching, under various pressures, the United States announced that President Obama would participate in the conference and promised on the basis of 2005 to reduce 17% of the greenhouse gas emissions by 2050, and 83% by 2050. Its promise not only arrived late, but was also far from the request from developing countries to developed countries.

Other countries in Umbrella Group kept the same viewpoint as the United States before the Copenhagen Conference. Although Japan, Canada and Australia approved the *Protocol*, they followed the United States in the negotiations with a negative attitude towards the reduction of emissions, made all efforts to evade their compulsories and responsibilities and urged the developing countries to accept limited compulsories and responsibilities on reducing the emissions.

2. Copenhagen: A Battlefield of Different Interests Groups

The Copenhagen Conference began on December 7'and ended on December19, of 2009. It lasted for two weeks and was one day longer than planned. During these two weeks, conference became silent battles. Fierce confrontations unfolded among different groups. The *Copenhagen Convention* was the fruit of difficult negotiations and discussions among the state parties who made great efforts and competed with different interest groups.

i. Interests and Stand Conflicts on Key Issues

During the Copenhagen Conference, different groups on climate changes began confrontations and contests on the reduction goal of developed countries, capital, technical support and agreement effect. From the following four parts we can see that the old problems in past negotiations were still key issues of disputes at this time.

Disputes on the reduction goal: Developing countries asked the developed countries to reduce 25% to 40% on the emission level of 1990. However, developed countries had no clarified schedule or detail action on when to carry out their promises. This was not acceptable for developing countries. Island nations issued that the temperature should be limited within 1.5 degree. If not, island nations would be faced with an existence problem. Island nations and the least developed countries asked the developed countries to reduce at least 45% of the emissions on the level of 1990 by the year 2020, and reduce 95% by 2050. They hoped the emerging developing powers would participate in the reduction action like the developed countries. This aroused conflicts among developing countries. The United States and other developed countries insisted on conditional reduction. European Commission President Barroso said both developing and developed countries should carry out compulsory reduction indicators; only when other countries acted together, did the European Union upgrade the mid-term reduction target to 30%.

Disputes around capital: The European Union announced at the conference that they would offer a total amount of 2.4 billion euro to developing countries from 2010 to 2012 as aid capital to help them face climate change challenges. However, there was still distance from the request of developing countries. The least developed countries thought that the aid capital offered by developed countries should reached 1.5% of their GDP, which would be more than 30 billion USD. The representative of "Group of 77 plus China" expressed that the promised capital of the EU was "not a big amount." The small island nations called for the international community, especially the developed countries, to take action first to significantly reduce greenhouse gas emissions and increase economic and technical help at the same time.

One focus around the capital issue was that the United States and developed countries hooked the reduction target of China with the capital assistance for developing countries together. They tried to transfer the contradictions to China and other emerging developing powers, which aroused conflicts between China and the U.S. On capital issue, the United States emphasized that the capital aid offered by the developed countries must be used on the least developed countries and must carry out "one agreement covering all major economic bodies' actions against climate changes and on the basis of offering their action transparency." Vice deputy of Chinese delegate Su Wei replied: "The emission reduction of developed countries was their international compulsories; but China, as a developing country, will take independent reduction measures."

Disputes on the effect of the agreement: Andreas Carlgren, Minister of Environment of Sweden EU's rotating presidency, expressed that "one agreement with legally binding" should be adopted on the Copenhagen Conference, which should also include the content of the *Protocol*. However, the representative of the United States expressed on different occasions that the result of the Conference might be a "political announcement." The gap between the U.S. and the EU was obvious. The high diplomat of Sudan in terms of "Group of 77 plus China" pointed out that Copenhagen Conference should not end with only a political announcement, but made detail regulations on the reduction target of the developed countries and their capital support. Small island nations called for all nations to adopt an agreement for their existence.

ii. Games on the Final "Battle of Drafts"

For different stands, interests groups issued their own drafts, which were called the "battle of drafts."

During the Copenhagen Conference, developed countries once attempted to adopt "Danish Draft" without any deep discussions with developing countries. This draft abandoned the content of the *Protocol*, respectively figured out reduction targets for developed and developing countries, forced developing countries to agree on quantitative reduction targets and measures, suggested to weaken the eminent domain of the United Nations over the capital aid against climate change and also stated that developed countries would decide on whether to offer capital aid on the basis of the detail reduction actions of the developing countries. This news shocked the international community and aroused strong indignation from developing countries that contested by abandoning the conference. Some medias even exclaimed that the Copenhagen Conference walked to the edge of rupture.

During the negotiations on climate change, China, India, Brazil and South Africa issued a joint draft. These four nations' stand could be concluded as: 1) insist on the climate change negotiations under the frame of the *Convention*, the *Protocol* and *Bali Roadmap* and suggest to figure out the compulsory reduction goal for developed countries mentioned in the first appendix of the *Protocol* for the period from 2013 to 2020 and ask the United States, that was out of the *Protocol*, to guarantee its reduction promise comparable with other developed countries; 2) it should be approved that the scientific viewpoint of limiting the global temperature increases within two centigrade;and 3) developing countries should take measures for reducing greenhouse gas emissions, but their independent actions should not accept the "Three-able Checks"(measurable, reportable and checkable).

The Pacific island country Tuvalu, in terms of the small island nations, officially submitted one amendment for the *Protocol*. Island nations asked that the Copenhagen Conference should on the basis of negotiations to approve a new agreement with the same legal position as the *Protocol*, including the limitation for the global temperature increases within 1.5 centigrade and bringing China, India and other developing countries with huge emission quantity into the reduction plan. This proposal gained support from the Alliance of Small Island States (AOSIS) and some of the developing countries, but developed countries, China and other developing countries were against the proposal; therefore this proposal could not get into the regular negotiations from the procedure.

Different drafts showed that during the Copenhagen Conference, viewpoints around climate change were becoming increasingly complicated. Different opinions surfaced between both groups of developed and developing countries. Opinions of different interests varied significantly, reaching no united opinion at the end of the conference. In the last period of the Copenhagen Conference, in order to avoid a fruitless end, after the negotiations and compromises among leaders of China, India, South Africa, Brazil and the United States, the *Copenhagen Agreement* was formed that was called the agreement with periods without legal binding.

iii. Copenhagen Agreement of Half Success-Half Failure

The *Copenhagen Agreement* was only a two-page political statement. Without the approval of all nations, it could not take legal effects, but was full of positive meanings.

The main content of the *Copenhagen Agreement* included: first, implement a dual-track system, insisting on the principle of "common but differentiated responsibility" clarified by the *Convention* and the *Protocol*. Second, reclaim the global temperature rising no more than two centigrade in order to reach the final target clarified by the *Convention*. Third, developed countries agreed to collect 100 billion USD every year before 2020 to assist poor countries facing climate changes. From 2010 to 2012, they would offer 30 billion USD to help those countries that were the most vulnerable developing countries facing climate changes. Fourth, all nations must work out their own reduction plans before January of 2010. Fifth, developing countries were accountable for reporting reduction procedures, including submitting reports to the United Nations every two years and accept international supervision without hurting the sovereignty. Sixth, promise to reduce greenhouse gas emissions and protect the forests.

The mainstream view on the agreement is, although the Copenhagen Conference did not realize the expected target with a satisfactory result, it did not fail. Secretary General of the United Nations Ban Ki-moon said, "This conference was successful and one important step towards a correct direction." Foreign Minister of China Yang Jiechi said that the conference gained "important and positive" results in three aspects: 1) strongly maintain the principle of "common but differentiated responsibilities" clarified by the Convention and the Protocol; 2) new but stable steps on compulsory reduction of the developed countries and the initiative action to reduce emissions of the developing countries; and 3) consensus was reached on global long-term target, capital and technical support, transparency and other key issues.

Surely, several nations and individuals expressed dissatisfaction on the conference and its result. President of EU Commission Barroso expressed after the meeting: "the agreement is far away from what we expected." Some developing countries, with Group of 77 as mainstay, thought that the *Copenhagen Agreement* neglected the interests of the developing countries. Some international environmental organizations also stated their dissatisfaction towards the conference. The dissatisfactory of the developing countries mainly resulted in the attempt to bring the negotiations to deviate from the "Bali Roadmap" and in the irrational requests towards developing countries, which aroused the upgrade of their sorrow and fury emotion.

Although there were some dissatisfactory feelings, objectively speaking, the Copenhagen Conference was a step forward. While facing climate change and the extreme weather, governments and all walks of life are taking reflection and investigation, looking for the root of the climate change and the solutions. "Only from this point of view, Copenhagen Conference was successful."

3. The Pessimistic Future of the Cancun Round of Negotiations

The result of the Copenhagen Conference differed from what the representatives of each nation expected and left many key issues to the Cancun Conference held in November 2010. The important task of the Cancun Conference lay in the promotion on the negotiations to gain a new agreement with legal binding.

i. Pressures and Difficulties of Each Nation After the Copenhagen Conference

With the approaching due date of the first period promise clarified by the *Protocol*, international and social pressures on all state parties significantly increased after the Copenhagen Conference. In 2010, many countries strengthened the emissions reduction on different levels and successively issued new reduction measures and a long-term plan. Even the United States, who refused to participate in the Protocol, shifted its attitude on the reduction issue and restarted its domestic legislative procedure for climate change.

Since October 2009, the legislative procedure of the United States fell into stagnation, but on May 12, 2010, Democratic Senator John Kerry and the independent senator Joe Liebermen issued climate act draft at the press conference held by the United States Senate hearing.

European Union Commission reported on May 26, 2010 that financial and economic crisis greatly decreased the cost of the EU's realization of the reduction target. Therefore, the European Union should consider upgrading the reduction target from 20% to 30% by 2020. Although the proposal must be approved by all party states of the EU, there was a promise at least.

At present, the key crux on climate change negotiations is that the developed countries have no defined promise on the quantitative indicators for the emissions reduction by 2020. Oral intention on reduction greatly was far from what was expected. The United States' draft for reducing 17% of greenhouse gas emissions on the level of 2005 by 2020 has not been adopted and lacked relevant domestic legal basis. Many changes lie in the political decisions on climate change in the European Union and it seems impossible to give up the additional conditions at present. Developed countries, including Japan, are waiting and watching the attitude of the U.S. and the EU.

Faced with various problems, the new executive general of the Convention Hilfiger Reese pointed out that in order to promote the negotiations, all governments of the state parties should carry historical responsibility on reduction indicators of the developed countries, aid developing countries, express start for the capital, institute for reduction check and legal agreements. These five "key aspects" work together to face climate changes challenges.

ii. Limited Achievements After Four Rounds of Negotiations in 2010

Before the Cancun Conference that was held at the end of 2010 in Mexico, state parties of the *Convention* and the *Protocol* respectively held four negotiations on climate changes, discussed the text documents for the Cancun Conference and also reset confidence among each other for the achievement of the conference. However, the achievements for these four rounds of negotiations were limited.

The fourth round of negotiation on climate change was held in Tianjin, China on October 4, 2010. This was the first time for China to undertake the United Nations' climate change negotiating conference and it was the last meeting before the Cancun Conference. It made progress, but it was still full of conflicts. On Tianjin negotiation meetings, each delegate discussed items listed in the schedule and all of them hoped the Cancun Conference would gain achievements. Su Wei, deputy of Chinese delegate, evaluated the Tianjin meeting was successful and matched the expectation at first as a working meeting with negotiation on draft as core. If state parties made progress on the draft, the Cancun Conference would prosper. It could be said that the text work on the draft made progress, not only reducing some parentheses, but also succeeded in reducing conflicts among each other and laying a good foundation for the final consensus. Hilfiger Reese, Executive General of *United Nations Climate Change Frame Convention* said, "We are approaching a set of systematic resolutions at Cancun."

From the overall prospective of these four negotiations, although it gained achievement, it did not eliminate the fundamental differences.

iii. Cancun Achieved Success with Difficulties

The 16th states parties' meeting of the United Nations Climate Change Frame Convention will be held from November 29 to December 10, 2010 in Cancun, Mexico.

This conference was no doubt very important for the climate change negotiations.

After 13 days difficult negotiations, the Conference, under the *Convention* and the *Protocol*, adopted a package resolution, i.e. the Cancun Agreement was the consensus agreed by 193 nations, except for Bolivia. Although outside expectations on Cancun Conferences were not high, it made periodic progress while there were many conflicts between the developed and the developing countries. Generally, the Cancun Agreement not only insisted on dual-track negotiation institutes and the principle of "common but differentiated responsibilities," but also made progress on different levels of realization of capital aid, technical transfer and other issues concerned by the developing countries. On the other hand, during the conference period, because of the negative attitude of the United States, Japan and other developed countries, the Cancun Conference was once faced with the danger of failure and the negotiations on the *Protocol* fell into a deadlock.

The recent climate change negotiations, including the Cancun Conference, frequently fell into difficulties. The major reason was that during the negotiations, there were more economic, especially political confrontations among nations. Therefore, no matter the inaction of the United States or the proposal of giving up the promises for the second period clarified by Japan and other countries, both covered the attempt for minimizing its international duty on emissions reduction and capital aid and maximizing their own interests. For now, because of the objective existence of political and economic conflicts, the future is still unknown for the negotiations on climate changes.

4. The Challenges to China

With the deepening of the climate change negotiations, the major pressure and challenges for China are: 1) the domestic pressure and challenges reflect in the coordination between economic development and environment protection. On the one hand, the economy needs sustainable development, but on the other hand, the pressure for emissions reduction is increasing. 2) with the emergence of China and the increasing request for resources for economic development, as a big consumer of resources is faced with increasing pressure from international public opinions. 3) in the present international structure, with the strengthening of the influence and becoming an important participant in the world, the role and influence of China is more and more important in the climate change negotiations, which means China should carry more international responsibilities and compulsories.

Before the Copenhagen Conference, China promised by 2020 to reduce 40% to 45%

of carbon dioxide per-unit GDP. This effort is initiative without any pre-condition, nor hook with other countries' reduction action. Therefore, China will regard the fight against climate changes as a strategic issue and classify it into economic and social development plan (the 12th Five-Year Plan). After the Copenhagen Conference, China accelerated the step to reduce greenhouse gas emissions and figured out relevant measures. The promise of China and its action is the authentic illustration of "responsibilities of China."

Chapter 8

Global Energy Politics: 2009~2010

Xue Li

Petroleum and natural gas accounted for 60% of global primary energy consumption, so energy politics on the international level, to a large extent, refers to the conflicts and cooperation concerning the petrol and natural gas exploration among nations. Since 2009, global energy disputes underwent several ups and downs, though with a decreasing intensity, while cooperations were deepening and widening. "That the two sides were compromising in the deal in order to maintain cooperation relationship and avoid destruction to both" had become a trend. This essay is dedicated to describing various energy conflicts and cooperation in different areas, explain the reasons for them and predict future trends.

I. The Characteristics and Catalogues of Global Energy

Energy is the driving force of an economy. The government is obliged to guarantee energy security of its country. Therefore, energy is a kind of special commodity, closely related to politics. Since petrol and natural gas make up a large portion of global primary energy consumption and is a rigid consumption, petrol and natural gas security has become the energy security focus of every country.

Energy politics is the political activities related to energy, normally referring to the political activities to assure one country or region's energy security and energy consumptions for political ends. Climate politics, as a special type of energy politics, has shown a concern for the benefits of the whole of mankind, and the energy security interests of different countries and regions as well. In most cases, the latter is more important.

Countries both fight and cooperate for energy security. Therefore, war and peace are the two means to realizing this goal. Peaceful means fall into three categories: exclusive development, cooperative development, or neither cooperation nor development. Since the

1960s, the oil-producing countries had started an energy nationalization movement. To avoid exploration risks, the international energy corporation gradually agreed to adopt a cooperative development path. Currently, cooperative development has become the mainstream method of international petrol and natural gas exploration.

Different from other industries in the petrol and natural gas exploration area and backed by national government, energy enterprises competed, made deals and compromised in the disputes with partner companies and energy producing countries. This is an inevitable companion in the global energy development. Therefore, the energy relationships among nations, in its nature, are a kind of transaction. Cooperation is the product of conflicts.

In terms of industrial division, the oil and natural gas industry could be divided into three parts: the upstream, middle reaches and the downstream. The upstream refers to the hydrocarbon exploration and development; the middle reaches indicate the multiphase transportation and storage of oil and natural gas; and the downstream means petroleum processing and petrochemical industries, including the wholesale and retail terminals. Hence, energy politics could be categorized as follows: the conflicts and cooperation among upstream countries, mainly referring to the ownership disputes concerning energy resources and oil and gas exploration and development; conflicts and cooperation among the middle reach countries, including sea transportation routes, crude oil transportation pipelines, and the refined oil and natural gas transportation pipelines of the downstream category; and the conflicts and cooperation of the downstream countries in aspects such as the refining process, petrochemical industries, wholesale and retail terminals of oil and gas products and so on. Examples that cannot be included in these three categories shall be analyzed as "others," such as climate politics and the energy diplomacy of Venezuela.

II. The Cooperation and Conflicts in Upstream Industries

The first step to insure energy security is to obtain as much energy resources as possible. On the international level, it could be achieved through three ways: territorial expansion, development agreement concerning the disputed regions, and obtaining oil and gas exploration and development permission in foreign countries. Therefore, the energy politics in the oil and gas upstream industry has two kinds of disputes: territorial disputes centered on the ownership of oil and gas resources and disputes and cooperation concerning the development of oil and gas resources.

i. Territorial Disputes on the Ownership of Oil and Gas Resources

With the science and technology development, some land and ocean, which were ignored or considered to have no economic value, now attract the world's attention. Countries take actions and seek to prove that they acquire sovereignty over these regions so that they could legitimately obtain the ownership of the oil and gas resources in these places. The cases of the Arctic regions and Malvinas Islands waters are typical examples.

1. Energy Disputes in the Arctic Regions

The main body of the Arctic regions is oceans surrounded by the territory of several sovereign states. The Arctic problem is mainly a maritime issue. Some countries take various actions and aimed to strengthen their Arctic territorial claims for the purpose of gaining as many interests as possible in the future. Canada is a typical example. On the one hand, after Russia planted a Russian flag on the seabed below the North Pole in 2007, Canada soon sent a patrol vessel to the Arctic waters, set up Arctic forces in 2008 and started annual military exercises. However on the other hand, they did not deny peaceful dialogues and cooperation.

Russia, another great power coveting Arctic sovereignty, is also preparing for two eventualities. For one, Russia informed Canada that they would resolve the ownership dispute of the Lomonosov Ridge based on the United Nations Convention on the Law of the Sea and scientific research. For another, Russia planned to build the most solid icebreaker to explore the Arctic.[60] In October, 2010, Vladimir Vysotskiy, the Commander-in-Chief of the Russian Navy, expressed in one of the governmental maritime conference that, "Russia is currently increasing its combat potential in the Arctic with new ships and additional station sites."[61]

Without a comprehensive treaty like the *Antarctic Treaty*, the disputes in the Arctic regions will last for a long time, though large-scale conflicts are unlikely to occur. Scrambles for the Arctic regions among nations are more preparative than confrentational.[62]

---

60 "*Russia Build Another Strong Icebreaker to Explore the Arctic,*" *Reference Newspaper* (China), Sep. 21, 2010.

61 "*Russia Planning to Increase Combat Potential in the Arctic,*" *Reference Newspaper* (China), Oct.4, 2010.

62 The Arctic shipping route that has been constantly listed as the headlines of various media is actually available for shipping only for a few days within one year. Thus it does not possess much business value. The most positive prediction is: "since 2030 (the earliest possible time), there should be a short period of iceless time in the Arctic Ocean in every summer." See *Six Reflections About the North Pole*, *Reference Newspaper* (China), Sep.1, 2010.

2. Energy Disputes in Malvinas Islands Waters

In December 2009, the Argentina parliament passed a law, claiming that Islas Malvinas Islands (known to Great Britain as the Falkland Islands) was part of Argentina. In early February 2010, Great Britain declared that the British Desire Petroleum was permitted to drill oil near the Falkland Islands waters. On February 15th of the same year, the Denmark vessel, Thor Leader, which was loaded with oil pipelines and headed for the Malvinas Islands, was detained by Argentina. The next day, the Argentinean vessels brought in controls on ships passing through waters to the islands. On the 17th, the destroyer HMS York of the British Royal Navy steamed off the Falkland Islands coast and joined the other three islands' regular patrol vessels. On the 21st, British Desire Petroleum started drilling on the Ocean Guardian drilling platform. On February 26th, Repsol-YPF, a joint venture by Argentina and Spain, announced their oil exploration plan around the Malvinas Islands waters, but admitted that the success rate might be as low as 10%. At the end of March, Desire Petroleum warned that early evidence suggested they might not be commercially viable.[63] In May, the Special Meeting of the Heads of State and Government of the Union of South American Nations issued a declaration, reiterating support for Argentina's sovereign claims over the Malvinas Islands and calling for peaceful resolutions to the disputes.

Neither Great Britain nor Argentina desired war. Gordon Brown, the British Prime Minister at that time expressed that they wanted to "try to avoid military confrontations." Argentine government also excluded the possibility of solving the dispute by military forces. This dispute suspended with the drilling result released by the Desire Petroleum, but might be provoked again in the future.

ii. Disputes and Cooperation on the Exploration of Oil and Gas Resources

In the upstream of oil and gas resources, it is common to witness the disputes, competition and cooperation concerning the energy resources exploration among the sovereign states. In the inter-state level, some radical government behaviors such as the energy nationalization and expel of foreign energy companies would often lead to energy disputes among the energy producing country, energy companies and the mother country of the energy companies. However, none of these events have occurred since 2009. On the

63 SONG Jieyun & FENG Junyang. *British Petroleum Company Disappointed at the Malvinas Islands Drilling Result*, Xinhua News Agency Report, Buenos Aires, Argentina, Mar. 29th, 2010.

domestic level, conflicts over energy exploration between central (federal) government and local government (or non-governmental armed forces) have gradually become an energy politics hotspot. The typical examples are Nigeria and Sudan. New developments in the oil and gas exploration field always remain to be a major component to the global energy politics, such as the two rounds of oil field bid in Iraq and the Bolivian achievements in attracting foreign investment.

1. Nigerian Energy Disputes

Multinational energy companies have their presences in dozens of oil producing countries and, generally speaking, they will not cause disputes or violent accidents. The energy disputes in Nigeria are mainly in the domestic level and have led to serious consequences: decreasing oil production, oil refineries running under their production capacity, global oil price fluctuations and the Nigerian government is now under great pressure from various foreign companies and governments to ensure the safety of their foreign staff.

As one of the most prolific oil producers in Africa for years, Nigeria is the only member of the Organization of Petroleum Exporting Countries (OPEC) of the Sub-Saharan African countries. The hydrocarbon resources in Nigeria are mainly embedded in the coastal basins (including the Niger River Delta and the coastal waters). These places are among the most oil-rich regions along the African coast. The Nigerian government once expected to produce as many as 4 million barrels of oil daily by 2010. However, since 2006, oil production in Nigerian has kept decreasing and failed to achieve this goal.

There are two main reasons accounting for the Nigerian energy disputes: wealth distribution and environment pollution. The remarkably huge sum of wealth coming from oil did not change the impoverished life of the people living in the oil-producing areas. The exploration of hydrocarbon resources and the accompanying environmental pollution deprived the local people of their land and original means to make a living (such as fishery). Consequently, an anti-governmental organization, the Movement for the Emancipation of the Niger Delta (MEND), launched a so-called "Oil War," with terrorist attacks, kidnapping (mainly aimed at foreigners), and attacks on oil facilities. For example, on October 1, 2010, MEND set off two car bombs, which caused 14 fatalities and another 40 victims injured. Energy investors need to fully evaluate the investment risks before investing in Nigeria.

2. Sudan Energy Disputes and Cooperation

Since the main disputes in Sudan are on domestic levels, there are two energy dispute counterparts that the Sudan government must deal with: The Justice and Equality Movement (JEM) in Darfur and The Sudan People's Liberation Movement (SPLM) in South Sudan.

In February 2009, the Sudanese government and Khalil Ibrahim, the leader of JEM, signed *the Agreement of Good Will and Confidence Building for the Settlement of the Problem in Darfur*, to achieve consensus over a series of key issues, such as establishing mutual trust, releasing imprisoned persons and realizing reconciliation. After that, much fewer conflicts related to energy have occured in Darfur. In 2009, the daily oil production of Sudan amounted to 490,000 barrels, the highest ever in history.[64]

In April 2010, the Sudanese presidential and parliamentary election was held smoothly. The current president, Omar Hassan Ahmed Bashir, won another term of office. The National Congress Party, led by Bashir, and The Sudan People's Liberation Movement (SPLM), led by Salva Kiir Mayardit, had an overwhelming victory in the North and South Sudan respectively. The two sides would form a coalition government and prepare for the southern Sudanese independence referendum. SPLM would take up 30% (a percentage settled on the 2005 *Comprehensive Peace Agreement*) of the seats in the new government.

The independence referendum in January 2011 showed that 98.83% of the voters supported the Southern independence. The Sudanese president, Bashir, declared an acceptation to the referendum result and the Southern Sudan shall be independent as of July 2011.[65] The division of oil fields along the North-South boarder line would be sensitive, but would not influence the general situation.

3. Competition and Cooperation in Iraq Energy Exploration

The goal of Iraq is to reach a daily oil production approaching 12 million barrels by 2015 and become the largest oil-producing country in the world. To achieve this goal, Iraq has completed two rounds of oil filed auctions. In the first international bidding round in June 2009, only one out of the eight large oil fields was successfully auctioned off. The joint British BP-Chinese National Petroleum Corporation (CNPC) won the bid for the giant Rumaila oil field in southeastern Iraq. In the second bidding round in December of the same year, seven out of ten oil fields were awarded to foreign investors. The winning bidders were a consortium led by China National Petroleum Corp., France's Total and

---

64 *BP Statistical Review of World Energy June 2010*, p.8.

65 *Southern Sudan Independence Referendum Result: 98.83% Voted for Separation, people.com* report, Khartoum, Sudan, February 7th,

Malaysia's Petronas, Russia's Lukoil Holdings along with Norway's Statoil ASA, a group of Royal Dutch Shell and Malaysia's Petronas, a consortium made up of Petronas and Japanese oil company Japex, and a group grouping Russia's Gazprom, Korea's KOGAS and Turkey's TPAO and so on. People's concern that "the U.S. and Britain would monopoly the hydrocarbon exploration in Iraq" did not happen. The British BP and Royal Dutch Shell both chose to form partnerships with foreign companies to bid. Not seen many U.S. companies were seen.

4. Bolivian Energy Exploration and Cooperation

On October 29, 2006, Bolivia completed the energy nationalization process, which enabled the state to gain more wealth out of energy. In 2008, the Bolivian government obtained an income of 2.3 billion USD out of national gas, while in 2005, the number was only 0.25 billion. Some foreign companies left Bolivia, while others remained to administrate the normal daily production of natural gas. However, new investment to the natural gas in Bolivia was reducing and the natural gas production increased slowly.[66] To encourage the natural gas production and export, the government has taken plenty of measures: a 2009~2015 medium energy investment plan with a total investment of 10.75 billion USD; permitting foreign investors to invest in regions specialized for state-owned petroleum enterprises; and Evo Morales, the president of Bolivia, personally invited countries like China and Russia to join in the hydrocarbon exploration in Bolivia. These endeavors have been paid back. In September 2008, Russia's Gazprom and France's Total signed an agreement with Bolivia, saying that they would invest 4.5 billion USD to explore the hydrocarbon resources in Bolivia. In November 2009, a Spain-Argentina joint venture, Repsol, announced that they would invest 1.5 billion USD in Bolivia, to increase their oil production and storage size of the country.

III. The Cooperation and Conflicts in Midstream Industries

In terms of oil transportation, there have not been any events that attracted the world's attention since 2009. However, Russia, Belarus, Ukraine and the EU have fallen into various disputes that call for attention in the transportation of natural gas. The oil and gas pipeline cooperation progress around the Caspian Sea region are also worth mentioning. For China, the operation and construction of several oil and gas pipelines are also the great

66 *BP Statistical Review of World Energy June 2010*, p.25.

achievements of international energy cooperation.

i. Russia-Ukraine Energy Disputes

The natural gas disputes between Russia and Ukraine has been constantly escalated since 2005. On January 1, 2009, Russia again cut off all gas supplies passing through Ukrainian territory. Starting from January 7th, the natural gas supplies to nine European and Asian countries were halted, which caused great dissatisfaction from the EU. This event, however, contributed to pushing the Russia-Ukraine negotiation forward. Later, on January 19th, the two countries signed a new natural gas supply and marketing contract that would cover the next 10 years. In early 2010, Yanukovych, the leader of the Ukraine Party of Regions, who was also supported by Russia, won the presidential election, which was favorable for a stable Russia-Ukraine relationship. In June 2010, during the Russia-Belarus energy disputes, Ukraine offered to increase the supply running through Ukraine, in order to neutralize the negative impacts that were brought on by the close of Belarus natural gas pipeline to Europe.

To eliminate the potential danger brought by the uncatchable Ukraine pipeline, Russia speeded up the construction of another twin pipelines bypassing Ukraine, namely, the Nord Stream and South Stream. The annual natural gas supply running through these two pipelines after completion would take up 2/3 of that now passing through Ukraine territory. Ukraine clearly knew what this meant. Therefore, they offered to modernize the current domestic natural gas pipelines to replace the South Stream. When running for the early 2010 presidential election, Yanukovych expressed Ukraine's wish to participate in the Nord Stream project. Russia's reaction towards this was: If the Ukraine Naftogaz Company merged with the Russian Gazprom, Ukraine would be included into the Nord Stream natural gas pipeline project automatically.

Two thirds of the natural gas needed by Ukraine came from Russia. It could be expected that after the Nord Stream and South Stream were completed, Russia would have an increasing influence over the European market and Ukraine; on the contrary, would lose the bargain chip to challenge Russia. Ukraine shall pay a long-term price for the short-term vision and behavior of its leaders in the past few years.

ii. Russia-Belarus Energy Disputes

Among all the Russian natural gas supplies to the Europe through pipelines, 80% is running through Ukraine and 20% through Belarus. The natural gas supplies in Lithuania are 100% dependent on the Belarus pipelines and a small portion of Poland and Germany import natural gas also come from this pipeline. Russia claimed that Belarus did not pay the necessary fees, according to the contract, while Belarus complained that Russia had set an exorbitant gas price and owed Belarus transit fees. For these reasons, the two sides endured a tense relationship in August 2007. On June 21, 2010, Russia again started reducing the gas supplies and Belarus closed the natural gas pipelines to the EU members. Both sides settled the disputes quickly. Russia resumed the natural gas supplies to Belarus on the morning of June 24th and transferred 228 million USD natural gas transit fees to Belarus.

With an intimate bilateral relationship, it is unlikely for the two sides to have a complete break-up. Russia choosing to play the energy card at this time was aimed at warning Lukashenko, the President of Belarus since 1994, because they did not want him to become pro-Western. Lukashenko is a veteran politician and fully aware that it is not easy to play the energy card. Therefore, he simply stopped before going too far and declared that Belarus would not have economic wars with Russia.

iii. Russia-EU Energy Disputes

The Russia-EU energy disputes mainly concern the *European Energy Charter* and the *Energy Charter Treaty*. The oil and gas export income has accounted for 50~60% of the total export income of Russia,[67] and the majority of the natural gas are exported to the EU, taking up 25% of the total gas import of the latter. Therefore, once Russia takes up the energy issue, the EU becomes extremely passive and uncomfortable. To solve this problem, the EU has wanted to include Russia into the framework of the *European Energy Charter* and the *Energy Charter Treaty*, in order to restrain Russia's energy diplomacy behavior. However, Russia held that the current energy market regulation system was unfair and joining the Charter could not guarantee its national interests. As a result, on May 23, 2009, Russia reiterated that they would not approve the *European Energy Charter* unless major amendments were made. Later in June, Dmitry Medvedev, the president of Russia, suggested that a new energy charter should be settled as the game rule of the global energy market. It could be seen that it was impossible for Russia to join the *European Energy Charter* within a short period.

Russia maintains that they are a reliable supplier to the European energy market. It is the transiting countries, such as Belarus and Ukraine, which cause the trouble and leave the

---

67 Основные положения энергетической стратегии России на период до 2020 года. http://www.mte.gov.ru/oficial/strateg_energ.htm, quoted from FENG Yujun, *Russia's Energy Development and Its Energy Cooperation with China*: P.11, not published yet.

EU with an impression of "unreliable." Therefore, Russia speeds up the construction of the twin pipelines, the Nord Stream and South Stream, to get rid of the negative impacts brought by these two unreliable transiting countries. However, after the completion of the two pipelines, Russia would obtain a stronger and more direct controlling ability over the EU energy market, which may increase the sense of uncertainty within the EU and promote the implementation of EU energy diversification policy (the signing of the Nabucco Gas Pipeline Agreement was a signal). Hence, it could be concluded that the game between the two sides centered on the European Energy Charter and the Energy Charter Treaty will continue.

iv. The Caspian Sea Energy Issue

Various powers compete and cooperate over the exploration of the hydrocarbon resources in the Caspian Sea region, which presents a full-length drama to the global stage of energy politics. Russia manages to control the Central Asia's oil and gas export passage with the pipeline system constructed in the Soviet Union era. Russia has a strong wish to maintain its advantageous situation. Therefore, it is Russia's position to oppose constructing new pipelines bypassing Russia and advocate elevating the capacity of the current pipelines, while the new pipelines should be connected to the current system as well. The oil and gas import countries and the Central Asia producers disagree with Russia. The Central Asian countries, abundant in oil and gas resources, want to increase the oil and gas production to a large scale and develop a diversified export market. Their principles are centered around resolutely destroying Russia's monopoly, but not refusing to continue cooperation with Russia. Undoubtedly, the oil and gas importers, such as the United States, the European Union, China, Japan and Korea, are in favor of the producers' position. It is the same situation with oil and gas transiting countries, such as Turkey and Azerbaijan.

As a result, Kazakhstan, the leading oil power in the Central Asia, is now constructing a crude oil pipeline to China in the east and a trans-Caspian Sea oil pipeline to Azerbaijan in the west, while still exporting crude oil through Russia. Turkmenistan, a gas-rich country in Central Asia, constructs pipelines to Iran and China, despite the pressure from Russia, and plans to provide gas supply to the Nabucco pipeline through the trans-Caspian Sea lines. In addition, they also agree to restore the Turkey-Kazakhstan-Russia gas pipeline, which has been halted due to the aging problem. This is a crucial step for Turkmenistan to gain a competing edge in the future energy game. Currently, its annual gas production is less than 70 billion cubic meters, while the domestic consumption plus the promised gas supplies to the four export pipelines amount to 200 billion cubic meters per year.[68] According to the agreements signed with other countries, they could rely on the large sum of foreign investments provided by the gas importers to increase the gas production of Turkmenistan and determine the allocation of the natural gas to each pipelines based on their needs.

v. Chinese Oil and Gas Pipeline Construction

Since 2009, China has made remarkable achievements in terms of oil and gas pipeline construction. On the domestic level, the most captivating event was the Sichuan-Shanghai Gas Pipeline project, which, with an annual capacity to transit 12 billion cubic meters of natural gas, was put into business operation in August 2010. The construction of pipelines for importing oil and gas are especially important: the construction of China-Myanmar oil and gas pipelines has started and the China-Russia oil pipeline as well as the China-Central Asia gas pipeline are planned to provide a stable bidirectional supply.

China has planned four routes for importing oil and gas: the China-Russia oil and gas pipeline in the Northeast; the China-Central Asia gas pipeline and the planned China-Russia natural gas pipeline in the Northwest; the China-Myanmar oil and gas pipeline in the Southwest; and the liquefied natural gas import sea routes along the eastern coast. Huge progress has been made in the construction of the three land importing pipelines, which apparently is a contribution to China's energy security. China-Central Asia gas pipeline is one that could ease the energy disputes around the Caspian Sea region and realize a prosperous situation through cooperation.

IV. The Cooperation and Conflicts in Downstream Industries

In the following aspects, "Mutual Complement, Cooperation and Mutual Benefits" is the mainstream. The manifestations could be divided into several types: the cooperation among oil-producing countries to enter the downstream market; the cooperation between oil producers and importers to enter their own disadvantageous areas; and the cooperation

---

68 Its annual domestic consumption in 2009 was about 20 billion cube meters. The annual transiting capacity to each pipeline is: 40 billion cube meters for China-Central Asia Pipeline, 80 billion cube meters for Central-Central Asia Pipeline and another 30 billion cube meters for Russia-Turkey-Kazakhstan Pipeline, 28 billion cube meters for the Turkmenistan-Iran Pipeline which started operation in 1998 and 31 billion cube meters for the Nabucoo Pipeline. The highest annual production in 2008 was 66.1 billion cube meters and a sharp production decrease in 2009 due to the cutoff of gas supply to the Central-Central Asia Pipeline.

among energy importers to achieve mutual benefits. China has a splendid performance in these aspects.

The energy cooperation between China and Russia has covered the whole stream of oil industry, the upstream, middle and downstream. As for the upstream, on February 18, 2009, China and Russia signed a 25 billion USD "loan for oil" pact. In terms of the middle reaches, the examples are the China-Russia oil pipelines described above. Regarding the downstream, a China-Russia joint venture Oriental Petrochemical 13 billion tons annual oil-refining project started construction in September 2010 in Tianjin.

Saudi Arabia is China's largest crude oil import partner. The bilateral relationship is currently not limited to crude oil transactions any longer. Sinopec Group has entered the hydrocarbon exploration area of Saudi Arabia and Saudi Arabia has participated in the oil downstream industries of China. In November, 2009, the Fujian Refining and Ethylene Joint Venture Project invested by China, the United States and Saudi Arabia, officially started business operation. The Qingdao Refinery Project is expected as the next step for Saudi Arabia to enter China's downstream oil industry.[69] During Chinese President Hu's visit to Saudi Arabia from February 10 to 12, 2009, new bilateral energy cooperation agreements were signed.[70]

V. The Cooperation and Conflicts in Other Sectors of the Energy Industry

Some energy politics cases may involve the upstream, middle and downstream of the oil and gas industries, such as the Venezuela energy diplomacy and global climate politics.

i. Venezuela Energy Diplomacy

For a long period, Venezuela was the top five oil supplier for the United States. However, Chavez, the president of Venezuela, argued that it was the U.S.'s intention to keep Latin America as its political and economical neighbor that largely caused the poverty and huge wealth gap in Latin America. Therefore, it was necessary for Latin America to get rid of the political and economical dependence on the United States and realize self-independence, development and social fairness. To achieve this goal, he has been

69 *Saudi Arabia's Aramco Resuming Negotiation with Sinopec over the Qingdao Refinery Project*, *China Business News*, Nov.12, 2009.

70 *President Hu Jintao Meeting with Saudi Arabia King, Signing Five Bilateral Energy Agreements*, Xinhua News Agency report, Riyadh, Saudi Arabia, February 10, 2009.

actively promoting the anti-U.S. energy diplomacy that includes: forging anti-U.S. forces, reducing contacts with the United States, nationalizing the major exploration projects whose share was mainly held by European or U.S. petroleum companies, establishing coalition fleets with Chinese ventures and construct or enlarge large-scale joint-venture refineries in places such as Brazil, Argentina, Cuba, Syria and China.

There are three distinctive features of Venezuela energy diplomacy: systematically taking advantage of energy resources for political ends, strongly anti-U.S., involving the upstream, middle and downstream areas of energy industries. The Venezuelan constitutional referendum result in the early 2009 allowed Chavez to run for office in 2012. Therefore, Venezuela energy diplomacy will continue for some more years.

ii. Conflicts and Cooperation in Climate Politics

The up, middle and downstream of hydrocarbon industries such as the energy exploration, development, transportation and consumption would pollute the environment, which is widely seen as the main cause for global warming. It has been the focus of climate politics to control the emission of green house gases. Climate politics is likely to become the leading pillar of the global politics in the 21st century. The 192 member countries of the United Nations have confirmed the principle of "common but differentiated responsibility" to cope with the climate change through discussion. However, the developed and developing countries still emphasize the different aspects of the same principle, and it is difficult to coordinate. The Cancun Conference held in December 2010 has drawn the lesson from the Copenhagen Conference and stressed less on the emission goals. However, the moderate and low-pitched strategy adopted by various sides just postponed this tough issue. Since this issue is closely related to the core national interests of both the developed and developing countries, breakthroughs concerning the settlement of the quantifying index of global green house gas emission are not expected to be seen in the United Nations Climate Change Conference in Durban, South Africa, in later 2011.

After all, climate politics have a definite influence on the energy policies in various countries. Plenty of countries have made laws concerning saving energy and reducing emissions and many have accelerated their exploration of green energy, such as wind power, solar power, hydrogen power and biomass energy, promoted clean coal technology, emphasizing developing relatively cleaner energy such as nuclear and natural gas.

Nuclear energy is a cleaner energy than natural gas and the only one among all the clean energies that could generate large-scale electricity stably with mature technology and lower costs than hydrocarbon resources. However, the disadvantages are the sensitive disposal problem of nuclear waste and the concerns among the public. Generally speaking, the advantages of nuclear power outweigh the disadvantages. Therefore, nuclear power has been put into practice in many countries. In September 2010, German chancellor Merkel, decided to extend the lifetime of 17 nuclear power plants. In April 2010, Italy planned to construct four nuclear power plants with France in the next five years. In February 2010, President Obama of the United States announced that an 8 million USD government loan would be offered to help building two new nuclear power plants and by October 2010, China had already established six nuclear power plants and another 12 are under construction, while 25 more are planned to be built in the future. It is expected that the Chinese nuclear installed capacity would approach 80 million kilowatts by 2020. Even countries with rich oil and gas resources, such as the United Arab Emirates and Kuwait, are determined to build nuclear power stations.

Japan's Fukushima nuclear power plant leak was the most serious nuclear plant accident in the past 25 years. It was categorized as a level 7 crisis, just like the Chernobyl nuclear accident in 1986. This was a huge strike to the global nuclear power development. However, the role played by nuclear power in tackling the climate change issue cannot be displaced. Therefore, conclusions could be drawn that the Fukushima nuclear leak accident will not reverse the global trend of developing nuclear energy, though the nuclear security standards are sure to be elevated, which would put off the construction of some nuclear power plants.

VI. Conclusion and Outlook of the Global Energy Politics

Overall, the 2009~2010 energy politics has displayed several features as follows:

Some countries have strengthened their sovereignty claims over regions with hydrocarbon resources ownership disputes, but have also maintained certain restraints on their positions and behaviors. In terms of the exploration and development of oil and natural gas resources, radical government actions, such as energy nationalization or expelling foreign energy corporations did not happen. The current disputes were mainly in the domestic level. On the international level, remarkable progress could be identified in the cooperative exploration and development. Countries with rich resources such as Iraq, Bolivia, Venezuela, Russia and Brazil have signed large amounts of exploration agreements with foreign investors.

In the middle stream of oil and gas industries, the disputes mainly occurred between Russia and Belarus, and Ukraine and Turkmenistan. Cooperation could continue because none of these countries has the intention to intensify the disputes. Some significant oil and gas pipelines would start operation within one year, while the construction of some others has been speeded up as well. Countries also signed agreements to construct more pipelines. China made fruitful achievements in this aspect. Among the four oil and gas import passages in the North, South, East and West, the construction of the three land passages has been greatly pushed forward.

In the downstream of the oil and gas industries, "Mutual Complement, Cooperation and Mutual Benefits" is the mainstream. China has performed skillfully and signed a large sum of cooperation agreements with many oil-producing countries. "Loan for Oil" has become a distinctive Chinese approach in global energy cooperation.

From 2009 to 2010, Venezuela energy diplomacy was a classic case in the energy politics. Climate politics changed the energy policies in many countries to a large extent and therefore constitutes an important component to energy politics. Fukushima nuclear power plant leak accident will not reverse the global trend to develop nuclear power, but would lead to an elevation of nuclear power development standards.

Looking ahead, the energy disputes concerning sovereignty and territorial ownerships will continue, and may even increase. The possibility of resolving the disputes by non-peaceful means is rare. In the regions abundant in oil and gas resources, such as the Middle East, Africa, South America and Central Asia, the countries who have already held a share will attempt to maintain their advantage, while the followers are certain to enlarge their investment, if possible. In this kind of competition, a series of political factors will continue to make a difference. With the rising status of new emerging countries in the global economic politics, they will play a more important role in the energy sectors.

Chapter 9

Paroxysmal Calamities and Governance in the World's Cities

Wang Mingming

At the beginning of 2010, powerful earthquakes occurred in succession in Central and South America, resulting in the tragic loss of life and property that was far more devastating than the earthquake in Sichuan, China in 2008. In the 2010 "World Disasters Report: Focus on Urban Risk," the International Federation of Red Cross and Red Crescent Societies remarked that urban residents who live in low-income countries are facing various "urban risks" due to rapid urbanization, population growth, and climate change.[71] Now, the city already has half of the world's population and the vast majority of created, spiritual and material wealth. The loss from urban disasters is far more serious than that in other regions and the threat to human life and property is unprecedented. Faced with global challenge like these, all countries need to think seriously about urbanization and natural disasters.

I. Global Urbanization

Urbanization process in developed countries progressed earlier than in developing countries. Britain's accelerated urbanization began in the early 19th century. In 1801, the British urban population reached 27.5% of the total, up to 51% in 1851.[72] In 1840, urban population in United States exceeded 10% of total and reached 51.2% in 1920. In 1947, Japan's urban population took up 33.1% of the total population, and reached 56.5% in 1965. In 1960, Korea's urban population took up 28% of total population and reached 50.2% in 1970.[73] Currently, the urbanization rate of the developed countries and some newly

71 International Federation of Red Cross and Red Crescent Societies: *World Disasters Report 2010: Focus on Urban Risk.* http://www.ifrc.org/Docs/pubs/disasters/wdr2010/WDR2010-English-2.pdf

72 Gu Yanfang: *Re-evaluation on the British Enclosure Movement and the Urbanization*, **Xinhua Digest**, 2008, No.21, http://www.doc88.com/p-69091444695.html

73 http://finance.sina.com.cn/leadership/mroll/20100419/12017778777.shtml

industrialized countries is up to 70% to 90%, and no longer continue to increase.

The period of accelerated urbanization in developing countries began in the 1980s to 1990s. After ten years of development, urban population in China increased from 30% in 1995 to 46.6% in 2009.[74] Now, the urbanization rate of less developed countries in the world ranges from 30% to 70%. In the acceleration period, these countries will hold all of the newly-born population.

Table 1 Urban/Rural Population Trend in Developed and Underdeveloped Countries (1950~2050) Population Unit: 100 million

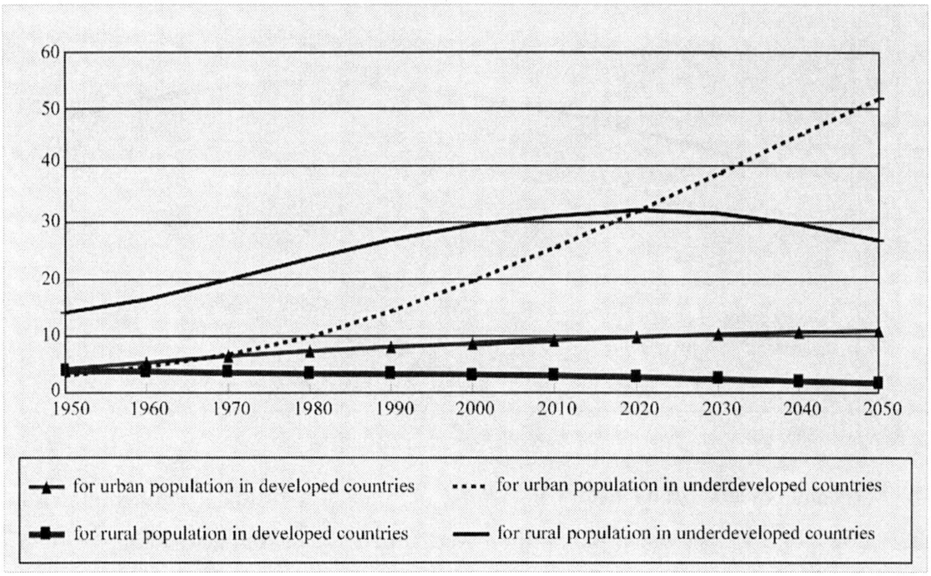

Before 2008, most of the world's population lived in rural areas. According to the United Nations Population Fund report, 2008 was marked as the "watershed" for urbanization process. For the first time in history, the urban population exceeded the rural population.[75]

On March 25, 2010, Population Division of the United Nations Economic and Social Affairs Department published the "World Urbanization Prospects Revision 2009," which reported that the world's urban population had been closer to 3.5 billion and a rural population of over 3.4 billion. The report predicted that with the growth of urbanization in developing countries, by 2050, the world's urban population will rise to 6.4 billion and rural population will be reduced to 2.9 billion. Asia's urban population will rise to 1.8

74 http://news.xinhuanet.com/fortune/2010-10/09/c_12639879_3.htm

75 United Nations Population Fund: "Linking Population, Poverty and Development". http://www.unfpa.org/pds/urbanization.htm

billion by 2050; African urban population will increase to 900 million; Latin America and the Caribbean urban population will increase by 200 million.[76]

Table 2 Global Urban/Rural Population Trend (1950~2050)
Population Unit: 100 million

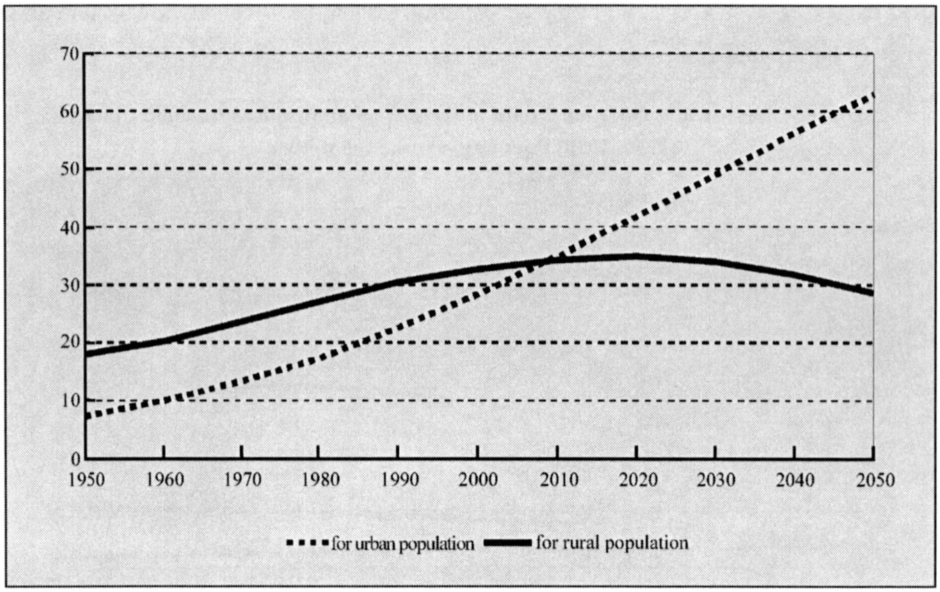

Resources: http://esa.un.org/unpd/wup/index.htm

According to the China National Bureau of Statistics, China's population reached 1.335 billion in 2009, of which 622 million were urban population, accounting for 46.6%; 713 million were rural population, accounting for 53.4% of the total.[77] The United Nations' World Urbanization Prospects Revision 2009 pointed out: "In the process of urbanization in the world, China's urbanization rate is particularly prominent. In 1980, there were 51 cities with a population of over 500,000. From then on until 2010, China has increased 186 cities with such capacity of population. A quarter of the cities with a population of 500,000 and over are located in China." One of McKinsey & Company's report entitled "Preparing for China's One Billion Urban Population" said that according to the current development trend of China's urbanization, China's urban population will reach 926 million by 2025, and exceed one billion in 2030. By 2025, China will have had 221 major cities with one million people and 23 cities with more than five million people.

76 UN Department of Economic and Social Affairs, Population Division: "World Urbanization Prospects: the 2009 Revision." http://esa.un.org/unpd/wup/index.htm

77 http://www.stats.gov.cn/tjgb/ndtjgb/qgndtjgb/t20100225_402622945.htm

Beijing, Shanghai, Guangzhou, Shenzhen, Tianjin, Wuhan, Chongqing and Chengdu will become the mega-cities with populations of over 10 million.[78]

II. Types of Urban Risks and Calamities

International Federation of Red Cross and Red Crescent reported in *World Disasters Report: Focus on Urban Risk* that: "The vulnerability of the cites in the face of danger can be seen everywhere: earthquakes make hospitals, schools and houses collapse; volcanic eruptions trap the city airport in chaos; floods turned clean city streets into a river full of debris; drug trades deteriorate the city down to a battlefield; infectious diseases spread rapidly with the help of overcrowded slums."[79]

2.1 Risk of Urban Disasters

The city has held a large urban population, infrastructure and economic activities. Thus, in the past decade, large-scale disasters tended to make the city suffer the most. For example, the victims of China's Wenchuan earthquake were mainly found in Beichuan County, Shifang City, Dujiangyan City, Mianzhu City; loss in Haiti in early 2010 concentrated in the Port City; 2,200 people were killed in the Yushu earthquake in April 2010, and 95% were living in the county; personnel and property loss in Zhouqu debris flow were also concentrated in cities.

Regarding the risk assessment of urban crisis, there were no widely accepted standards or methods. Some government and non-governmental organizations are bound to collect data and establish such standards in the future. The commercial insurance company Munich Re Group has a database for a certain amount of unexpected disasters and an index system according to the business need of the company, becoming a high-recognized risk-rating agency. It has designed risk indexes for the top 50 most populous (with two million populations) and the most economically prosperous (accounting for a certain percentage of GDP) cities. The index made a thorough analysis of 30 cities in middle-income countries and 20 cities in high-income countries, and for the first time took a variety of disasters into account, including earthquakes, storm surges, floods, volcanoes, forest fires, frost, etc. The index is composed of three variable parts: the amount of disaster, vulnerability and property value of the loss. Vulnerability

---

78 http://news.xinhuanet.com/fortune/2008-03/25/content_7854598.htm

79 http://www.ifrc.org/Docs/pubs/disasters/wdr2010/WDR2010-English-2.pdf

involves most of the city building structures and materials, urban disaster prevention facilities, plans, laws and regulations. Vulnerability of property value estimates are based on average family property and industry and commerce services GDP. The most important factor in this assessment is in property prices and the frequency and intensity of the risks. By means of this indicator, Tokyo ranks with the highest risk, followed by San Francisco. 17 out of the top 20 are high-income countries.

Table 3 Top 20 Cities with High Risk Index

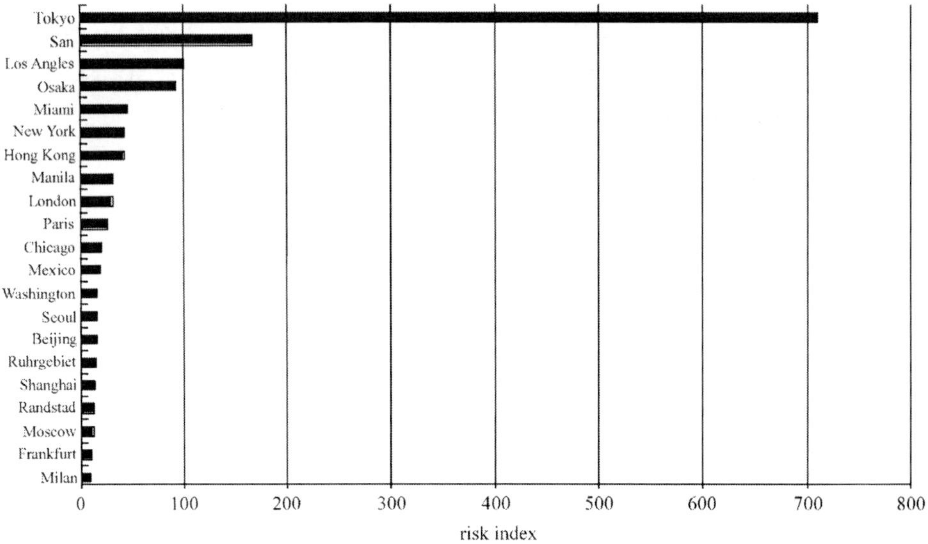

Resources: Munich Reinsurance Company (2004)[80]

From the proportions property value took up in GDP caused by disasters, the loss in developing countries is undoubtedly much higher than that of developed countries. For example, the M 6.7 Northridge earthquake occurred in California, USA in 1994 caused economic losses accounting for one percent of local GDP; 1972 M 6.2 earthquakes in Nicaragua caused economic losses of 40% of national GDP; M 7.5 earthquake in El Salvador in 1986 caused economic losses accounting for 30% of national GDP. Munich Reinsurance Company's data show that from 1985 to 1999, economic losses caused by natural disasters in the world's richest countries accounted for 2% of national GDP, while in the poorest countries, the proportion reached 13%.[81]

---

80 Munich Re: "Statistics and Natural Hazard Risk for 50 Selected Megacities," January 2005. http://www.munichre.com/app_pages/www/@res/pdf/media_relations/press_releases/legacy/pm_2005_01_11_01_en.pdf

81 Tiffany M. Luck, "World's most Earthquake-vulnerable Cities", May 23, 2008. http://www.financialpost.com/careers/World+most+earthquake+vulnerable+cities/532784/story.html

2.2 Types of Urban Disasters

International Disaster Epidemiology Research Center for Disaster (CRED)[82] consider that the disaster is an unforeseen, sudden event that can cause huge casualties and property loss, and beyond the capacity of handling. The organization divided disaster into two categories—natural disaster and technological disaster. Natural disasters have been divided into five categories, covering 12 types of disaster in 32 branches. Five major categories include biological hazards, geological hazards, climatic disasters (such as drought), and hydrological and meteorological disasters (such as storm surges). Technological disasters are divided into three categories: industrial accidents (chemical spills, facilities collapse, explosion, fire, harmful gas leaks, and toxic and radiation hazards), traffic accidents, and other accidents (fire, explosion, building collapse etc.).

In 2007, CRED, together with Munich Re, Swiss Reinsurance Company, the Asian Disaster Reduction Center and the UNDP, co-founded a new disaster statistical method with the aim of consolidating global and regional disasters statistical standards. The new method proposed that natural disasters having access to international disaster database are required by the following conditions: a death toll of over 10; at least 100 people affected by disasters; declaring an emergency; calling for international assistance.

Similar to general disasters, urban disasters can be divided into one of the following categories: geological disasters (earthquakes, mudslides, landslides, etc.), climate/weather disasters (floods and droughts, storms, extreme temperatures, marine disasters, etc.), accidents (various forms of pollution, food safety, industrial accidents, fires, etc.), urban violence (riots, large-scale crime, kidnapping, etc.), and disease disaster (plague, etc.). A number of hazards are unique to the city, such as accidents and urban violence. Some others are common to both the urban and rural, however more harmful to urban environment.

2.2.1 Geometry Disasters in Cities

Though the magnitude of the Sichuan earthquake (in 2008) was lower than the

82 An institution developed from Department of Public Health of the Catholic University of Leuven located in Brussels, Belgium in 1973. The organization initiated from researches on epidemic began, and gradually developed into a professional academic research institution researching on natural disasters, including health problem. In 1980, it developed into a research center of the World Health Organization. In 1988 it established a global database of natural disasters, which was employed by the International Red Cross Red Crescent Societies for annual report data. For more information, please visit: www.cred.be

earthquake that occured in East Kunlun (in 2001), Sichuan saw more damage than East Kunlun. It is because the former affected multiple towns, while the latter happened in rural areas. From history, it can be seen that earthquake has brought the most damage to cities among all natural disasters: one-fourth of Lisbon's population (70,000 people) died in an earthquake in 1755; one-fifth of Tangshan's population died in 1976's earthquake, together with 97% of the buildings in the city were destroyed.

The threat of earthquakes to cities includes collapse of building, fires, and tsunamis; and there is a co-relation between the quality of the building structure and the risk of its collapse. The common reasons to the damage brought by the two earthquakes in Port-au-prince and Yushu are: 1) High magnitude and shallow focal of the quake; 2) inadequate seismic ability of buildings; and 3) high population density in the affected area. In the 20th century, the total casualties from earthquakes are about 1.2 million, in which half of the casualties (about 0.6 million) were from China. Since 1949, the death brought from natural disasters is about 550,000, in which 370,000 of them comes from earthquakes.

Threat of debris flow to a city comes from improper siting or the destruction of natural habitat. As the size of a city expands, areas that were not suitable to build are used as foundations of buildings and structures, some of the buildings even located in areas with high risk of floods and mudslides.

Another threat that cities are facing is the subsidence of land. It creates cracks in the ground, as well as the internal of buildings. It also causes the dislocation of the ground level point and the loss of the ground safe altitude. The natural source of subsidence is the motion on the crust and soil compaction. On the contrary, artificial subsidence is usually caused by over exploitation of underground water and minerals. Although the subsidence progress is slow, the consequences will occur suddenly and are irreversible. Most land subsidence happens on unstable settlements, and it may bring damage to the structure of buildings and their foundations. It can be seen that urban developments in settlement areas require more investments in infrastructures. While settlement area usually occurs in coastal areas, sea water will drain back when the land subsidence reaches sea-level, causing salinisation of soil and underground water.

Settlement can be seen in about 50 countries and regions, such as in Mexico City, Mexico, the Sam Joaquin Valley in Long Beach, California and Houston, Texas in the United States, Tokyo and Osaka in Japan, Bangkok in Thailand, Cheshire in the United Kingdom, Waunakee in New Zealand, Latrobe Valley in Australia, etc. Though settlements are usually counted within meters, some areas have been settled for over 10 meters. Settlements can be found in 45 out of 50 states in the United States and account for 4.4

million square kilometers. In Japan, 12% of habitable area (equivalent to 1128 square kilometers) is below sea-level.

2.2.2 Climate

With expansion of its size and population, cities are now experiencing its own climates. Climate disaster refers to the damage brought on by or affected by typhoon, storms, cold weather, winds (including dust storms), temperature, drought, lightning, hail, frost, and fog. As proprieties and people are densely populated inside cities, the amount of damages brought by climate disasters is usually large and other disasters such as fire, contaminations and diseases will usually followed.

The most common disaster occurring in cities brought on by climate is flooding. As tall buildings are densely located in cities, the heat-island circulation effect will facilitate the heat convention upon the ground, and cause weather storms. Pollutants in cities facilitate water condensation in the air and create a comparatively more rainfall than rural areas. Since the drainage system in cities can reach its capacity, higher rainfall may interrupt supply chains in cities and may eventually create chaos.

As a combination of global warming, urbanization, reduction of green lands, the rising temperature in cities is becoming a more prominent phenomenon. This brings threats to the population and creates pressure to utility supplies of cities. An example of this was the heat wave in North India in June 2010. The region suffered from the longest heat wave since the 19th century. New Delhi reached 45 degrees celsius and the lowest temperature remained at 32 degrees. On the same day, the temperature in the north-east region maintained 40 degrees and caused more than 200 deaths, with heat-stroke patients filling the hospitals. In mid-June, heat waves reached various Middle East countries such as Kuwait, Iraq, Israel and Saudi-Arabia, in which the temperature in Kuwait recorded 54 degrees, marking an historical record. At the end of June, temperature in the mid region of Russia achieved a record 37 degree celsius. In Europe, a heat wave also created high temperatures: Italy reached over 40 degrees, France and Spain obtained over 35 degrees, and Germany was recorded at 40 degrees. In America, both Washington and New York have reached over 38 degrees.

Also, dust and smog are not easy to spread and diffuse out of the cities as the wind speed near ground is slow and air current is stable. With urban developments, the amount of dust and pollutants from vehicle exhaust accumulates, in addition with low wind speed and high relative humidity, dust and smoke will surround the city and form photochemical smog. Hence, transportation system is affected, and insulation of the power field is weakened, satellite communications become unstable and it will eventually affect the health of the population. In the beginning of August 2010, smog created by a fire in sub-urban area covered Moscow, Russia for days. Households shut their windows, pedestrians wore masks and the underground transportation system was filled with smog.

On the other hand, some coastal cities may suffer from soil erosions. A report from the OECD has exposed the weaknesses of 100 metropolitans when they face huge rainfalls that occur once every 100 years. The study indicates that among the 20 most densely populated regions that will suffer from rainfalls, half of them are located in Asia. It is estimated that in 2070, 17 out of the 20 cities come from low-income nations (in which China accounts for four and Bangladesh accounts for two).

2.2.3 Accidents

Accident defines as natural or artificial incident that happened against the wills of humans and causes damage to life, damage to the economy, or pollution. It includes fire hazards, explosions, traffic incidents, leakage of hazardous substances, electric and water hazards, etc.

Fire hazard was a specific hazard only occurring in cities. Like London in 1666, Chicago in 1871, and Thessaloniki in 1917, fires can level entire cities. Nowadays, it is unlikely to see large scale fires in wealthy cities, as low-income areas and unregulated constructions are the major sources of fire hazard. A study from South Africa has analyzed 18,504 fires occurred in Cape Town between 1995 and 2004. This indicates that although fire hazards are in small scales nowadays, the damage and loss brought by fire are tremendous. Most fires occurred in slums, usually caused by lighting candles and lights or burning charcoals and woods. Such as the fire in Hout Bay near Cape Town in February 2004, 1,200 houses were destroyed and more than 5,000 people became homeless.

Accidents in the industrial sector bring losses to enterprises and the surrounding residents. On July 16, 2010, an oil pipeline exploded near Dalian in China, and a massive amount of crude oil leaked into the sea and created an ecological disaster, and hundreds of millions of yuan were spent in compensation. On July 28, 2010, workers broke a propane pipe in Nanjing, which caused leakage and explosions. Thirteen people were dead and more than 120 were injured. On October 4, 2010, a leakage from an aluminium waste tank in a factory located in Veszprem, Hungary caused nine deaths and more than 150 injuries, and more than 100 million square meters of toxic wastes (including heavy metals such as lead) flooded to three nearby villages and rivers.

2.2.4 Urban Violence

Violence in urban areas is becoming a phenomenon in developing countries with high speed urbanization. In Latin America and areas south to the Sahara, the height of violence can be compared to civil wars. A report from UN-HABITAT shows violence in cities had increased by 30% between 1980 and 2000. While 60% of cities' population has suffered from crimes, the most suffered are those with one billion populations living in slums. Many African countries are developing a phenomenon that the riches are living in power supplied residential areas, but the poor remain in slums without laws and enforcements available.

Urban violence is usually categorized into economic, social, and political violence.

Economic violence includes activities aimed to gain financial profits such as drug trafficking, kidnapping and robberies. These activities are co-related with the uneven income distributions in society, including poverty. Countries in Latin America tried to "sweep" the underground economy by removing and isolating the poor from the urban areas. However, this caused an increase in violent crimes, as the poor rely on illegal trades and services in underground economies.

Social violence refers to the brutality between individuals, families, and communities for power, and this usually occurs among gangs while they attack each other. In Nairobi, 60% of the population lives in 5% of residential areas, and residences habitat with various gangs and smuggle weapons from Somali and Uganda to fight for power. Another source of social violence is unorganized criminal offences. In China, a killer slaughtered six primary schools and kindergartens between March and May 2010 and caused 18 deaths and more than 70 injuries.

Political violence is defined as the violent act to obtain or maintain political power, such as the anti-government campaign in Bangkok in March 2010, which caused at least 54 deaths and the campaign against fiscal cuts in Athens on May 6th, where thousands of protesters threw stones and tried to occupy the congress. Police threw tear gas to the protesters and the riot caused three deaths.

2.2.5 Diseases

Disease is one of the most common urban disasters, as illness can spread quickly in densely populated areas. Between 1420 and 1485, seven plagues occurred in London, in which the Black Death claimed 1/3 of the population around the London area and almost halted the of population movement from village to city. Until now, the threats of disease to city population still exist, such as the SARS virus in 2003, and the H1N1 spread in 2009, which infected 160,000 people around the globe in only three months.

Low-income residences in metropolis in low-income nations are suffering from a lack of fundamental sewage and waste treatment facilities, and the rate of diarrhea within the infant population is extremely high: 38% in Pakistan, 23.9% in Cameroon, and 32.3% in Congo. Within 10 million deaths in children under five years of age, two million are caused by diarrhea. Compared between industrialized and undeveloped nations from 1990 to 2006, the deaths of children under five years old has decreased from 10,000 to 6,000 in the former, while the latter has only dropped from 103,000 to 79,000. In countries like Benin and Congo, rate of malnutrition of children in cities is higher than that in villages (46% compared to 16%). The "Lancet" magazine estimated that about half of the population in Asia, Africa, and Latin America are suffering from one or more diseases related to contaminated water supply or insect spread diseases. Nevertheless, cities are at a high risk of infectious diseases even in developed nations. In the case of tuberculosis, the amount of cases in New York is four times higher than the national average, even higher than the rate in the UK or China.

III. Urban Calamities Management

Although Western countries began to attach importance to disaster and crisis management since the 1970s, the international community did not start a system of special study until 1989, when an international disaster reduction activity was launched. In the United States Academy of Sciences, after Dr. Frank Pres' initiative proposal, the United Nations passed a resolution to determine the decade from 1990 to 2000 as the United Nations' "International Disaster Reduction Decade." In May 1994, the conference on disaster reduction held in Yokohama, Japan made a mid-term retrospect on last decade's disaster reduction course. Yokohama Strategy and Plan of Action confirmed and strengthened the "International Disaster Reduction Decade," which aimed at reducing the loss and turbulence caused by technological and environmental disasters while reducing natural disaster. In June 1994, the second session of the General Assembly for human habitation, held in Istanbul, also stressed the two agendas of "an appropriate shelter for all" and "urban housing acceptable for urban residents."

On October 13, 2010, the International Day for Natural Disaster Reduction, the UN launched 2010~2011 World Disaster Reduction Campaign, emphasizing the theme of "Let the city resist disasters: My city is ready." "City" refers to a broad sense of the urban areas, including "local government responsibility" at different levels of district, provincial, city, town or village. The campaign aims for at least one commitment out of "ten elements of urban disaster-resistance 2011" from 100 mayors and mobilizing hundreds of local government make as much of a commitment as possible to the safety of the public schools and hospitals.[83]

2.3.1 Vulnerability Gap: The Phenomenon and Causes

International Red Cross and Red Crescent Societies raised the concept of the vulnerability gap in *Global Disasters Report: Focus on Urban Risk* in 2010, pointing out that poor urban residents in developing countries are the main victims of sudden disasters. Compared with middle-income groups and residents in developed countries, they are facing with a huge risk. For example, even though tropical storm frequency and intensity suffered by Japan is higher than in the Philippines, and the population in Japan is denser than in the Philippines, the number of the Philippines killed in tropical storm is 17 times that of Japan.[84]

Table 4 Loss of Four Income-level Countries in Tropical Storm

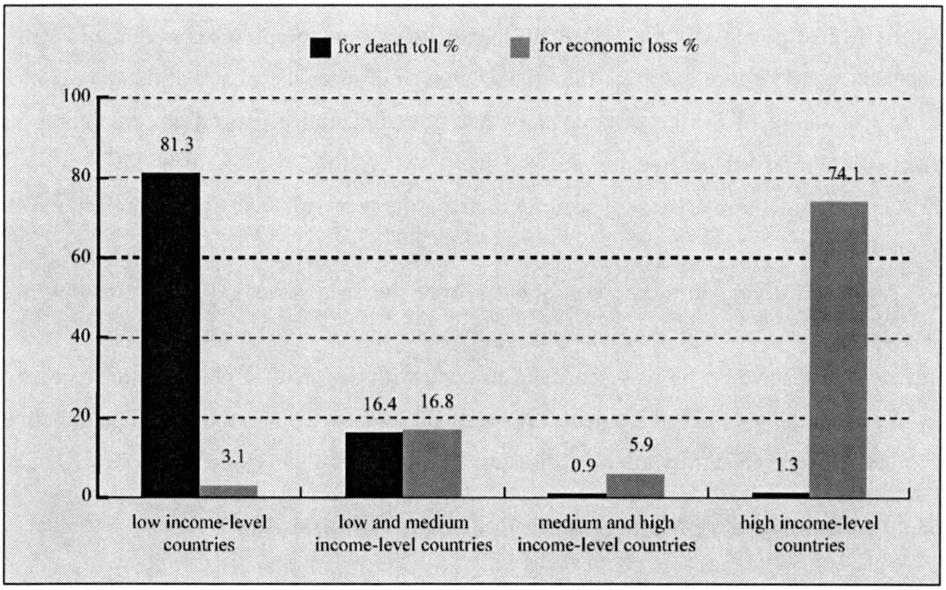

Illustration: high-income countries most frequently attacked by tropical storms are Japan, South Korea and U.S.

In January 2010, a magnitude 7.3 earthquake in Haiti killed more than 22 million people. In February, a magnitude 8.8 earthquake in Chile released energy equivalent to 500

83 http://www.un.org/zh/events/disasterreductionday/campaign.shtml

84 http://www.ifrc.org/Docs/pubs/disasters/wdr2010/WDR2010-English-2.pdf

times of the earthquake in Haiti, caused the country's total economic losses of 10% of GDP, and only the death of 800 people. On September 4, New Zealand's South Island earthquake, with a magnitude of 7.1 caused damages to over 100,000 houses, but only a few people were injured. Six months later, on February 22, 2011, New Zealand's South Island broke a 5km-depth M 6.3 earthquake, killing more than 200 people.

The biggest difference between Haiti and Chile and New Zealand is poverty and backwardness of Haiti. Chile is a moderately developed country. In 2009, Chile's per capita GDP was 14,341 USD, ranking the second in Latin America, just after Argentina with 14,561 USD. New Zealand is well known as a high-income western country with per capita GDP of more than 30,000 USD. In contrast, Haiti is the world's poorest countries, with per capita GDP of less than 560 USD. 54% of Haitians' daily cost of living is less than one USD, and 78% of the population lives on less than two USD a day.[85] Thus, urban poverty population is the main cause of the vulnerability gap.

Theoretically speaking, when the urban population accounted for half of the world's population, and the urban slum population accounted for 1/3 of the urban population, the significance of global urbanization is no longer just a demographic, economic and social urbanization, and also means that the urbanization of disaster risk. Lack of this recognition led to the failure of the governmental or non-governmental organizations in finding an effective solution to the housing for the poor, water, food, health, fire, flood control, anti-violence and other aspects of security, making the poor still living in the highest risk of urban disaster.

As people living in slums are isolated from the rest of society, they miss normal educational services and employment opportunities, with no means to earn money. Therefore they have no funds or capacity to cope with disasters or post-disaster recovery. On one hand, the poor urban residents are easily hit by disasters; on the other hand, there is no other self-help capability after the disaster. This is where their vulnerability lies.

2.3.2 Urban Disaster Management: Reducing Vulnerability

As the city's populations affected by disasters are mainly poor residents, the poor urban resident should become the starting point of reducing hazards. The effectiveness of state and city leaders' policies lies in the reduction of impact on the poor in the disasters. These efforts include the development of rational land-utilization plans, housing standards, roads, electricity, drinking water, sanitation, public transport, communication, education,

85 http://siteresources.worldbank.org/INTHAITI/Resources/Haiti.AAG.pdf

health services and waste disposal facilities provided to this vulnerable group.

With the development of cities, the number of poor continues increasing and size of the slums continues to grow. As congregates of the poor are usually outside the city's plan of residential lands, there is no existing infrastructure and poor conditions in security and sanitary environment. Many countries have simply expelled the slums, which was later proved to be ineffective and contrary to human rights and the spirit of the law. Therefore, granting the legal status and administrative divisions should be the first step to governance and improvement. Now, most developing countries have changed or are changing the approach of forcing the removal and deportation of the slums. Since the 1990s, the Brazilian government attached the governance on slums with tackling poverty and social problems, and took legal actions on some eligible slum lands.

The improvement on the living conditions of poor urban residents should play a leading role in reducing disasters, which includes bettering the housing conditions of slum dwellers, construction on the water supply and drainage system, and garbage collection and disposal system, in order to transform the slum into real urban communities with basic urban infrastructure facilities and living facilities. General Comments on adequate housing right, adopted in 1991 by the United Nations, stated that adequate housing standards was by no means simply confined to a living area with a wall and a roof, instead it must at least include the following elements: security of tenure, livable housing opportunities, a variety of services within easy reach, providing the appropriate infrastructure and cultural environment.[86] So far, some countries have achieved success in the slum-upgrading program. For example, in Rio de Janeiro's slums, the vast majority of households has access to running water and is connected to the national grid. According to UN-HABITAT report, due to the efforts of China and India, Slum Target in Millennium Development Goals has been achieved, with 227 million people's living conditions having been successfully improved.[87]

At the same time, non-governmental organizations also played an important role in the governance of slums. For example, Slum Dwellers International – (SDI) is an international alliance made up of 28 urban organizations from Asia, Africa and Latin America. The main purpose of SDI is to help poor communities design affordable housing, collect information and data for local government's decision-making in the disaster relief process, and provide assistance to slum dwellers' land requirement to the government, offer slum infrastructure

86 http://www.un.org/chinese/hr/issue/housing.htm

87 http://www.ifrc.org/Docs/pubs/disasters/wdr2010/WDR2010-English-2.pdf

planning and consulting to the government and contractors.

October 4, 2010 was marked as the United Nations' World Habitat Day. World Habitat Day in 2010 shared the same slogan with the Shanghai World Expo: "Better City, Better Life." According to UN Secretary-General Ban Ki-moon, Habitat Day appealed to governments, civil societies and private sectors worldwide working together to help the nearly 1 billion people living in urban slums to a better city life. Although the Millennium Mitigation Plan to improve slum conditions has been achieved, improvement in slum population cannot keep up with the population growth. In the era of deteriorating climate change, crustal movements frequent-bursting, and increasing environmental pollution, it is a serious and urgent task to reducing and preventing disasters by means of serving the poor.

Chapter 10

The Situation and Tendencies of International Migration: 2009~2010

Li Xiaoli

Under the background of continuously enlarging globalization, new changes and development bring about international population movement. The general trend of economic migration has been influenced by the economic crisis and its growth rate is constrained. The lifting threshold for migration, wars and other political factors make refugees' number remain high and there are numerous difficulties facing the issue of the placement of refugees. As the significant phenomenon of economic and numerous social developments, international immigrants' moving direction and dynamic development directly reflect the global economic status, political and social development of the countries and it is an important reflection of the international political order and environment.

1. General Situation of International Migration

Since the 21st century, the number of international immigrants has been increasing significantly. Based on the statistics offered by the International Migration Organization, after 10 years' accumulation, the number of the international immigrants of the entire world increased from 150 million in the year 2000 to 214 million, accounting for 3.1% of the entire world population. There is one immigrant among every 33 persons with 49% of feminine.[88]

At present, Europe is the main gathering place for most immigrants, with a number of about 70 million. With the economic and political integration of the European Union, the interior part of Europe formed the largest free migration area. In 2009, among the increased population of Europe, more than 60% of them were immigrants.

88 Reference to International Migration Web: http://www.iom.int/jahia/Jahia/about-migration/facts-and-figures/lang/en.

Asia is the most populous area in the world and its immigrants' number is second only to Europe. The fast economic development of Asia promotes the regional immigrant growth. Especially influenced by China and India, which are two populous immigrant nations, Asia is not only the largest labor-output area, but also the area with the most interior immigrants.

The number of immigrants in America has surpassed 570 million, with significant characteristics of the "south to north" phenomenon. More and more people from Latin America and the Caribbean area move to the United States, Canada and the developed countries in Europe, migrating in a "south to north" pattern. The United States and Canada continuously keep their dominant position as receivers of permanent immigrants, which made the North American area the chief gathering place for immigrants in the world. The international immigrants of the U.S reached 42.813 million in 2010, ranking first in the world.

African immigrants move mainly among African countries. Most of them are influenced by temporary work distributed in South Africa and Maghreb of West Africa.

Australia is the region with the highest proportion of immigrant population. Australia and New Zealand are two traditional immigrant destinations. Influenced by the climate, the first group of ecologic international immigrants was from island states around Australia.

A significant number of illegal immigrants exist among the global immigrants and they impact nearly all countries and regions. Estimated by the International Migrants Organization, illegal immigrants account for 10% to 15% of the total immigrants around the world.

1.1 Reversal of the Continuously Increasing Trend of International Immigrants

Since the 1990s, the global economy continuously remained prosperous and the international political structure has greatly changed. The average increasing rate of global immigrants was 2% year by year and the number of the moving population was generally rising.

The global economic expression resulted in the financial crisis of the United States, which directly impacted international immigration. Pressured by the economic crisis, the regional industrial structure had to implement adjustments that promoted the redistribution of the international labor and the number of immigrants started to decline.

Developed countries generally fell into depression and the unemployment rate grew fast. In the interior part of Economic Cooperation Organization, with 34 market economic countries as states parties since 2002, the legally permanent immigrants kept increasing significantly over five years, with an average increase rate of 11%. In 2008, because of several countries suffering from the decrease in international immigrants, the number of legal immigrants started to decline. Compared with the previous year (2007), the quantity of immigrants fell by 6%.[89]

In 2009, the scope and influence of the economic crisis enlarged and the immigration request around the world continued shrinking. It constrained many people's will to migrate and the number of most of the countries decreased. The international migration population continued a declining trend.

In developed European and American countries and the traditional immigration destination countries, the number of immigrants showed varying degrees of decline. This was the first time over the past three decades that the number of immigrants to the United States decreased. In the first quarter of 2009, the number of applications from the largest traditional group of immigrants for the United States, immigrants from Mexico was 137,000, reduced by 13% from the amount in 2008. The amount of immigrants to Australia reached the peak at the end of 2008 and then declined significantly. By June of 2010, 232,700 people obtained permanent and long term residential permits to Australia within one year, which was 31% less than the same period of the previous year and made the lowest record for the decline of the immigrants over the past 16 years. In 2010, the immigrant applications to New Zealand declined to the lowest level in history. The applications for the first six months were an average 30% less than 2009. In UK, Poland, Czech Republic and other new members of the European Union, the number of registered labor sharply declined by 55% from 2008.

Asia, South Korea, Thailand and Malaysia, which attracted many immigrants, successively took measures to constrain immigrants and stopped or suspended the issuing of work permits to foreign labors.

The harsh environment for immigrants made some of them return back to their mother countries. The International Migration Organization received reports from many countries on the back stream of immigrants, including Spain, Czech, United Arab Emirates and the United States. The Indonesian government estimated that over 60,000 people that once immigrated to Malaysia, Korea and other countries would return. Thousands of Indian labors would have to return from Dubai and the number of immigrants back from the

---

89 Referring to the website of OECD (Organization of Economic Cooperation and Development): http://www.oecd.org/dataoecd/12/53/45612345.pdf.

United States to Mexico reached 139,000, which were even more than the immigration applications for the United States.

1.2 The Number of Forced Immigrants Remains High

Around the world, a considerable number of international immigrants were forced to leave their hometown, among which there were refugees as result from war, conflicts and persecutions of race and religion, displaced persons and international ecological migrants suffering from natural disaster. For these forced migrants often concerned with complicated political factors and national interests, their resettlement was very difficult and the number of forced migrants accumulated to a considerable number. In 2009, the number of forced migrants under the management and concern of the United Nations reached 43 million, increasing 3.1% from 2008.[90]

1.2.1 Refugees

In 2009, the population under United Nations High Commissioner for Refugees and Relief and Works Agency in Near East—slight changes appeared in these two major organizations: because of the raise of the natural birth rate, the Palestine refugees in the Relief and Works Agency increased; and the amount of refugees under the management of the United Nations High Commissioner for Refugees declined. The total number of refugees of these two organizations was 15.2 million, equaling to the amount of 2008. Among the migrants of the world, the proportion of refugees declined from 8.8% in 2000 to 7.6% in2010.[91]

In 2009, there were 377,000 migrants that, because of political reasons, moved into 44 industrialized countries looking for asylum, and the number equaled to that of 2008. 45% of these persons looking for asylum came from Asia and the Middle East, 29% was from Africa and the persons of Europe and America accounted respectively for 15.5% and 9%.

Of the 44 industrialized countries, asylum seekers increased in 19 of them and declined in 25 of them. The quantity of applications for asylum from Southern Europe averagely declined 33% and applications from Italy and Turkey reduced by more than 40%. Among these asylum seekers, there were 26,800 people from Afghanistan, increasing 45% than in 2008; 24,000 from Iraq and 22,600 from Somalia. 134,900 of them applied for

---

90 United Nations High Commissioner for Refugees: 2009: Global Trends, Division of Programme Support and Management 15 June 2010 UNHCR

91 Reference to: http://www.iom.int/jahia/Jahia/about-migration/facts-and-figures/lang/en.

asylum from the United States, which had been continuously the first for four years. People seeking asylum from the United States, France, Canada, UK and Germany accounted for 48% of the total asylum seekers in 2009.

1.2.2 Displaced People

The term "displaced people" mainly referred to migrants forced to leave their hometown because of domestic conflicts, natural disasters or other reasons. Because of their similar situation with refugees who lived under conflicts and unstable environments, lacking of efficient national and governmental management, the United Nations and the international community listed them into the population concerned by international refugee organizations from the viewpoint of humanitarian relief.

In accordance with the statistics from Internal Displacement Monitoring Center (IDMC) of Norway, the number of displaced persons concerned by this center has been increasing in recent years. By the end of 2009, in 54 nations around the world, displaced people who were forced to leave their hometowns because of armed conflicts, violence and human rights violations reached 27.1 million, increasing by 28.6% than the previous year.[92]

By 2009, it was estimated that in 21 African countries there were 11.6 million internal displaced people, accounting for more than 40% of the total in the world and, which equaled to the amount in 2008. Sudan was the country with the most serious internal migration phenomenon, with about 4.9 million displaced persons; the second was Democratic Republic of Congo with 1.9 million and then Somalia with 1.5 million.

The regions where displaced population increased were mainly located in America, South and Southwest Asia. Because of domestic armed conflicts and anti-terrorism war, displaced people of South and Southwest Asia reached 4.3 million, increasing by 23%. The displaced persons in American regions increased and the total number was estimated at about 5 million, increasing by 11%. The violence brought about by Colombian drug groups forced many people to move to neighboring countries, which had an impact on the whole region. Colombia, together with Sudan, became the countries with the most serious problem of displaced persons with the longest duration.

There were about 2.4 million internal displaced persons in Europe and Middle Asia, among which Turkey ranked the first whose displaced population accounted for 40% of

---

92 Internal Displacement Monitoring Centre Norwegian Refugee Council: Internal Displacement Global Overview of Trends and Developments in 2009, May 2010, p.8.

the total of its region. In the Middle East, there were about 3.8 million internal displaced people. The displaced population in these two regions reduced respectively by 3% and 4%.

1.3 Reduction of Illegal Immigrants

The global economic crisis greatly influenced and shocked the living environment of the international immigrants. In most of the developed or comparatively rich countries, immigrants generally worked in construction, hotel, restaurant, manufacturing and other industries with strong periodicity characteristics. Compared with local people, the unemployed rate for immigrants rose faster and the existence for illegal migrants would be more difficult. Developed European and American countries, based on their own national interest and political needs, took strict limitation regulations over immigrants, which, to some extent, constrained illegal migrants.

The Spanish economy was seriously influenced by the financial crisis. Requests for labors from all of its industries declined and the existence for illegal migrants was very difficult. Illegal migrants to Spain reduced significantly. In accordance with the data from the Spanish Ministry of the Interior, in the first seven months of 2009, the number of the illegal migrants arriving in Spain was 4,475, reducing by 40% than the same period of the previous year. Compared with 2006 when the illegal migrants reached its peak, it reduced by 73%. In the regions where there was once a serious problem with illegal migration, the rare phenomenon even appeared that there had been no illegal migration records for several months.

Throughout the world, the United States was always an attractive place for illegal migrants. Since the financial crisis, this kind of charm faded. Recorded by the United States Migration Policy Research Institute, since the economy fell into depression, the net inflow of illegal immigrants was dwindling. Its illegal immigrants were estimated to keep at about 12 million. The border between the United States and Mexico was the direct channel for illegal migrants getting into the United States. The depressed economy and enhanced construction of border buffer zone made illegal migration even more difficult. In accordance with the statistics recorded by the United States Department of Homeland Security, in the fiscal year of 2009, 463,000 illegal migrants were captured. Compared with the same period of 2008, it was 131,000 less, reducing by 17%.

It is noteworthy that there is no obvious back stream to the mother countries of illegal migrants although the quantity was considerable. Most of the illegal migrants have strong viability and although the situation is difficult, few of them initially chose to go back to their hometown. The reduction of illegal migration and the enhanced expel and repatriate measures of the governments were the major reasons for the decline of illegal immigrants.

2. Dynamics of the International Migration Environment

The wide spread global economic depression not only impacted the economic development of countries, but also significantly changed the international migration environment. Based on the consideration of employment, security, social welfare and other factors, the people of some countries changed their attitude toward immigrants. From the viewpoints of politics and challenges against the rising unemployment rate, the governments shifted to rightist on migration issues and unpleasant political environment for immigrants appeared.

2.1 Recovery of Xenophobia of European and American Countries

In most of the countries with a higher number of immigrants, the economic crisis caused great pressure for employment and in the daily lives of its citizens. The xenophobia on immigrants, which was once hidden behind the economic boom, gained ground again. One investigation of U.S.-German Marshall Fund in November of 2009 showed that among the interviewees from U.K., France, Italy, Germany, Poland and Holland, a minimum 80% of them hoped to enhance the border control. In addition, a minimum 73% of them hoped to take more strict measures to punish the employment of illegal immigrants.

Immigrants in Germany are approaching 9% of its total population. How to treat seven million immigrants has become a widely discussed public topic. In April of 2010, in one sample investigation organized by the Friedrich Ebert Fund that had a political party background, many German people thought immigrants occupied their social welfare and work opportunities and the traditional culture of Germany influenced by foreign culture reached a "dangerous level." Their attitude towards immigrants started to turn to narrow nationalism. One third of the German people hoped immigrants would return to their home country. On the political stage of Germany, some of the politicians, to gaining votes, simply met the xenophobia motion and only seemed to publicly express their oppositions against immigrants became.

Inside Italy there was also serious xenophobia motion. In February of 2010, to the request of the Italian House of Representatives, the Federation of Italian Region took one investigation among 2,000 young people ranging from 18 to 29 years old. The report revealed the following: 39.6% of the investigated youth hold a defined open attitude towards foreign people; 46% of them had xenophobia motion and 20% of them hoped foreign people would leave Italy as soon as possible; the youth who had zero-tolerance towards immigrants accounted for 15.3% of them; and 10.7% of them accepted only Italian and European people. Doxa, the Italian Statistics and Public Opinion Research Institute, conducted a survey called "Italian Barometer of International Solidarity." The result showed the following: 83% of the invested people thought that the existing immigrants in Italy was beyond the capacity for accepting new comers; two thirds of Italian people worried about the immigration issues, believing that immigrants impacted their security and guarantee of the life; 25% of them held hostile attitude towards immigrants.

In traditional immigration countries like the United States, the voice of rejection on migrants raised. Since more and more children of illegal immigrants obtained American nationality by birth and enlarge the migrant family, more American natives started to worry that immigrants would encroach on their rights and benefits and asked to modify the principle of citizenship access by birth in the Constitution. On April 23, 2010, Governor of Arizona, Jan Brewer, signed Act SB1070, allowing local police to check and arrest suspected illegal migrants without a search warrant, clarifying that employment of illegal migrants would be punished, regarding people who could not offer valid documents for their legal identification as criminals. This act aroused fury and strong protests among Mexican groups in the United States.

The Canadian government was faced with political pressure from the public to reduce the number of immigrants allowed into the country. The Centre for Immigration Policy Reform, a non-government policy research institute established by senior officers of the pre-government, consultants and other political or commercial celebrities, proposed one suggestion: while groups of Canadians were losing their jobs, it was unreasonable to bring migrants to meet the request of labors. It asked to reduce 250,000 migration quota each year and 175,000 temporary foreign labors to avoid the xenophobia against immigrants like Europe.

In Australia, the inflow of migrants from India, China and other countries, coupled with the low birth rate of the local people, aggravated the anxiety on "proportion of races." Macroplan, one Australian population consulting company, made an estimation based on its own statistics: based on the increasing trend of immigrants, the foreign immigrants and the aging of the native people would accelerate the structural change of citizens in Australia. Within 15 years, native population born in Australia would be a minority group.

2.2 Further Tightening Migrants Policies in Developed Countries

Under the general international environment of economic depression, the request for foreign labors of western developed countries was greatly impacted. Some of the major developed countries adjusted the policies to match the need of internal economic development and successively took measures to enhance the choices of immigrants.

2.2.1 Lifting Threshold to Constrain Migrant Inflow

In recent years, several developed countries that once brought in a large amount of immigrants lifted the threshold and took tightening policies on migration. They also enhanced the control over technical and family immigration.

In 2008, U.K. implemented a "points based system" on non-EU immigrants, but it was not efficient to limit immigrants. In 2009, the immigrants of U.K. reached 196,000, with 33,000 more people than 2008. The study abroad industry left a considerable number of foreign people staying in U.K; more than 362,000 foreigners obtained a student visa, increasing by 35% than the previous year. After David Cameron from the Conservative Party of U.K. became prime minster, he criticized the pre Labor Party government's loose control over immigration and promised to promote new migration policies, Based on several adjustments on technology and policy, Australia adjusted its policies for technical immigrants, announced to replace positions that were in shortage and the key positions named in the technical positions list and limited immigrants for low-tech jobs. The new governments of the Labor Party of Australia abandoned the migration-based economic increase strategy taken by each pre-government since the Second World War; it insisted that "the request of immigration development must match with the economic environment" and promised to realize the sustainable development of Australia by reducing immigrants.

Canadian immigration management organizations gradually tightened the vocation scope for technical immigrants in recent years and upgraded the demand on language, both of which reduced the number of applications for technical immigration.

Holland Immigration Bureau started to upgrade their conditions of approval for immigrants in 2008 and closed the disguised channel for immigration by several limit regulations, including the raise of the age of married immigrants.

The party in power of Denmark tried to limit the lowest salary for immigrants as much as half of the lowest salary for native people and control immigration via economic levers.

2.2.2 Using Economic Levers to Enhance Immigrants Selection

Viewing the changes of immigrant-welcoming countries in recent years, one common feature can be seen that all policies lean to investment immigrants and these countries use economic levers to limit the amount of incoming immigrants. After the financial crisis in the United States, the debt crisis and the break of the capital chain spread all over the world. Importing investment immigrants cannot only bring capital, but also control the quantity of immigrants, which is regarded as a good measure by all nations.

In order to attract investment immigrants, in recent years, the United States swiftly enlarged the investment district and the special economic zones approved by the U.S Migrants Department are developing explosively and the amount of foreign investment immigrants increased significantly. In accordance with the statistics from the State Council of the U.S., in the fiscal year of 2009, immigrants who got permanent residence by investment increased from 1,443 to 4,218 people, three times more than the previous fiscal year.

U.K., Germany, France and other European countries that once kept a conservative attitude towards immigration issues started to pay more attention to investment immigrants. In order to publish the temporary limitation quota for non-EU immigrants, the U.K. started to amend *Boarder, Immigrants and Civil Law of U.K.*, attempting to tighten the inflow of high-tech immigrants by creating a new law and keeping a comparatively stable policy for investment immigrants. The U.K. hoped to create new jobs by investment immigrants to promote the economic development.

Some immigration countries in the Pacific-Asia area also successively adjusted their policies on investment immigrants. Following the lower demand on investment immigrants in July of 2009, New Zealand governments implemented new investment immigration policies in November of the same year. The applicant can gain permanent citizenship as long as they invest 500,000 New Zealand dollars (NZD) to start an undertaking or business. In April of 2010, Australia implemented the new investment immigration policies to upgrade the demand for the investment proportion of the applicants. Singapore has become a popular state for immigration in recent years and its threshold has been lifted by the demand. Based on the new standard issued by Singapore Economic Development Department, since January 1, 2011, the capital for investment immigrants increased from 1.5 million NZD to 2.5 million and, by economic standard, blocked many immigrants.

Under the environment of the global economic depression, Canadian governments carried out targeted adjustment on immigration policies. In 2008, the vocation for technical immigrants was reduced to 38 categories. In 2010, it further tightened the quota for technical immigrants and accelerated the approval for investment immigrants for different countries. In order to attract investment immigrants from China, the quota for China was greatly increased.

2.2.3 Making Use of Opportunities and Enhancing the Fight Against Illegal Immigrants

The global economic depression, in the political aspect, created a helpful environment for some countries to fight against illegal immigration. Many of the governments, excusing for obeying the public opinion, took measures to expel and instituted heavy penalties to enhance the fight against illegal immigration.

The Obama government, to gain support on extensive immigration reform laws from the Democratic Party and establishing authority for the government on immigration law enforcement institute, fought strongly against illegal immigration, strictly checked enterprises suspended to hire illegal labors and criminal groups for illegal immigration and accelerated to expel the illegal immigrants who violated laws. In the fiscal year of 2009, the amount of the expelled illegal immigrants created the highest record in history: 392,000 illegal immigrants had been expelled in one year with only 195,000 of them violating laws.

The enhanced fight against illegal immigration in neighboring countries pressured Canada, who started to create new immigration laws and wanted to legislatively fight against traffic in persons through the Canadian immigration institute, to deal with the increasing trend of illegal immigration and guarantee the security of the nation and a completed and fair immigration institution.

EU brought about a joint activity named Hermes against illegal immigration while Spain was in turn of rotating presidency. The activity has been carried out since October 2010 and the member states of EU began large-scale check around bus stations, subway, railway stations and other places where the illegal immigrants frequently visited. It examined the capability for the EU states for cooperation and coordination on fighting against illegal immigration. Nations like Belgium and Spain that once implemented loose immigration policies or generously treated illegal immigrants changed their attitude from "tolerantly accept" into "strictly fight." Governments announced that they would no longer implement amnesty policies towards illegal immigrants and carry out new immigration laws that brought forward harsh demands on family-reunion immigration, prolonged the custody for illegal immigrants and accelerated the expel. In order to increase work opportunities for natives, U.K. enhanced the remediation on illegal labor market while strengthening immigration policies at the same time and double-punished the employers hiring illegal immigrants.

2.3 Gap between Employment Rates Enlarged and Immigrants Fell into Survival Dilemma

Economic depression effected industries like construction, manufacturing and catering services and immigrants all over the world felt the shock of unemployment. The gap between employment rates for natives and immigrants enlarged in many countries.

In accordance with the statistics Organization of Economic Cooperation and Development, the unemployment rate of young immigrants in its member states was high. In 2009, the unemployment rate of young immigrants was 15% in America, 20% in Canada and the average rate for 15 of the EU states reached 24%.[93]

In Canada, even technical immigrants with technological skills could hardly find jobs matching within their majors. Disguised discriminations towards immigrants further expanded unemployment rate. In Toronto, Canada in 2009, the unemployment of new immigrants who migrated 5 to 10 previous reached 15.1% and the unemployment rate for the young immigrants from 15 to 24 years old was 30.2%.

The problem for unemployment among immigrants in Finland was serious. In May 2010, the unemployment rate for Finland people was approximately 8.7%, but the unemployment rate for the 143,000 immigrants was much higher than natives. Among immigrants as refugees from Afghanistan, Iraq and Somalia, the unemployment rate for Afghanistan and Iraqi immigrants was as high as 61%; 55% of the Somalia immigrants lost their jobs; 28% of the Russian immigrants, the biggest group of immigrants, were unemployed.

Immigrants in Austria were more vulnerable to becoming victims of the depressed labor market. Reports from State Statistic Bureau of Austria showed in 2009 that the unemployment rate for foreigners living in Austria was 10.2%, while the unemployment rate for the natives was only 4.1%.

---

93 Reference to the website of the Organization of Economic Cooperation and Development: http://www.oecd.org/dataoecd/12/53/45612345.pdf.

In Portugal, the number for unemployed foreign immigrants continuously increased. By February of 2010, the registered unemployed foreign immigrants in the Portuguese Job Center reached 42,400, increasing by 34% compared with the same period of the previous year.

Invisible discrimination also brought difficulties for the immigrants' work. In May of 2009, University of British Columbia (UBC) in Canada created a survey in Toronto that assembled most of the races and nationalities in the country and the result showed that under the similar resumes, 16% of the British natives could get the opportunity for interviews, but for the new immigrants of other nationalities, only 5% of them could gain the opportunities.

In Ireland, one research appointed by the Equality Authority demonstrated that job seekers with foreign names were 50% less likely to get interview opportunities than the seekers with typical Irish names. Accounting and retail industries discriminated African, Asian and German immigrants. Employers in Finland frequently refused immigrants using the excuse that they lacked Finnish language skill.

3. Conflicts and Problems Relevant to International Migration

International immigrants had strong national, regional, cultural and social features and their mergence with natives was a long-term and complicated procedure. The huge inflow of immigrants made up for a deficiency of labor in an economic aspect and promoted the social development. However, it brought structural change of the population and impacted the recognition of national concept, legality of the national states and the social stability. The global economic crisis worsened the structural contradictions between the dependence on immigrants in some industries of developed countries and the unemployment of the native people. Influenced by political power, the "conflicts" between immigrants and mainstream society increased.

3.1 French Immigrants Conflicts Aroused Political Turmoil

In the international immigrant events of 2010, the most reactive was when France expelled Roma people from East Europe. The immigrants in France reached 6,685,000 and they had become one of the major social problems for the French public. Under the shock of the economic crisis, the attitudes towards immigrants started to change. The governments drew support from the public and implemented hard immigration control measures. They expelled 29,000 illegal immigrants in 2009. In July of 2010, in Saint-Aignan, a city in Northwest France, military policemen shot a Roma because he was suspected of stealing and resisted arrest, which caused a riot of Roma people to break out in the street. The Sarkozy government continuously insisted on the harsh policies and carried out a series of punishment measures, including the cancellation of half of the residential places of Roma within 2010 and expelling illegal Roma immigrants who violated laws once. More than 1000 Roma people were successively expelled to Romania and Bulgaria and more than 100 illegal camps were removed.

The concentrative actions of French governments on expelling Roma incurred great criticism. The United Nations Committee on Elimination of Racial Discrimination, European Union Committee, the Pope and hundreds of non-government organizations in France expressed their concern and attitude by statement, correspondences and marches. Faced with international and internal political pressures, French governments kept its harsh attitude. On October 12, 2010, French parliament adopted an act to deprive the French nationality from criminals who were born-immigrants by 294:239 votes.

The basic motivation of France to deport Roma people was to rectify social order and maintain social security and stability through strict immigration policies and management. However, this reflected the reality from a profile that immigrants in France were marginalized from the social and economic life. Since 2005, multiple riots under immigration background outbreak in France and formed "immigration conflicts" in many aspects of region, culture and national recognition and immigration was more and more regarded as the root of social problems. Although it did not strongly disturb the stability or social security, the subtle contradiction was tantamount to the "time bomb" for the government and society. The deport action of France in the free migration area in the European Union challenged the political principle of EU and tarnished France's political image.

3.2 Failure of Immigrants Mergence in Germany Highlighted Social Problems

The immigrants' mergence into mainstream society was a sensitive problem that was difficult to completely solve. Under the shock of the global economic crisis, the difference of recognitions and disharmony problems between immigrants and mainstream society broke out in some of the developed countries. Whether immigrants could merge into mainstream society became the focus of the public.

The threshold for Germany to accept international immigrants was comparatively low. In the early times when the economy was prosperous, it attracted a lot of immigrants. After years of accumulation, the population of immigrants or with immigration background increased fast. In accordance with the statistics from the German Federal Statistical Office, in 2009, the population of Germany reduced by 235,000 from 2008. Its total population was 81.9 million, with 15.7 million of them having immigration background, approximately accounting for one fifth of the total population.[94] For a long time, Germany did not realize the difficulties that would emerge the merge of immigrants and major policies. However, since then, many social problems have accumulated. 10% to 15% of immigrants refused to merge into German society.[95] One invisible gap of recognition lay between immigrants and mainstream society. Generally, the educational and the professional training levels of civilians with immigrant background were low: 14% of immigrants had no graduation certificate of compulsory education and 44% of them had no vocational qualification. Gerd Hoff, educator at Freie Universitaet Berlin (Free University of Berlin), believed that the lack of immigrants' education "increased the instability of the society and threatened the democracy."

Turkish immigrants formed the largest group of immigrants in Germany and, for a long time, offered sufficient low-cost labors for the social and economic development of Germany. Because of the influence of Islamic background, German society could not completely accept Turkish immigrants. In August of 2010, director of Deutsche Bundesbank, Thilo Sarrazin, published his book that criticized Muslim immigrants. It incurred huge reflection in Germany and was criticized by all walks of life, including the Prime Minister of Germany. The domestic opinion poll showed that only 35% of the public did not agree with Sarrazin, but only 30% supported him. 56% of the public ascribed the problem that the immigrants could not merge into the society to immigrants themselves, while only 11% of the people ascribed the problem to the government.[96] This event, to some extent, aggravated the antagonism of Muslim immigrants, weakened the fragile relationship between each other and seriously weakened the national recognition. Prime Minister Merkel admitted that the efforts attempting to build up a multi-cultural society fell into complete failure and it increased the crisis of political turmoil to the state and the society.

3.3 Difficulty for Asian Immigrants in the U.S. to Merge into Mainstream Society

The United States is a traditional nation of immigrants, which was once called the "melting pot" for nations because it was a medley of the world nationalities and it took

94 Reference to: http://www.destatis.de/jetspeed/portal/cms/Sites/destatis/Internet/DE/Navigation/Statistiken/Bevoelkerung/MigrationIntegration/MigrationIntegration.psml.

95 Reference to: http://www.oushinet.com/179-2605-93655.xhtml.

96 Reference to: http://www.zaobao.com/special/feature/pages/feature100905.shtml.

diversified approaches for immigrants to merge into mainstream society. However, to realize the complete mergence with immigrants was also a challenge. In America's 200-year history, immigrants from Asia accumulated to 11.5 million. Divided by geography, the concept of "Asian –American" was formed in the United States. In recent years, Asian immigrants diligently worked to gain the "Model of Minority." Favorability of the American natives towards them increased and the considerable number of Asian ministers in the Obama government upgraded the social awareness for Asian immigrants.

However, while American society admitted the contributions of Asian immigrants, the implicit discrimination against Asian immigrants and a political trust gap still existed.

Divided by vocations, polarization lay in the Asian population: in New York, where Asian immigrants were concentrated, their employment rate was higher than the average level, but 41% of them were living with low-income areas and 20% of them lived below the poverty line. In the economic crisis, the average unemployed time for Asian immigrants in California was as long as 27 weeks, while the average unemployed time for Latino and white men respectively accounted for 40% and 42% of that of the Asians.

A psychological gap lay between Asian immigrants and the mainstream society of the United States. In January of 2010, appointed by Committee of 100 (an Asian immigrant organization), Harris Interactive, Inc. carried out an opinion survey to see if the public of the United States doubted the loyalty of Asian immigrants. The survey revealed that 45% of the public believed that Asians would be more loyal to their mother countries. Nearly 60% of the Asian immigrants thought they had suffered from racial discrimination. Like the Arabic immigrants, Asian immigrants were vulnerable to suffer from doubt of spying. At least 28% of the interviewees expressed that they seldom or never got in touch with Asian immigrants. The political influence of Asians was lower than other national groups. 82% of Asian immigrants thought that the Asian power in Washington was weak.

Cultural differences between East and West have impacted the merge of Asian immigrants into American society. The report of Victor, professor at Duke University, published by Manhattan Institute of New York illustrated that, because Asians ranked last in the index of cultural merge, the integrated index of immigrants from mainland China ranked the seventh in ten of the major immigrant groups for their merger into the American society and it was a middle-down reaches in the global ranking.

4. Tendency and Outlook of International Migration

International population migration resulted in political, economical, social and other complex reasons. The major reason for initiative migration was economic and social reasons, while forced moves mainly resulted from political and natural reasons. The decline of immigrants all throughout the world was the direct result of the global economic crisis. With the world economic recovery and international political situation, the trend is probably changed. It is projected that in 2011, the quantity of global immigrants will catch up with the development trend of the global economic recovery.

In developed countries with a considerable number of international immigrants, neither the employment structure of the population, birth rate and other social basic environment change from the root, nor the rigid social needs for supplementation of labors. The economic crisis temporarily constrained labor immigrants. With the world economy walked up from the valley, the immigrant population in developed countries is expected to regain the increasing trend.

For the national interest, developed countries insisted on a high threshold of immigration policy and it plays an important role for guiding the flow of international immigrants in the future. On the one hand, high threshold promotes the degrees of freedom for immigrants to lean towards high-quality talents with skills and investment immigrants. It will be easier for top and successful talents to get into developed countries, which exacerbates the international human resources competition. On the other hand, the high threshold artificially limits the flow of common labors, creating a social environment for illegal migration and increased crisis of enlargement of illegal immigrants and the difficulties for managing immigrants. With the tightening of immigration policies for each nation, polarization of international immigrants worsened. Developed countries made use of their economic benefits, social welfare and environmental resources to attract talents all over the world, which made developing countries stay in an unfavorable place for human resources competition. Although this can constrain the immigration to some extent, it probably increases the crisis for illegal immigration in a wider scope.

After years of high-speed economic development, India, China and other emerging economic equities accumulate social wealth fast and their contributions to the world economy continuously grow. The contribution rate for China reached 50% in 2009.[97] The pursuit for wealth, living standard and self-realization of their people cultivate the dream for people from different levels to go outside their mother countries. The enlargement of economic activity and the demand for expansion of capital promote the trend for immigration to other countries. Under the background of decline of international

97 http://www.gov.cn/ldhd/2010-10/10/content_1718832.htm.

immigration, the immigrants from India and China do not reduce, but increase. In the following period, if there is no big political turmoil, economic activity and immigrants from emerging powers will remain at a high level.

It is noteworthy that the global economic crisis and political situation changes probably incur regional turmoil. In the Middle East, Africa and other places with rich resources, the infiltration of national interests and political powers have evolved into conflicts for resources control. Many refugees who are forced to move and the displaced population are forming a new wave of refugees.

Having experienced the economic crisis, the international community had a deep understanding of the role of immigrants in economic development and politics. More and more countries realized that international migration is not an isolated social phenomenon. That regions and states enhance the migrant management and develop comprehensive cooperation are efficient approaches for standardizing and resolving migration chaos. The international community should establish a more efficient international cooperative frame for migration issues to avoid the political crisis brought on by international migration.

Chapter 11

The European Sovereign Debt Crisis and International Relations

Lang Ping[98]

As the Chinese proverb goes, "adversity sees the true feelings." The European sovereign debt crisis, which began in Greece, has undergone many significant fluctuations from its beginning, spreading, escalating to alleviating. The adversity came, but where "the true feelings could be seen." From the perspective of international relations, the European sovereign debt crisis was a period where different interest groups clashed with each other. For the European Union, this crisis was the most serious challenge they had experienced since the establishment of the Euro zone. The future of European integration was ultimately determined by the political willingness and resolution of eurozone countries. Economically, the European sovereign debt crisis seems to have eased. However, it might pose profound influences to the political arena. Whether they could overcome this crisis would not only have a huge impact on the social and political stability of European countries, but, more importantly, determine the future of Europe, or even change the future global political economy pattern.

I. The Origins and Dynamics of the European Sovereign Debt Crisis

The European sovereign debt crisis could source its origin back to Greece. In November 2009, the newly-elected Greek government revealed that the previous government had hidden the government's true deficits and debt data. In December, the world's three main credit ratings agencies, Fitch, Standard & Poor's and Moody's, downgraded Greece's sovereign credit ranking, and Greece became the Euro zone country

98 Lang Ping, Assistant Researcher of the Institute of World Economics & Politics, Chinese Academy of Social Sciences; Research fields: International Political Economy and Contemporary Global Issues.

with the lowest credit ranking. As a result, the Two-Year Greek bond yields surged to 3.39%, the highest level since March of 2009.[99] However, the financial experts widely believed that the debt crisis of Greece, a small country with the GDP accounting for only 2.6% of the European total, would not have great general influence.

However, the situation deteriorated sharply in 2010. In early 2010, the Greek government stated its 2009 fiscal deficit had reached 13.6% of GDP and the debt-to-GDP ratio of 2009 approached 115.1% and was likely to surpass 120% by the end of 2010. Investors began to abandon Greek sovereign bonds for fear of Greek default. On April 23, 2010, the Greek government formally requested the EU and IMF for bailout package. Four days later, Standard & Poor's downgraded the Greek sovereign debt to "BB+"- and marked the outbreak of the Greek debt crisis.

With another peak in Greek bond yields, other four PIIGS[100] members (Portugal, Italy, Ireland and Spain) were stricken by a credit crisis as well, but to different degrees. Reality showed that investors' concern over the sovereign debt of one country in the eurozone could be transferred to another eurozone country. On January 11, 2010, Moody's warned that Portugal, like Greece, was on the path to an economic "slow death." The sovereign debt credit ranking of Portugal would be downgraded, if Portugal failed to take effective measures to control deficits.[101] On April 27, 2010, Standard & Poor's downgraded the Portuguese sovereign debt credit ranking, which caused general concern among the investors that Portugal would soon become the next Greece.

This grim reality pushed the EU decision makers to fear that the crisis might spread to other larger economies, especially Spain. On February 4, 2010, the Ministry of Economy and Finance of Spain revealed that the 2010 Spanish public budget deficits were likely to take up 9.8% of GDP, causing Spain to become the third highest country in terms of fiscal deficit, after Greece and Ireland.[102] In April 2010, Standard & Poor's downgraded Spain's sovereign debt ranking. Different from small countries such as Greece and Portugal, Spain is the fourth largest economy in the eurozone, with a population of 46 million. The European Union was bound to be heavily hit if Spain was submerged into the crisis.

---

99 The higher the bond yields, the higher interests that the country had to pay for the debt, indicating the poorer the credit of the country issuing bonds.

100 Five European countries, Portugal, Italy, Ireland, Greece and Spain, were coined as "PIIGS".

101 "*Moody's: Portuguese and Greek Economy Might Lead to a Slow Death*", Sina Finance, January 13th, 2010, http://finance.sina.com.cn/stock/usstock/economics/20100113/23247239690.shtml

102 "*Spanish 2010 Fiscal Deficits Accounting for 9.8% of GDP and Likely to be the Next Greece*", reports on Chinanews, February 4th, 2010.

The financial situation in Ireland became disturbing as well. In 2009, the fiscal deficit in Ireland accounted for 12% of the GDP, right after Greece, among the eurozone countries. Before the eruption of Greek debt crisis, Ireland had already suffered from debt crisis. Thanks to a series of measures taken by the government, Ireland seemed to overcome a very difficult time. However, their reality was far from optimistic. In August 2010, Standard & Poor's downgraded Irish credit ranking.

Besides, even countries like Belgium that were commonly believed to have a sound economic development were predicted to have high budget deficits in the next three years. Within a short period, the GDP of countries in the shadow of debt crisis took up 37% of the total eurozone GDP. Greece was no longer the leading role of the crisis and the Greek debt crisis evolved into a European debt crisis.

Germany and France, two leading economies in the eurozone, were also under the pressure of the crisis. On August 24, 2010, according to the statistics provided by Federal Statistical Office of Germany, in the first half of 2010, the German budget deficit increased to 42.8 billion euros, several times higher than before, accounting for 3.5% of GDP and largely overstepping the 3% red line stipulated in the *Stability and Growth Pact*. France, always insisting that there were no downgrading risks for French sovereign credit, suddenly lost its confidence. On May 30, 2010, Francois Baroin, French Budget Minister, indicated that the French government ought to conduct practical economic reform and cut fiscal budget, to maintain its top sovereign credit ranking. With the prevailing fear that Europe may experience a severe financial crisis, the euro sharply depreciated against the USD and the European stock market crashed. The whole eurozone was faced with the biggest challenge in the 11-year history of the euro.

On May 10, 2010, EU and IMF finally came up with a 750 billion-euro plan to aid Greece, to avoid furthering the spread of the crisis. With the bailout plan and plenty of aid measures offered by the European Central Bank, European Union and governments in the eurozone, the European sovereign debt crisis seemed to be eased in July 2010. First of all, Greece successfully sold out its short-term bonds and the market confidence appeared to be restored. Secondly, good news followed the European bank industry. On July 23, 2010, the Committee of European Banking Supervisors released the results of the 2010 EU banking industry stress test, which showed that the basic condition of most banks in the eurozone were better than expected and the risks were under control. However, as the saying goes, "Rome was not built in a day." The alleviation of the crisis did not mean the end of the crisis. The 2011 European debt crisis continued to worsen and the situation in countries like Portugal were still worsening.

The outbreak of the European sovereign debt crisis was mainly attributed to the continually worsening fiscal deficits of the five PIIGS countries, represented by Greece. In terms of external factors, it was the eruption of the U.S. subprime mortgage crisis that stimulated European countries to adopt fiscal rescue plan, boosting economy through an expansion of public spending, which led to a rapid growth in government fiscal deficits. Domestically, the Greek government's dishonesty, masking debt with Goldman Sachs, and the speculation behavior of international investors were also the contributing factors to this crisis. But, again, "Rome was not built in a day." The large amount of fiscal deficits and government debt of these countries were accumulated over a long period of time. Historically speaking, in the past decade, owing to the decreasing core competence and lack of resilience of labor markets, these countries had constantly undergone expanding deficits. Besides, the government had to borrow foreign funds in order to maintain the traditional high welfare system. For 11 years from 1999 to 2009, the annual fiscal deficit to GDP ratio of Greece had exceeded 3%, while that of Italy and Portugal surpassed 3% for six and five years respectively. After joining the EU and eurozone, it was quite easy for these countries to obtain large amounts of transfer payments, and a huge sum of foreign investment kept flowing in. With sufficient funds, the Greek government had no stimulus to cut fiscal deficits. When the crisis happened, since the eurozone countries only had a unified currency policy, but no fiscal union, countries trapped in crisis could not respond or adjust by means of fiscal transfer.[103] Of course, the reality that the EU failed to offer prompt aid also caused the deterioration of the crisis.

II. Roles of Different Players in the European Sovereign Debt Crisis

Greece was the first victim of the European debt crisis and put on a "euro defending war" with other eurozone countries. To defend the euro, the European Union member states were faced with two major dilemmas: the first was the confrontation centered on the Greek debt crisis, and whether or not to rescue Greece and how. Secondly, these countries released their own fiscal austerity plan to protect their own economy from the crisis. The former was aimed to help Greece and other eurozone countries to overcome the emergency, while the latter was supposed to push the economic development of eurozone countries

103 YU Yongding, "*European Sovereign Debt Crisis and the Future of Euro*", *Finance Comment* No. 2010.054, World Economy Research Center of the Institute of World Economics & Politics, Chinese Academy of Social Sciences, August 12th, 2010.

forward. The difficult interactions, on the one hand, revealed the political resolution and willingness of European countries to further enhance European integration. On the other hand, it also uncovered the complicated interest conflicts and confrontations among the European countries. Besides, the United States, on the other side of the Pacific Ocean, was involved as well. Both the American governmental officials, scholars and media were actively engaged in the defending war.

1. Greece in Debt Crisis

During the five months from the eruption of the crisis to Greece's formal request for aid from the EU and IMF, the Greek government had experienced an attitude transition. The confident Greek government was finally forced to ask for help. Greece, deeply trapped in credit crisis, had to admit that the confidence of global investors could not be restored with Greece's own efforts.

At the beginning of the crisis, the Greek government was confident in solving domestic fiscal problems independently. At that time, concerns from the European organizations were not welcomed. George Papaconstantinou, Greek Minister of Finance, stated that they would not ask for or expect financial help from the European Central Bank, and the Greek government did not want foreign groups to engage in its fiscal consolidation.[104] Some market experts worried that, without foreign aid, it was almost impossible for Greece to pay back their high debt with its own strength.

To further rebuild confidence in the market, Greek Prime Minister, George Papandreou, announced a series of more practical measures in his televised speech on the evening of February 2, 2010. A slight change in Greece's attitude towards foreign aid could be identified. On February 11, 2010, Greek Prime Minister, George Papandreou, suggested that Greece was looking forward to the political support from European Union and did not want IMF to be involved. He also expressed his wishes that Germany and France should further bail out countries like Italy and Spain, which were influenced by the debt crisis as well.[105] On February 22, 2010, Louka Katseli, Greek Minister of Economy, said, during an interview, that financial aid was not necessary, but the European Union shall settle certain mechanism arrangement to stifle market speculation.[106]

---

104 "*More European Countries Might Be Trapped in Credit Crisis After Greece*", *Economic Information Daily*, January 12th, 2010.

105 "*European Union Reached Consensus on Rescuing Greece, Detailed Plan to Release Next Tuesday*", *First Financial Daily*, February 12th, 2010.

106 SHANG Jun, "European Commission Denied Plans of Raising Funds to Rescue Greece", reports from Brussels on Xinhua website, February 22nd, 2010.

Though Greece was always reluctant to request assistance, with the escalating financial market turmoil, the Greek government realized that it was almost impossible to satisfy financing demands by means of the market. On April 23, 2010, Greece formally asked the European Union and IMF for help. The shift of the Greek government's attitude, from insisting "independently" solving the problem in the very beginning to requesting loans in the condition of accepting strict fiscal austerity plan despite severe domestic opposition later, was a helpless choice the Greek government had to make. Greek Prime Minister, George Papandreou and his party, the Socialist PASOK Party, took initiatives to bear the responsibility of tackling the crisis, and therefore, gained more support than the main opposing party, New Democracy, both in the Parliament and the public. It was generally acknowledged in the outside world that the current poor Greek fiscal condition was caused by the previous ruling party, the New Democracy, and the crisis arose because the New Democracy party had masked the problem to a degree beyond control. Due to the reasons listed, the fiscal austerity plan raised by the Papandreou administration was approved by the Parliament without much difficulty. To some extent, it was a comfort to the current Greek government.

2. To Rescue or Not

With the sharp deterioration of the European debt crisis, European Union countries felt the urgent need to strengthen budget rules. First of all, they reached consensus over strictly controlling budget deficits. On May 12, 2010, the European Commission unveiled plans to effectively exercise its power to supervise a national budge by a strengthening oversight over the entire European economy. [107] The EU Economic and Monetary Affairs Commissioner Olli Rehn noted the reason why the European Union initiated this policy was to guarantee that the spending plan of the EU member states could be consistent with the European goal. On May 21, 2010, the meeting of European Union finance ministers arrived at a very clear and wide consensus of backing financial and non-financial sanctions over the debt-laden euro zone countries.[108] The following question was whether or not to rescue these countries.

As the crisis continued to deepen and spread, the European Union changed attitudes towards whether it was necessary to continually aid Greece. At the beginning of the crisis, out of the concern for the Greek economic condition, the European Commission and

---

107 Reports from Brussels by the Associated Press (AP), May 13th, 2010.

108 Reports from Brussels by Agence France Presse (AFP), May 21st, 2010.

European Central Bank once again expressed their strong positions and took initiatives to act. But at that time, Greece believed that they did not need foreign aid. European Central Bank chief economist Juergen Stark also urged Greece to solve its fiscal deficits with its own efforts.[109] However, the European Union could not continue to remain calm with the worsening crisis. On April 11, 2010, leaders of European countries agreed to rescue Greece after fierce discussion, but differed greatly on which institution to take a leading role in the rescue.

In March 2010, after Greece formally requested for aid, European countries were split into two campuses concerning whether or not to rescue. The opponents, represented by Germany, believed that, according to the no-bail-out clause in the context of the Economic and Monetary Union (EMU), the eurozone members were not allowed to provide aid to other members that were trapped in rising public debt. There was no exception with Greece. The majority of European countries, represented by France, however, supported the plan to bail out Greece. In terms of how to rescue, Germany proposed the leading role of IMF, while countries like France wanted to keep IMF away, out of the concern that the independence of the euro was likely to be undermined and the United States might take the advantage to interfere with European affairs. As Germany refused to rescue, France compromised and proposed a combination of bilateral loans from individual eurozone countries and IMF aid. On March 25, 2010, eurozone countries agreed to create a financial safety net with IMF. The agreement was the result of the second mutual compromises made by the two campuses. Germany accepted that most funds shall be raised from the eurozone economies rather than IMF and recognized the aid mechanism of eurozone countries, in the condition that IMF must be involved and eurozone countries ought to consent to a stricter budget system.

In the process of making the EU bailout plan to rescue Greece, Germany seemed to be the only obstacle in eurozone to rescue Greece. The German position was greatly influenced by domestic public opinion. Germany had a reputation for frugality and Germans had long been dissatisfied with the extravagant lifestyle of Greece. Therefore, they were unwilling to rescue a country like Greece that was reluctant to reform. German public opinion and the overwhelming majority of electorates frequently opposed to Germany rescuing countries. However, as an EU official said, rescuing Greece was not only saving Greece.[110] When the Greek crisis

109 "*More European Countries Might Be Trapped in Credit Crisis After Greece*", *Economic Information Daily*, January 12th, 2010.

110 Reports by Bloomberg, March 19th, 2010.

deteriorated to a degree that posed a serious threat to the whole European political and economic order, the German government had no choice but to stand by other European countries to defend European interests together.

3. Germany and the United States during the Crisis

Among the European countries, Germany was one that never suffered from the debt crisis. However, as the economic powerhouse of the European Union, Germany became one of the key countries in the crisis. As one of the most strong and influential EU countries, Germany's position was shaping the future of the European Union. It was commonly believed that Germany was the beneficiary and contributor to the European debt crisis. Germany was criticized by its European allies, the American president, bankers and the media. German people, who insisted on austerity, consuming domestic products, and strictly controlling debt, seemed to become the targets of public opinion overnight.

When the Greek crisis continued, there first appeared criticism against German economic policies within the European Union, which mainly came from France. The French Minister of Finance, Christine Lagarde, argued that Germany pushed the eurozone into deflation. She criticized the German government for overstressing export and strengthening competence through reducing labor cost, which, she suggested, were not sustainable. Besides, some other European high officials accused the export-oriented economy of Germany of achieving its own economic growth at the cost of other eurozone countries. One EU report indicated that the European Union should impose pressure, forcing Germany to weaken its competition edge and raise salaries in order to increase domestic needs.[111]

On the other side of the Pacific Ocean, the United States also pointed a finger at the German fiscal austerity policy. American President Barack Obama maintained that this policy might postpone the global economic recovery. Timothy F. Geithner, U.S. Secretary of the Treasury, said during an interview that Europe should not only cut expenditures, but also emphasize economic growth. Countries like Germany that had a huge trade surplus were supposed to boost domestic demands. To be more specific, the deterioration of the European debt crisis could be released if Germany was willing to spend more money and vigorously stimulate domestic demands. The response of German chancellor Angela Merkel was that it was the right thing for Germany to

111 "*Low salaries at the Cost of Other Countries*", *TAZ (German Newspaper)*, March 16, 2010.

increase export, and that the annual 10 billion-euro budget deficit cut by Germany would not hinder the global economy.[112]

A Commentary in the *Los Angeles Times* believed that Greece's crisis was Germany's gain. The reason why Chancellor Angela Merkel delayed the bail-out plan was not simply pandering to her fragile coalition and frustrated electorate. Instead, the Greek crisis turned into a huge opportunity for Germany. The country had dramatically boosted its exports thanks to the weak euro, which could help German to recover from the 2009 economic recession as soon as possible.[113] Some other comments in the *Washington Post* even argued that Germany's frugality bemoaned for inhibiting eurozone growth. Currently, the real problem for the eurozone was Germany's years of anemic domestic demand. It had to be changed to ensure the euro's survival. "The Germans were catering a big party that was going on in the euro area, selling the food and offering the credit to the party guests," said Thomas Mayer, chief economist for Deutsche Bank. "But the guests got drunk and ate too much, and now Germany is stuck with the bill. What this tells us is that the euro model must be adjusted. Yes, the Greeks are going to have to make reforms, but the Germans are going to have to change, too."[114]

America's criticism also echoed the leading role of Germany. At present, whether the EU countries facing the danger of bankruptcy could be saved and the destiny of the euro and EU were all determined by Germany. The former German Foreign Minister, Joschka Fischer, once said, "Because of its size, location, and history, Germany has a specific role to play within that unique structure - sandwiched between national and European interests - that is the EU. If Germany no longer acts as the driving force of European integration, then European integration is a thing of the past."[115] Since the foundation of the German Empire in 1871, Germany had been fighting for the leading role of Europe, which was a reason behind the start of the two world wars. Germany itself also suffered a great deal. After the re-unification in 1990, Germany was busy with breaking down domestic burdens. Now the sovereign debt crisis sweeping the Europe provided a golden opportunity for Germany to play a larger role in Europe.

---

112 "*Soros: Germany Is the Leading Role of Euro Turmoil*", Sina Finance, June 24, 2010, http://finance.sina.com.cn/stock/usstock/c/20100624/09278169341.shtml.

113 Thomas Meaney and Harris Mylonas, "Greece's crisis, Germany's gain," *Los Angeles Times*, March 15, 2010.

114 Anthony Faiola, "Germany's frugality bemoaned for inhibiting euro zone growth," *The Washington Post*, Sunday, February 28, 2010.

115 "*Germany Building a New Empire*", *Morning News (Russia)*, June 16th, 2010.

III. The Future of Europe After the Sovereign Debt Crisis

The European debt crisis was developing into a European political crisis. Strike waves began to sweep across Europe as European governments promised to adopt economic austerity policies. Turmoil fueled by social instability had seriously damaged the European social order and political stability. If the austerity policy failed to lead the European economy out of crisis, regime change might take place in some European countries. As for the Europe Union, the debt crisis unveiled plenty of problems in the European integration process, from cultural tradition to regime design and from political nationalism to supra-nationalism. If these problems could not be solved, the debt crisis might become the watershed of the European integration process. European Union's status in the international political economy structure was likely to be challenged.

1. Strike Waves and Governments' Predicaments

The debt crisis started in Greece, and so did the strike wave. The Greek strike wave continued to grow and escalate as the Greek government declared to conduct a tight fiscal spending policy. Other European countries were disturbed and deeply concerned about the strike waves as well. On May 29, 2010, tens of thousands of Portuguese protestors marched in Lisbon against the government's austerity measures. On June 9th, Spain was hit by the first large strike since the Spanish Socialist Workers' Party gained power in 2004. On June 13th, tens of thousands of Germans took to the streets of Berlin to protest and accuse the government of helping the rich by robbing the poor and demanded the government to cancel the plan to cut social welfare spending. On June 25th, a nationwide strike in transportation sector took place in Italy. On September 7th, a nationwide strike was organized by the French Trade Union and people demonstrated on the streets surpassed one million; on the same day in Britain, the London underground strike affected millions of passengers. On September 23rd, the French Trade Union led the second nationwide strike within one month. Altogether there were 231 demonstrations and more than 2.9 million people marched across the streets. On September 30th, workers in many European countries demonstrated in the streets to protest against the fiscal austerity policies.

The power base of government was shaken by the economic austerity and social instability. Many European governments were confronted with serious political crisis. German Chancellor Angela Merkel's ruling coalition suffered severe setbacks in the regional elections and lost many seats in the upper house. The election result changed the

German political map and Merkel had to be restrained by the opposition party when implementing her major policies. On June 7th, Merkel announced the largest fiscal austerity plan since World War II. Many German commentators believed this plan was the final problem and the ruling coalition was heading for a breakdown.[116]

In May 2010, the UK's general election resulted in a coalition government of the Conservative Party and the Liberal Democrats Party and ended the 13 years' leadership of the Labor Party. The inefficiency to overcome the crisis was one of the main reasons for the British Labor Party's defeat. The high unemployment rate, bankrupting of large amount of enterprises and the general concern of high debt that Britain held finally led to fierce anger with the government. For the new government, there would be a referendum about the election reform one year later, and the ruling coalition was supposed to be re-shuffled.

In Italy, due to the party split, the Italian Prime Minister Silvio Berlusconi, lost Parliamentary majority in early August 2010, which increased his difficulty to further carry out the austerity policy. The joint-statement released by the presidents of Italy's 20 regions stressed that the local government might not be able to function as a result of the tight budget. Now that the Parliamentary majority was lost, the supporting rate decreased, and the cabinet scandals and party splits intensified, Berlusconi was likely to dissolve parliament and hold forthcoming elections.

In Spain, the Cabinet led by Prime Minister Jose Luis Rodriguez Zapatero was also in the edge of stepping down. According to the latest Spanish poll result in May 2010, more than 50% of the electorates were dissatisfied with the government's measures to tackle the crisis and wished for advancing the election. Currently, the supporting rate for the Socialist Party under the leadership of Jose Luis Rodriguez Zapatero was only 35.1%, falling behind the largest opposition party, the People's Party, by 10.5%. On September 30, 2010, Spain witnessed the first large-scale strike since 2002, which marked the breakdown of the traditionally close relationship between the trade union and the Socialist Party government.

2. Say Goodbye to High Welfare?

One of the main reasons for the Greek sovereign debt crisis was the traditional Greek lifestyle. Under the high social welfare system, Greek people led an extravagant life. Popular opinion held that "millionaires live as billionaires." It was estimated that government officials, in a strict sense, accounted for 10% of the Greek labor forces nationwide. If the staff in some public service offices, such as the Pension Administration

---

116 Tristana Moore, "Is Germany's Government Headed for a Breakdown?" *Time*, Jun. 24, 2010.

organizations, were included, the ratio would be higher. This kind of lifestyle demanded high welfare expenses from the government. Since the social welfare system in Greece had become a major burden for the economy, some experts predicted that if fundamental and concrete reforms were not adopted, the system would collapse within 15 years.[117]

The policies brought up by the European Union to get rid of the crisis had an enormous impact on the traditional Greek lifestyle. Greece was likely to say goodbye to high welfare forever. According to the eurozone rescue conditions, the Greek government launched another round of tight policies. However, people in Greece rejected the Greek Prime Minister's advocacy to live a tighter lifestyle for the sake of the country. Protestors claimed that they refused to pay the bills for the government's mistakes. Therefore, in addition to the fiscal austerity policy, Greek Prime Minister Gorge Papandreou, promised to fight against corruption and cronyism at the same time. The Greek Prime Minister also said, "Corruption cost Greece 8% of its GDP per annum. For the sake of the public interests, they must strengthen administration upon national affairs... Every person should shoulder the responsibility."

As the cradle of European civilization, Greece once spread the value system of freedom and democracy to the whole European continent. Greek culture was the foundation of European culture and Greek spirits influenced the whole of Europe. Greek people were proud of this for a long time. Now faced with the European debt crisis, Greece would be the first country in Europe to conduct "cultural revolution." The massive official government team, severe tax evasion and corruption were all the targets of the austerity plan. Though Greek people were reluctant to change, and some even viewed it as an insult, Greece had no other choice. Greece was only a fraction of Europe, and there were many other European countries that were heavily burdened with the high welfare system, especially the Southern European countries such as Portugal, Spain and Italy. To look into the future, this debt crisis would not only change the traditional lifestyle of Greece, but also many other European countries sharing the same problems, and might cause another round of "cultural revolutions" among European countries.

3. Challenges in European Integration Process

The Greek debt crisis was the most serious crisis in European history. Though the European Union had experienced plenty of difficulties in its integration process, none of

---

117 "Greek Government Accused of Wasting Public Funds, Billions of Euros for Welfare", reports from Chinanews, April 30th, 2010, http://news.ifeng.com/world/detail_2010_04/30/1474985_0.shtml.

them had threatened the future of European integration as much as the current debt crisis. Months after the crisis, the European Union acted slowly and failed to come up with an effective solution besides constantly requiring Greece to cut its fiscal expenditure. Both the "president" and "foreign minister" of the European Union, and the European Commission or the European Central Bank, could do nothing but see the situation continue to worsen. The numerous resolutions and statements issued by the European Union were lacking in concrete contents. Consequently, the crisis spread rapidly and the euro depreciated continually. This crisis then posed a huge threat to the European integration process.

On the surface, the "inefficiency" of European Union was rooted in its regime defects. For one thing, in the early EU laws and regulations, such as the Maastricht Treaty, underlined the "no-bail-out" clause, making it illegal to use one member country's resources to assume the debts of another. Meanwhile, there were no countries within the European Union that had the willingness or capacity to share the burden. For another, the European Union was lacking in mandatory binding rules to regulate fiscal policies when unifying the monetary policies in the eurozone. They wished to realize economic balance through the fiscal self-discipline of each country. The founders of the eurozone even claimed that such a regime arrangement could reduce the risks of "moral hazard" among the member states to the lowest degree and therefore force them to achieve fiscal self-discipline. The reality turned out to be the exact opposite. Greece obtained large amounts of transfer payments and foreign investment flow after joining the European Union and eurozone. With sufficient funds, the Greek government had no stimulus to cut fiscal deficits. Since the European Union only had monetary union, but no fiscal union, the Greek government in crisis could not solve the problem by means of fiscal transfer.[118] These mechanism factors were also contributing to the EU's inefficiency in responding to the crisis.

Fundamentally speaking, however, the Greek debt crisis had gone far beyond financial and economic aspects. It displayed the profound conflicts between political interests of sovereign states and that of the European Union. According to the early designers of the European Union, the European integration was following a pattern of economy integration followed by political integration. They aspired to achieve a final unified regime through economic integration. However, from the reactions of European countries to this crisis, it could be concluded that domestic political concerns were still the top priorities in government policy-making. German chancellor Merkel's reluctance to bail out Greece was

118 YU Yongding, "*European Sovereign Debt Crisis and the Future of Euro.*"

because of the strong opposition among the electorates within the country. The decision-making of the European Union was directly influenced by Germany's domestic politics. As for the reasons why France rejected IMF's interference, some people argued that it was because French President Nicolas Sarkozy feared that the IMF Chief Strauss-Kahn, who was also French, might gain public support if he performed well in the Greek crisis and threatened his future renewal of term of office.[119] As suggested, in terms of political integration, European countries were unwilling to transfer political sovereignty, which was also the reason why they refused to transfer the power of foreign policy to an "EU Ministry of Foreign Affairs." However, according to the integration theories, political integration shall be achieved ahead of currency integration. Only in this way could currency stability be assured. Since the European Union had chosen the opposite path and it was difficult to push the political integration forward, it remained a major challenge for the political ability and resolution of the EU leaders to maintain the stability of euro.

A Chinese proverb goes "He who does not advance loses ground." The Greek crisis did unveil many problems in the process of European integration, but this did not mean that the European sovereign debt crisis was a definitely a negative decision for the European Union. For the European countries, the dissolution of the eurozone would bring about huge political costs. No one eurozone country wanted to see or accepted it, especially Germany and France, the two engine countries in the process of European integration. To see the current development of the crisis, the market confidence had been restored to some extent and the European debt market remained stabilized. Perhaps in the economic level, as the Spanish prime minister recently suggested, the European debt crisis ended. However, in the political level, whether the crisis was approaching an end was dependent on the economic recovery and political stability of European countries, both of which required the European Union and its members to carry out practical measures and respond to the problems unveiled during the crisis, from economy to politics and from concepts to culture. Only in this way could the world find a better future after the crisis, could the European integration process be strengthened rather than jeopardized, and could the Europe be able to maintain its ground in the fierce international political economy competition.

---

119 Zhang Ming, "European Sovereign Debt Crisis: Evolution, Prospects, Roots and Risks", Working Paper No. 2010W12, World Economy Research Center of the Institute of World Economics & Politics, Chinese Academy of Social Sciences, August 16th, 2010.

Part V Interrnational Organizations and Political Parties

Chapter 12

2010 International Organizations: Mechanism Construction and Global Governance

Li Dong yan

From 2009 to 2010, a prominent feature shown in the operation of the formal multilateral intergovernmental organizations, in particular international political and international security organizations as well as comprehensive international organizations is to further promote institutional reform and institutional building. These reforms improve the organization's capacity and efficiency and further promote the governance of global issues. To further illustrate the changes in roles of these international organizations and groups in the world, this report will classify the research subjects into three categories: the United Nations Organization, the regional organizations and the cross-regional groups, such as the G8, G20, G77 and Non-Aligned Movement. The main contents of the study is regarding to changes in the mechanisms of international organizations and the impact on international political and security situation.

I. United Nations: Reform Continuing

Even though over the year, General Assembly did not put forward major reform measures, the institutional reforms and adjustments in various departments are being carried on in a "quiet" manner. One of the most attracting reforms remains to be reform of UN Security Council, which is the most divisive issue between Member States, as well as the most difficult reform to complete. The establishment of "The United Nations Women's Department" is a fruitful achievement of the reform to maintain system consistency. In addition, this session of the General Assembly, for the first time held debates on the topic of UN peacekeeping reform, in hopes of encouraging Member States to propose optional guiding principles and strategies for future peacekeeping operations.

1.1 Security Council Reform Entering Into the Phase of Intergovernmental Text Negotiations

On February 19th, 2009, the General Assembly launched the intergovernmental negotiations on Security Council reform, which have been conducted for several rounds, mainly focusing on five major issues of Security Council members category, the veto, regional distribution of seats, size of an enlarged Security Council, working methods of Security Council and the relationship between the Security Council and the General Assembly. Intergovernmental negotiations encouraged countries pursuing for permanent seat in Security Council and countries that are in support of the expansion of UN Security Council. Ali Treki, President of the 64th Session of the UN General Assembly said that intergovernmental negotiations "broke the model which the Security Council reform has been rigidly adhere to for the previous 15 years".[120]

From the end of 2009 to early 2010, Chairman of the intergovernmental negotiations on the reform of the Security Council and its Member States have made frequent exchange of letters to express their points of views, and held several rounds of negotiations. In May 2010, Mr. Tanin, Chairman of intergovernmental negotiations submitted to all members with a letter with "Text", in which all proposals from the Member States have been summarized, and some recommendations have been made. This "Text" involved the previously mentioned issues regarding to Security Council members category, the veto, regional distribution of seats, size of an enlarged Security Council, working methods of Security Council and the relationship between the Security Council and the General Assembly. Thus intergovernmental negotiations would have a relatively concentrated "Text" for discussion and revision during negotiations. Optimists see it as a crucial victory toward more substantive negotiations among governments.

However, at this stage, all parties still held inconsistent attitudes towards the expansion of the Security Council and the gap has not narrowed. African countries still insist to get two seats on the Security Council with veto power. Muslim countries held that any expansion plan without representatives on behalf of their interests in the Security Council is unacceptable. China adheres to the principle that Security Council expansion should give priority to developing countries. United States has not recognized the Security Council expansion plan including more seats for developing countries. The so-called negotiation "Text" remains to be immature, containing a number of controversial

120 http://www.unmultimedia.org/radio

suspensions and pending proposals.[121] More difficult and arduous task of reforming the Security Council will be left to the new United Nations General Assembly, which will face increasing pressures. Fundamentally, developing countries support Security Council reform and expansion and look forward to increasing the representation of developing countries in the Security Council. Over the past year, the United Kingdom and France have repeatedly made clear their support for Germany, Japan, India and Brazil pursuing permanent seats in Security Council. Obama administration has expressed support for Indian joining in the permanent members. In rising countries, India, Brazil and South Africa act very actively, presenting an unavoidable issue to both the G20 or the BRIC in the future cooperation.

1.2 The Birth of "UN Women"

As one of the eight UN Millennium Development Goals, "Gender equality" is an issue closely related to development, security and human rights, an issue that "may never be overstated". One of the most significant outcomes of institutional reform of UN in 2010 was the establishment of "UN Women", wholly-called "the UN Entity for Gender Equality and the Empowerment of Women". The establishment of UN Women as part of consistency reform in UN system reflects the support from Member States to the institutional reform of gender equality in the United Nations and the expectations of UN on a greater role on gender equality issues. The birth of this new entity is considered to be a major achievement in the reform of United Nations.

In a number of UN consistency reforms, the successful completion of the integration of women institutions dues to the widest support from all Members, the smallest divergences among them and and therefore the smallest difficulty and resistance on this issue. The establishment of "UN Women" is expected to increase the capacity and efficiency in solving global issues of gender equality issues so that resources can be more concentrated and become a boost to the implementation of the Millennium Development Goals of "gender equality". Secretary-General Ban Ki-moon highly praised of the establishment of the institution and believed that "UN Women" will greatly promote gender equality throughout the world, expand opportunities for women and fight against discrimination on women.[122]

---

121 Letter from the Chair of the Intergovernmental Negotiations on Security Council Reform, 26 May 2010, http://www.un.org/ga/president/

122 UN Establish New Institution to Promote Gender Equality, July 3rd, 2010, http://world.people.com.cn

1.3 General Assembly's Thematic Debate on Peacekeeping Strategy Reform

In order to commemorate the 10th anniversary of publication of "Brahimi Report", the General Assembly held a debate on peacekeeping issues on June 22nd, 2010. This is the first time UN General Assembly held thematic debate on peacekeeping so as to listen to the recommendation from all parties and to explore the options for future peacekeeping reform. The United Nations peacekeeping operations are keeping expanding from the publication of the Report. On four continents, more than 100,000 peacekeepers are on duty in 16 UN peace-keeping tasks. In order to provide a new strategic direction and reform plans for the future peacekeeping operations, the UN started a new round of discussions on peacekeeping since 2009. Related departments issued research reports on the future UN peacekeeping strategy. General Assembly's thematic debate pushed the discussion on peacekeeping-related issues to a new high.

Research report from peacekeeping department stressed that the UN peacekeeping strategy should reflect the United Nations as a peacekeeping actor of strategic advantage, that the United Nations is the exclusive organization which enable the five permanent members and all other powers, including the emerging regional powers to participate in peacekeeping operations. Only the UN is capable of providing politically-diversified peacekeeping operations. UN peacekeeping operations must win the support of the five permanent members and all other powers.[123] UN also called for the establishment of a new global partnership which includes the Council, the Secretariat, peacekeeping personnel and host countries, including the United Nations subsidiary bodies and relevant organizations, funds and international financial institutions, bilateral, multilateral and regional organizations and non-governmental organizations. Facing complex peacekeeping missions, UN won't solve the political, military and financial challenges on its own without establishing a new global partnership.[124]

Peacekeeping thematic debate held in June 2010 at the UN General Assembly was focused on the contents of the report carried. The main contents include peacekeeping capacity building and partnership; peacekeeping operations, political will and political support, as well as interaction between peacekeeping operations and domestic political process of conflicting party; relationships of sustainable peace-building and development.

---

123 Building on Brahimi: Peacekeeping in an era of Strategic Uncertainty, http://www.un.org/zh/documents/view

124 A New Partnership Agenda: Charting a New Horizon for UN Peacekeeping, http://www.un.org/chinese/peace/peacekeeping/

In the debate regarding "peacekeeping partners", the support of the major powers is considered to be the key to success in peacekeeping operations. It is also believed that from the political, military and financial perspectives, the input from major powers in peacekeeping is most crucial"[125]. Developing countries providing the most peacekeepers also call for developed countries not only invest in financial peace, but also in personnel. Emerging developing countries such as India, China and others are expected to provide greater support in peacekeeping operations. Those who expect China to play a greater role in peacekeeping believe that China can take advantage of its permanent membership in Security Council, the rapid development of its economic and military strength, as well as its impact on other developing countries to eliminate disagreements on the issue of peacekeeping, and contribute on establishing a "inclusive alliance of global peacekeeping".[126]

II. Regional Organizations: New Development in Integration

Regional and sub-regional organizations as important actors on the international arena are indispensable components of constructing multi-layer global governance and global partnership. Over the past year, the major regional organizations have made great efforts in expanding cooperation, deepening the institutional construction and promoting the integration process, and have made historic progress in some aspects.

2.1 Roadmap by ASEAN to Realize Community

"ASEAN Charter" came in to effect in December, 2008. As the first documents with universal legal significance, it established the common objectives, principles, status and organizational structure of ASEAN, binding on all member states. According to the "ASEAN Charter", the ASEAN Community is composed of the three pillars of the ASEAN Economic Community, the ASEAN Political and Security Community and ASEAN Socio-Cultural Community, which shall be established in 2015. On the fourteenth ASEAN Summit March held in Thailand in March, 2009, ASEAN member states signed the "ASEAN Community Roadmap Declaration 2009~2015", drawing a complete roadmap for

---

125 Fred Tanner: "Addressing the Perils of Peace Operations: Toward a Global Peacekeeping System," *Global Governance*, Volume 16, Number2, Apr.-June 2010, p.213.

126 Fred Tanner: "Addressing the Perils of Peace Operations: Toward a Global Peacekeeping System," *Global Governance*, Volume 16, Number2, Apr. -June 2010, pp. 213~214.

the establishment of ASEAN Community in 2015.

The process of ASEAN community is clearly not an easy thing, but the most important change is that ASEAN is diverting from a regional economy-oriented organization towards a highly integrated institutionalized regional community in economic, political, security social and cultural aspects. It also requires of the common values of its member citizens and their recognition of "ASEAN" identity [127]. Followed by "ASEAN Economic Community Blueprint" in 2008, ASEAN Summit in 2009 issued "ASEAN Political and Security Community Blueprint" and "ASEAN Social and Cultural Community Blueprint". The goal of establishing a "political and security community" aims at building ASEAN into an alliance sharing common values, adhering to common rules and norms, enjoying common solidarity and cooperation, peace and stability, and jointly shouldering responsibilities. The goal of establishing a "social and cultural community" aims at building ASEAN into build an alliance with the gradual convergence in level of development, social welfare, social justice and civil rights. It stressed the recognition of "ASEAN" identity by the citizens of ASEAN member countries. In addition to economic integration, ASEAN also adopted a number of new initiatives in political, security, social and cultural fields in 2010 so as to promote community-building process, including institution-building legal construction, human rights mechanisms construction, and cooperation in non-traditional security area.

2.2 "Lisbon Treaty" Bringing Reforms to EU

EU has made important progress in institutional reform from 2009 to 2010. On December 1st, 2009, "Lisbon Treaty" came into effect, becoming another historic treaty following "Treaty of Rome" and "Maastricht Treaty" in the EU history. Also known as "Reform Treaty", "Lisbon Treaty" entering into force has injected new impetus for the years of stagnation of European's integration process and marked a new era of European integration process. According to "Lisbon Treaty", EU implemented a series of new institutional reforms, including reforms in foreign and security sectors.

First, EU carried out major reforms in its leadership structure. According to "Lisbon Treaty", the EU set up a permanent European Council presidency and integrated the two original positions of European Common Foreign and Security Policy High Representative and European Commission External Relations Commissioner into one, setting up a new EU Foreign and Security Policy High Representative, who has overall responsibility for EU

127 http://www.aseansec.org

foreign policy. This has obvious significance to EU. In the area of defense, EU defense ministers held an informal meeting in February, 2010, which was the first defense ministers' meeting after the commencement of "Lisbon Treaty". The conference concentrated on discussions of strengthening the EU military force, enhancing crisis management capabilities and promoting the EU common security and defense policy and reached some consensus.

The establishment of European external action service (EEAS) was another fruitful achievement in terms of foreign institutional reform over the past year. When emphasizing the need for such an agency, Ashton said: "We have to adapt to an increasingly complex, changing world. In order to play our role, we have to integrate powers in economy, politics, security, and crisis management in support of a common political strategy." In her expectation, EEAS should become an institution with European characteristics, able to cope with new challenges of the 21st century, to strengthen the coherence and effectiveness of Europe's global role, and to offer the best to Europe.[128]

2.3 Integration Process in Latin America

Latin America's regional and sub-regional organizations are flourish, such as the existing South America Union, the Rio Group, the ALBA alliance, Association of Caribbean States etc.. During the past year, U.S. and Colombia relations, Venezuela and Colombia relations have seriously affected the unity of the region, exposing the vulnerability of Latin American regional integration. Even in these cases, efforts have been made to strengthen regional solidarity and promote the integration.

South American Union was formally established in May, 2008. Its predecessor was the South American Community of Nations, comprising 12 nations of Argentina, Bolivia, Brazil, Colombia, Chile, Ecuador, Guyana, Paraguay, Peru, Suriname, Uruguay and Venezuela. The vacancy of Secretary-General of the Organization has long been a negative effect to the organization's operation. At the Special Summit of South American countries held in May, 2010, the former Argentine President Nestor Kirchner Carlos was elected first Secretary-General for the Union with the main task to coordinate the organization's internal affairs and formulate agenda. Undoubtedly the assumption of duty of the Secretary-General would contribute to the cooperation and development of the organization.

---

128 Catherine Ashton, High Representative of the Union for Foreign Affairs and Security Policy / Vice-President of the European Commission. Introductory remarks at presentation of the proposal for the European External Action Service (EEAS), Brussels, 25 March 2010, http://europa.eu/rapid/pressReleasesAction.

In February 2010, the Rio Group summit and Latin America and the Caribbean Union Conference were held in Cancun, Mexico. Conference adopted the "Cancun Declaration", by which members unanimously agreed to set up a new regional organization - Latin America and the Caribbean Community of Nations, to promote the regional integration process. In 2008, Mexican President Felipe Calderon has proposed to build a League of Latin America and the Caribbean without the participation of United States or Canada, which received wide recognition by the Caribbean countries. Currently, the establishment of the regional alliance has officially launched and the new alliance is expected to complete planning work and put into operation on Venezuela summit in 2011 or on Chile summit in 2012. Mexican President Felipe Calderon said the new alliance will be a common space for all the Latin American and Caribbean countries and conducive to promote the regional integration.[129]

Plan for Latin America and the Caribbean Community sent a positive signal. A Latin American and Caribbean Community without the participation of U.S. and Canada is bound to face many uncertainties, however, as expected by its members, the establishment of the new community will no doubt promote the regional integration process and enhance its right to speak in the international community.

III. Cross-regional Groups: Seeking for New Position

Unlike ordinary international organization, these groups usually have no fixed agendas, permanent secretariats, and executive authorities. In recent years, they have caused widespread concerns. In 2009 and 2010, the groups that catch most attentions are the G8 and the G20. Though some international organizations that begin in the Cold War (such as non-aligned movement groups and the G77) are not comparatively active, they are constantly adjusting their strategies, aims, and objectives to meet the current situations. As a result groups like the G8, the G20 and the G77 are facing the challenge to change and reposition themselves.

3.1 Change of Roles of G8 and G20

In September 2009, the G20 summit in Pittsburgh has replaced the G8 as the main forum to tackle global economic co-operations. People started to discuss the end of the G8

---

129 *Latin America and the Caribbean Community of Nations Will be Established*, Xinhua News Agency, 24th Feb, 2010, http://news.xinhuanet.com/video/

and the rise of the G20. After this year, it is hard to say that the G8 has overtaken by the G20. To be precise, these two groups has changed their roles and accountable for different roles on the stage of global economics.

The G8 has changed from a global economic forum into a group that concerns major global issues. After lost its influence in global economics, the G8 has hindered its focus on economics and put their attention to social development, peace and safety, and climate change. In the G8 Canada summit in June 2010, the discussion has shifted to global developments and issues related to world peace and world's safety such as the nuclear issue in Iran, situation in Korea, climate change and energy problems. 10 leaders in Algeria, Egypt, Ethiopia, Malawi, Nigeria, Senegal, South Africa, Colombia, Jamaica, and Haiti were invited to join the meeting, and it can be seen that the G8+5 will not continue. These have shown that G8 has changed its roles and moving forward to a new direction.

On the other hand, the G20 has not giving up their role as a forum in the developed world. Though the G8 has continued to reconcile its blast to global economics, it has re-positioned itself and put more focus on four main areas including global economics, climate changes, development and democratic bureaucracy and try to lead the world. It can be seen that the G8 still has a role in promote liberty, democracy, human rights and rule of justice. Stephen Harper, the Canadian Prime Minister, expressed that the share of values is the core of the success of the G8, and it allows the group to act and coordinates in quick response[130]. It can be seen that the G8 has a common ground in issues related to MWD, anti-terrorism and organized crime, and global climate change.

As a major summit in global economic co-operations, the G20 has contributed to tackle the global economic crisis and reform the international monetary policies since the summit in September 2009. At the same time, it has become institutionalized and moved from a loosened summit onto a systematic global economic co-operation institute. Followed by the G8 summit, the 4th summit of the G20 was held in Toronto, Canada, at the same location as the G8 summit. A declaration has announced before the summit and the members has stressed further measurements are needed to be taken to promote the global economic recovery.

Differed from the previous G8 summits, the agenda of the last G8 summit had focused on the global economic environment, international monetary reform, international trade and financial regulations. Compared to the G8, the G20 is a combination of developed and developing economies and represents the world's largest economies, which has more

---

130 http://www.g8.utoronto.ca/scholar/g8.-2009.pdf

influence and representations. It can be seen that the institutionalization of the G20 will become a major topic, varies solutions and discussions are in process, and the importance of the group will continue to rise. However, as the G20 is still in infancy, the lack of consistency and cohesion, interest, values raised uncertainties to its formalization. The direction of the G20 in the post-global economic crisis will be a popular topic.

3.2 Re-positioning of the Non-Aligned Movement and the G77

The Non-Aligned Movement and the G77 established during the Cold War are the two groups formed by most of the developing countries. Though they are loosely organized and not formalized, the number of member countries is large and they are actively involved in the UN and other international organizations. At the same time, China has always been together with the G77 in the UN and forms a G77+China group.

These two groups have a similar heritage in political values, such as anti- imperialism, anti-hegemonies, and anti-colonialism; on the other hand, they promote a fair and equitable international political and economic order and protect the rights of independence and sovereignty of developing countries. Both groups support the equality between countries, non-intervention of nations' internal affairs, and against the dual standards of human rights and controls of weapons. Also, they support the Palestinian and against the sanctions against Iran and Cuba. They have the same opinions on climate change the Millennium Development Goals, which is to press the developed nations to stick to their promises to developing nations. These two groups support the reform of the UN and against the trend that developed nations lead the UN and establish the international democracy.

However, as time and the international environment change, the function and necessity of two groups are being doubted, at the same time they are facing challenges from the new groups such as the G20. The two groups share a common problem: the way to continue to perform on the international stage. As seen in 2009 and 2010, they started to adjust and fit themselves into the new environment.

On 15th July 2009, the 15th summit of the Non-Aligned Movement was held in Egypt, and the "Sharm el-Sheikh Declaration"-a document exploring a 3-year plans and objectives of the Movement under the new economic and political environment has passed. It can be seen as the effort made by the Movement to adapt to the current situation. Under new circumstances, the core principal and values of the Movement become maintaining world peace and security, promoting multilateralism, becoming sustainable, and supporting values promoted by the UN including liberty, equality, unity, tolerance, and mutual respect. Later on, a special summit of the Movement was held in Manila in 17th March, 2010, in which it has discussed the approach to encourage dialogue between religions and cultures, emphasis that conversation facilitates peace and development.[131]The summit also discussed issues aimed to resolve the financial crisis, nuclear proliferation, food safety, and energy supply; at the same time, it focused on problems that members are facing including social justice, poverty, infectious disease, and other negative effects brought by globalization. It can be seen that both the Non-Aligned Movement are putting effort adjusting the changes to political missions and values.

The G77 are also adjusting their focus. Apart from dealing with global financial and trade issues, the group are contributing the climate change, reform of the UN, Millennium Development Goals, and South co-operations.

IV. Trends and Implications

To sum up the activities of major international organizations, the following three aspects are worth noting.

4.1 Expansion of International Organizations beyond the Geographic Boundaries

In recent years, the number of member states and observers of major international organizations have increasing expanded beyond the geographical boundaries. Horizontal cooperation between international organizations has become more closely, such as the cooperation between African Union and Arab League and the cooperation between the ASEAN and EU. ASEAN is ready to invite the United States and Russia to participate in the East Asia Summit in 2010, and also ready to approve Canada, Turkey and EU's accession to "Treaty of Amity and Cooperation".

Another expansion model of international organization turns to be the development of single-functional into integrated-functional. Some security-functional organizations began to focus on climate change, finance, food and other issues. As mentioned earlier, global peace and security, climate change, international development and democratic governance have all become the focus of the G8. ASEAN is working through the implementation of "ASEAN Charter" and the "three community blueprint" to build itself into an economic, political and socio-cultural integrated community. Non-Aligned Movement as a political organization observing independent, neutral principle to fight against imperialism,

131 Manila Declaration and Program of Action on Interfaith Dialogue and Cooperation for Peace and Development, Manila, Philippines, 16~18 March 2010

colonialism and hegemony, has now turned to a political organization paying close attention to the political, economic and social issues of its member states and a wide range of critical global issues. Influenced by this trend, "BRIC" will inevitably face the issue of enlargement, while G20 cannot limit itself to international economic and financial fields.

4.2 Competition and Cooperation in Global Governance

With the development of groups such as the G20 and deepening of integration of the EU, ASEAN, AU and other regional organizations, the effect and influence of international organizations in response to global issues keep rising. The cooperation among the United Nations, regional and sub-regional organizations and regional groups keep expanding. During the year, debates on how to improve and refine a multi-layered system of global governance including all nations and international organizations would become more heated. It's obvious to see G20 as the representative of the world's most powerful economic power in an optimistic way, but many medium and small countries are still in support of the United Nations with the universal representativeness, which also regard the G20 as a self-proclaimed club only entitling membership to big powers. Opponents argued that United Nations while having a broader representativeness and legitimacy, lack of consistency, efficiency, and coordination capacity, and thus making G20 take on hopes to play a central coordinating role, and "replace the United Nations in some of the functions".[132] On March 25th, 2010, the United Nations University held the workshop on "Global Governance: G20 and the United Nations" to discuss how to ensure that the G20's actions and decisions will strengthen the United Nations rather than undermine the United Nations, and how to establish a framework for the relationship between the United Nations and the G20. This discussion not only reflects different academic points of view, but also reflects the current competition between global organizations and groups on global governance.

In September 2010, the new General Assembly began in such atmosphere. In the opening ceremony of the general debate, the former Swiss Federal President, the 56th General Assembly President Joseph Deiss draw attention to the threat of marginalization facing the United Nations. He said, "the role of the G20 and other entities are undeniable. ... However, currently there is a critical and urgent need, that is, to build up a bridge of cooperation between different actors. ... which can only be achieved by the United Nations and General Assembly."[133] Deiss' speech shared concerns of some nations on the chances

---

132 http://global.dwnews.com/news.

133 http://www.unmultimedia.org/radio/chinese/

that the United Nations may be weakened and marginalized by the G20 and other international organizations.

From the future trend, although there are competitions between organizations and groups, it's no simple story of who can take the place of whom. United Nations, regional organizations and other groups have their advantages as well as their own helplessness. There is no doubt that they will play different roles on the global stage. By means of coordination, cooperation and complementarity, they may become integral parts in the multi-layer system of global governance.

4.3 Advantages and Disadvantages of the Development Trend of International Organizations on China

Development of international organizations poses both positive and negative influences on China. On the one hand, China is expected to play a greater role in international organizations. Ban Ki-moon's said when he visited China: "China's global influence is expanding. The United Nations needs China's further participation and greater support."[134] According to the UN members' scale of assessment from 2010 to 2012, China's normal scale of assessment raised from 2.667% in 2009 up to 3.189%, peacekeeping costs from 3.1474% up to 3.9390%. The adjustment in the two scales of assessments makes China rank eighth and seventh in all member states. This trend creates more space for China to enhance its status and role in multilateral international organizations and global governance.

On the other hand, China also faces challenges from many different types of international organizations. The followings are more prominent: first, the intention of other major powers and neighboring countries to restrict China through international organizations is becoming more and more obvious, particularly in the Asian-Pacific regions, such as ASEAN trying to constrain China together with United States, Russia, India and Australia, India insisting on the exclusion of China a full member of SAARC. Second, international organizations and groups are exerting greater pressure on China in regards of climate change, the Security Council reform and territorial disputes. Third, the G8 and EU have significantly developed economic cooperation and development with regional organizations of developing countries, posing a greater competitive pressure to China as well.

---

134 *Ban Ki-moon's Lecture in China: UN Needs China's Further Participation,* July 2nd, 2008, http://www.china.com.cn

Chapter 13

New Trends in the World's Party Politics

JIN Xin

The political situations of most countries in the world have been stable, while some have been trapped in instability since 2010. The debt crisis had a profound influence on the world party politics development. The election results of various counties were stalemated. The term "Hung Parliament" frequently appeared in some countries Governing Coalition consisting of various parties and thus, with different theories and propositions, came into power. The fate of some parties was closely related to the economic and social governance and the self-construction and modernization pace of parties accelerated. There appeared new trends in the world political party development, which posed enormous impacts to the global and regional situations.

I. Fundamental Characteristics of Political Parties in Different Regions

1. The developed countries were deeply disturbed by the financial crisis Poor economic and social situations undermined the status of ruling parties in many countries and the Opposing Parties began fierce confrontations and political games over concepts and policy decisions

1.1 The Opposition Party in the United States, Japan and Australia frequently exerted pressure to the Ruling Party for their incompetence in coping with the financial crisis. The difficulty for Ruling Parties to implement policies increased and their political influences decreased

After U.S. President Barack Obama took office, a series of policies aimed to reform health insurance, promote economic recovery and expand employment were implemented. The comprehensive reforms involved many sectors and interests groups, however, the results were not satisfactory. The U.S. economic recovery was not stable, the unemployment rate remained at a high level of around 10%, the national debt exceeded 13 trillion USD and there was a growing dissatisfaction among the public. Particularly, the high employment became the targets of the Republicans who criticized the Democratic Party for their inability to lead the American people out of the financial crisis. Some Republicans even labeled Obama as the "Unemployment President." The health insurance reforms initiated by the Democratic Party further intensified the conflicts with the social class and interests groups represented by the Republican Party. During the several voting processes concerning the health insurance reform in Congress, almost all of the Republicans voted against it. In addition to the government's inability to deal with the crude oil leak accident in the Mexican Gulf, Obama's approval rating declined. In November 2011, the Democratic Party was defeated in the mid-term election and the Republic Party took control of the House of Representatives, which weakened the political influence of the Democratic Party on the Congress.

The 2010 Japanese political changes caught to world's attention. On June 2, 2010, the Japanese Prime Minister, Yukio Hatoyama, announced his resignation after being in office for only eight months. He stepped down over failures to fulfill his election promises, including the relocation of Okinawa's U.S. air base and losing public trust for political fund scandals. On June 4, 2010, Naoto Kan, the former leader of the Japanese Democratic Party and the Deputy Prime Minister of the Yukio Hatoyama's Cabinet, was elected as the new Prime Minister. Only one month after the establishment of Naoto Kan's cabinet on July 11th, Japan began the 22nd Senate election, where the Japanese ruling coalition was defeated and the opposition party obtained more than half of the seats of the Senate. Another "distorted parliament," namely, the Senate and the House of Representatives were separately ruled by the opposing and ruling party. There were three reasons why the Democratic Party lost the election: firstly, Naoto Kan, the leader of the Democratic Party and the Prime Minister, should have organized profound discussions within the party, developed a well-developed regime design and expounded to the public thoroughly before officially proposing the suggestion of raising consumption tax; secondly, the Japanese citizens were disappointed at the ruling capacity of the Democratic Party. The typical example was the declining political authority of the Democratic Party as a result of the fund scandal in which the high officials of the Democratic Party were deeply involved; and finally, the disunity within the Democratic Party that undermined the power of the Party. There was no doubt that the Liberal Democratic Party of Japan, the largest opposition party, was the biggest winner of the election, which also laid a solid foundation for gaining power in the next election of the House of the Representatives.

On June 24, 2010, Kevin Michael Rudd, the leader of the Australian Labor Party and the former Prime Minister of Australia, also announced his resignation, having had the shortest tenure of any Prime Minister in nearly 40 years. Julia Gillard, the former Deputy Leader of the Australian Labor Party and the Deputy Prime Minister was unanimously elected as the leader of the Labor Party and thus became the first female Prime Minister of Australia. On August 21, 2010, two months after Gillard took office, Australia started Federal election. Tony Abbott, leader of the main opposition party, the Liberal-National Party Coalition, harshly attacked the Labor Party for the mistakes they made in climate change and natural resource tax reforms, and further claimed that a large amount of waste had been caused by the economic stimulating measures of the Labor Party. The criticisms received good feedback. Among the 150 seats in the House of Representatives, the Liberal-National Party Coalition gained 73 seats, while the ruling Labor Party only won 72 and the other five were divided among the Green Party and four independent candidates. No one party met the requirements for majority government, resulting in the first hung parliament since the 1940 election. Supported by the Australian Greens MP and three independent MPs, Gillard barely beat Abbott, the leader of the Liberal-National Party Coalition, with a slight edge of 76:74 and thus obtained the power to form the cabinet. However, the Green Party and independent MPs held the power of balance between the Australian Parliament and the government, posing great challenges to the ruling of the Labor Party.

1.2 Slight changes took place in the European political landscape. The financial crisis did not maintain the trend of the declining Centre-Left Parties, while that of the Right-Wing Parties were further enhanced.

Since 2010, the election results of some European countries indicated that the "strong right and weak left" political party pattern was not reversed, but continued to develop in a way favorable for the right-wing parties. Elections were first held in Hungry, followed by Great Britain, Czech Republic, Netherlands and Sweden. Without practical and effective measures to tackle the financial crisis, the centre-left political parties were continuously defeated in the elections, while the right-wing parties came into power in countries like Great Britain, Hungry and Czech republic. Consequently, the "strong right and weak left" European political party pattern was enhanced.

In April 2010, the Hungry Parliament held the sixth election since the drastic changes in Eastern Europe. The result showed that the largest opposition party, Fidesz, won a two-thirds general election victory, while the Socialist Party, which had ruled Hungry for eight years, suffered a humiliating defeat. The political landscape of Hungry underwent huge changes and never in history was such an overwhelming victory of a single party witnessed. The main reason why Fidesz, a right-wing political party, could enjoy absolute predominance was that the former ruling party, the Socialist Party, failed to address the financial crisis effectively. Hungry was heavily stricken by the financial crisis. The electorate gradually lost confidence in the Socialist Party as the unemployment rate soared to 11% and the international loans amounted to 25 billion USD. Fidesz criticized the Socialist Party for betraying the national interests of Hungry and proposing policies to protect the national interests of Hungry, such as protecting domestic lands and products and renegotiating loan conditions with IMF. The policies and measures initiated by the Fidesz echoed people's wishes for reform and change and finally enabled it to take office.

On May 7, 2010, the election result of the British House of Commons was unveiled. The main opposition party, the Conservative Party, won 306 out of 650 seats and became the majority party in the Parliament. The ruling party, the Labor Party, obtained 258 seats and lost its privilege as the majority party. Another opposition party, the Liberal Democratic Party, obtained 57 seats. Since none of the parties achieved the 326 seats needed for an overall majority, the new government could not be formed immediately and both the Labor Party and Conservative Party wanted to win supports from the Liberal Democratic Party. After fierce coalition talks, on May 11th, the Conservative Party cooperated with the Liberal Democratic Party and formed the first coalition government after the Second World War. It had been 13 years since the Conservative Party had gained power and the 44-year-old David Cameron served as the Prime Minister, the youngest prime minister in the past two centuries. The third largest party of Britain, the Liberal Democratic Party, finally jointed the central government after ruling in regional parliament and participating in regional political affairs for 70 years. The reason why the Conservatives could win the election was mainly because of the bad performances of the former Prime Ministers of the Labor Party, Tony Blair, in the very last period of his tenure, and Gordon Brown. During the 13 years' leadership under the Labor Party, the reforms in education and health care were not satisfactory and people were criticizing the government for sending troops to Iraq and Afghanistan. As the financial crisis erupted, the Labor Party government borrowed huge amounts of foreign debts. The voters distrusted the Labor Party as the high fiscal deficits soared, economic recovery was too slow and the scandals within the Labor Party were frequently exposed. At the same time, the Conservative Party called for reforms, which were greatly welcomed by the electorate. Therefore, the Conservative Party was elected as the largest party in the Parliament. The coalition between the

Conservative Party and the Liberal Democratic Party broke the traditional British political pattern, two major parties ruled in turns and one party dominated at a time.

On May 28, 2010, Czech Republic held the fifth Parliament election since its independence. Altogether, 25 political parties participated and five of them obtained more than 5% of the votes and thus could enter parliament. Among the five parties in the parliament, none of them could form a government independently. The Social Democratic Party was the biggest winner of the election, with a supporting rate of 22.1%, 2% higher than the Civic Democratic Party that followed in second place. The Social Democratic Party only won 56 out of 200 seats in the House of Representatives in the Parliament, while the centre-right Civic Democratic Party had 53 seats, "Tradition Responsibility Prosperity 09" (TOP09) party won 41 seats and Public Affairs had 24 seats. No one of the three other parties obtained more seats than the Social Democratic Party. However, they added together to 118 seats and finally formed a three-party coalition government under the leadership of the Civic Democratic Party. Overall, the centre-right parties defeated the left-wing political parties. Social Democratic Party received the highest number of votes, but was excluded from the ruling government.

On June 10, 2010, the Netherlands election result was released. The right-wing People's Party for Freedom and Democracy (VVD) became the biggest party with 31 seats, followed closely by the Labor Party (PvdA) with 30 seats in the House of Representatives, and thus obtained the prior right to form the government. This was the first time in history that the Liberal Party became the majority party in the Dutch House of Representatives since its establishment in 1948. The far right political party, the Party for Freedom, with an extreme anti-immigrant stance, leapt to the third largest party in the parliament. The election result showed that Dutch politics were bound to be dominated by the right-wing positions.

Elections in Sweden are held every four years. On September 19, 2010, the new general election results came out. The centre-right coalition, consisting of the Moderate Party, the Centre Party, the Liberal People's Party and the Christian Democrats defeated the centre-left Red-Greens coalition formed by the Social Democrats, the Left Party and the Green Party and won the power to form the cabinet. The main reason why the center-right governing coalition won was that the governing capacity of the center-right coalition government had been approved by the electorate. Since 2008, the governing coalition addressed the financial crisis appropriately. While the majority of the European Countries was either experiencing economic stagnation or severely trapped in the sovereign debt crisis, Sweden successfully achieved economic recovery, enjoyed sound development and became the country with the highest economic growth rate among the OECD countries.

By the end of 2010, the left-wing political parties only ruled 5 out of 27 European Union countries, including Spain, Portugal and Greece, the lowest percentage in history, while the influence sphere of right-wing political parties expanded to the majority of European Union countries such as Great Britain, France, Germany and Italy. Apparently, the political power distribution was favorable for the right-wing. In countries like Spain and Portugal where the left-wing parties ruled, since the Communist Party of Spain and the Portuguese Socialist Party failed to tackle the financial crisis and sovereign debt crisis properly, their political status and images were damaged and the ruling foundation was undermined. The approval rating kept decreasing. The opposition parties took the advantage to pose pressure no the ruling party and the government. The confrontations and political games between political parties intensified.

There were many reasons why the European left-wing parties were trapped in the predicaments, among which the most critical factor was that the left parties were "losing self": their theoretical guidelines were swaying and policies tending to become similar to that of the right-wing. From the 1990s to the outbreak of the financial crisis, new liberalism prevailed in Europe. Under the great pressure of globalization and the intensified competition among nations, left-wing parties gradually compromised and conceded to the new liberalism in terms of their theoretical guidelines and policies. Politically, they seek the "third road" between the traditional social democratic and liberalism. Economically, they were inclined to emphasize market efficiency and, in terms of social policies, reform measures such as cutting social welfare caused dissatisfaction among the electorate with traditional stance. The left-wing parties did not insist its traditional values of justice, unity and mutual-help, but sought common policies with the right-wing parties. Consequently, their political images were blurred and the traditional votes lost direction.

2. The political democratization process of developing countries is tortuous and diversified. "Street politics" are frequently displayed in some countries, therefore there is a long way before the party politics mature.

In Southeast Asia, Thailand suffered great political chaos in 2010. On March 14, 2010, the Red-Shirts, supporters of former Prime Minister Thaksin, waged large-scale protests in Bangkok, trying to force the Democratic Party to step down and hold a re-election. After the negotiation with the government failed, the conflicts between the Red-Shirts and the government escalated. On May 20th, the Democratic Party Leader, Prime Minister Abhisit, used military forces to dispel protesters and ended the street protests that had lasted for several months. This political struggle finally ended with more than 80 deaths and about 3,000 injuries, becoming the most serious political unrest since 1992. Although the Thai government controlled the situation, there is still a long way ahead to realize social reconciliation.

In South Asia, on May 2, 2010, the United Communist Party of Nepal (Maoist), the biggest opposition political party occupying nearly 40% of the seats in Parliament, claimed that they were not satisfied with the slow process of the new constitution making, and thus started a national strike, requiring to dismiss the government, change the Prime Minister and form a new government under the leadership of the United Communist Party with national consensus. On June 30th, the Prime Minister declared to resign. Later, the United Communist Party of Nepal (Maoist), the Communist Party of Nepal, and Nepal Congress Party competed fiercely for the leadership in government. The Prime Minister election lasted for months, and it was extremely difficult to re-elect the Prime Minister and establish a new government, which seriously hindered the development of the country. Since the three parties of Nepal lacked mutual trust and all desired for an absolute predominance, the future development in Nepal would not be smooth.

In Africa, military coups took place in Niger and Guinea-Bissau. In Niger, the army captured President Tandja who intended to seek another term of office by revising the constitution, declaring the establishment of the supreme council of restoring democracy and designating Danda, who was independent from any army or political parties, as the Prime Minister of the military government. In Guinea-Bissau, the vice army chief detained the army chief and temporarily arrested the Prime Minister Gomes Junior. There were two main reasons for why military coups took place in Africa: first, the multi-party system did not fit Africa. Some observers maintained that although some countries seemed to adopt the democratic multi-party system, they were still dominated by strongman politics in reality and the executive power was far greater than the legislative power. The reason for the coup in Niger was that the President Tandja dismissed the Congress and the Constitution Court, held a referendum by taking advantage of his executive power, and also adopted the new constitution that allowed presidents to get re-elected to infinity, so that he could renew his office for the second time, which caused the dissatisfaction of the Opposition party and the people; second, the poor population demanded changes. Niger ranked the 182nd in the 2009 United Nations Human Development Index, and many people lost confidence in their government and the party in power and hoped the ruling party and government could be replaced and lead them out of poverty. This, to some extent, created favorable conditions for military coup d'état.

In West Asia and North Africa, at the beginning of 2011, in Tunisia, the regional riot caused by the self-burning of an unemployed young man soon escalated to huge social unrest and violent conflict against President Ben Ali and the ruling power, the Constitution Democratic Union Party. President Ben Ali, who had been in power for more than two decades, fled to Saudi Arabia -and the ruling power was dismissed. This political crisis soon spread to the Middle East and North Africa. Egypt, Yemen, Jordan, Libya, Algeria, Syria, and Oman were all hit by large-scale mass demonstrations, demanding the long ruling power step down and carry out political reform. The Egyptian President Mubarak turned out the power under great political pressure, and the National Democratic Party faced a big blow. The anti-government political turmoil in Libya brought about a civil war and the military intervention of Western countries.

3. Governing parties of the Socialist countries attached great importance to strengthening governance capability, and frequently put forward new initiatives in political, economic and party construction.

Democratic People's Republic of Korea (DPRK) was the focus of the international community in 2010. In the political realm, DPRK strengthened their position and function of the Party, and paced up the process of introducing the new leader. On September 27, 2010, the son of Leader Kim Jong-il, Kim Jong-un, was awarded the General of People's Army. On September 28th, the Workers' Party of North Korea held a party conference after several years, electing the supreme governing body of the Workers' Party of Korea, and elected Kim Jong-il as the General Secretary and the Chairman of the standing committee of the central party political bureau and Central Military Commission. Also, Kim Jong-un was elected as the Vice Chairman of Central Military Commission. On October 8th, Yang Hyong Sop, the Vice Chairman of DPRK Supreme People's Assembly Standing Committee, confirmed to the public that Kim Jong-un, as the son of Kim Jong-il, would be the third generation leader. On October 10th, DPRK held the 65th anniversary of the establishment of its Party, and Kim Jong-un accompanied Kim Jong-il to review the military, which showed that Kim Jong-un formally stepped on the political stage of DPRK.

In the economic realm, the DPRK government made enormous endeavors in strengthening economic development and improving people's livelihood, which attracted the world's attention. Economic reform moved on step by step. In agriculture, the government called on people with various occupations to work in the fields, and the agencies and military forces also started planting, aquaculture and other occupations. In industrial development, DPRK defined power, coal, metallurgy and railway transportation as the four departments of economic priority. Kim Jong-il frequently visited the shops to check whether the food supply was assured. DPRK also actively promoted international cooperation. Kim Jong-il and his delegation of representatives from the Workers' Party of Korea had visited China twice. He expressed his wishes to strengthen cooperation with China during his visit to Northeast China.

In March 2010, the Communist Party of Vietnam held the tenth twelfth plenary session. They thoroughly debated over the *2010~2011 Economic and Social Development Strategy, XI Political Report,* which was to be submitted to the Eleventh Central Committee, and discussed issues such as the personnel preparation of the Eleventh Central Committee, the number of representatives to present, and quota allocation. To further promote democratization inside the party, the Communist Party of Vietnam also steadily promoted the trial of direct elections for the three levels Party Representatives Conference, carried out the work of direct elections for the standing committee, chairman, and vice chairman in 5% to 7% of village-level Party Representatives Conference all over the country, and trials for direct elections were conducted in 230 counties and 10 provinces as well. In January 2011, the Communist Party of Vietnam held the Eleventh Central Committee, and elected the new central committee and central politburo. Nguyen Phu Trong replaced Nong Duc Manh as the General Secretary of Central Committee, which symbolized a smooth power transition inside the Party. The Eleventh Central Committee also put forward the economic development goal of an annual increase rate of 7% in 2011 to 7.5% by 2015.

The Lao People's Revolutionary Party took multiple measures to guarantee smooth economic and social development. In May 2010, the Lao People's Revolutionary Party held the tenth plenary session of the eighth Central Committee and discussed the political report (draft), the draft amendments of constitution, and the seventh Five-Year Plan (2011~2015) for social and economic development for the Ninth National Congress of Central Committee and the personnel arrangements. In March 2011, the Lao People's Revolutionary Party held the Ninth National Congress of Central Committee and Zhu Mali again was elected the General Secretary. The LPRP proposed to continue to reform comprehensively, basically solve the poverty problem in 2015 and withdraw from the list of poor countries in the world in 2020.

The reform in Cuba also progressed. In August 2010, on the Cuba People's National Congress, the State Council President Raul Castro pointed out the need to deepen structural readjustment and mentality reform in social economic sectors, and declared some important reform policies. First, to abandon the "lifelong secure jobs regardless of performance" which had existed for 50 years, and reduce the number of staff in public sectors step by step.

Second, to further open the privately owned business. In September, the National Secretary of the Central Trade Union declared to lay off one million staff in public sectors. The reduced state-owned businesses should adopt the salary system of distribution according to workload. In April 2011, the Communist Party in Cuba held the Sixth National Conference and Raul Castro was elected the First Secretary of Central Committee. The economic reform measures were passed, including the opening privately owned sectors, establishing taxation system, building independent enterprises, eliminating unnecessary subsidies and so on. The international community believed that these actions indicated that Cuba would change the old economic development mode and demonstrated Cuban leaders' determination to reform.

II. Foreign Political Parties New Strategies of Improving Party Construction

Against the background of intensifying globalization and international competition and the rapid shift from industrial society to informationalized society in the new century, the traditional theory and social foundations for the survival of parties have also changed. To tackle these new challenges for parties' development, major parties in different countries began to take innovative measures. They tried to maintain and expand the parties' influence and set up a new image of modern parties by expanding the social foundation, adjusting guidelines and policies, innovating organizational development and strengthening the ties between the party and the people.

1. Expanding the Social Foundation of the Party and Building a Completely Open Party

With the deepening of economic globalization, many countries witnessed great changes in social structure and class structure. To win more support from the people, many major parties began to place less stress on the class property of a party and more on its openness, diversity and affinity to people. In September 2010, the biggest opposition party of Denmark held a National Congress where it no longer emphasized that it represented the interest of the lower-middle people, but that it was the party of all Danes, a party citizens from all fields, all walks and all areas could trust. This proposition fitted in with the fundamental interests of all Danes. This party also sent a positive signal to the business cycle that it was not a rival of businesses and it would commit itself to creating more favorable conditions and providing more policies and services to help them improve international competitiveness. German SPD also redefined itself as a "Left Party for All People" in Hamburg Guideline, the party's new guiding principle, stressing that only with the support of all classes could it become a party with vitality toward the future. The French Socialist Party also pointed out that it would expand its social foundation and win the support of middle voters, making the party stronger, more democratic, more open and more representative for the whole society. Parties in Indonesia pursued pragmatism, responding to the request of vast middle voters by emphasizing diversity, tolerance, democracy, equitability, development and prosperity. The Hindu Nationalist Party also played down its factional property and highlighted its nationalist property, holding that it represents the interest of all Indians.

2. Adjusting Party Guidelines and Policies to Win Wide Recognition of People

Facing negative impacts of globalization and the consequential new economic and social problems and changes, parties in many countries were speeding up the process of adjusting guidelines to pay more attention to balancing economic development and social justice and winning more support from the people. In the UK's General Election in 2010,Prime Minister David Cameron, the leader of the Conservative Party, adjusted the party's guideline on time. It not only stuck to traditional values like privatization, market economy, business competition and social responsibility, but also borrowed the concepts of social justice and common well being from middle-left Labor Party, asserting that it was more sympathetic to the public and more concerned with their interest. The Conservative Party also included environmentalism pursued by the Green Party and the Liberal Democrats into its own ideological system to appeal to people's increasingly stronger awareness of the environment. It attaches great importance to people's well being. For example, in the 28 policies carried out before the General Election, 12 directly concerned livelihood and social problems, winning great support from the lower-middle class. The Labor Party learned its lesson of losing the election at the annual conference. The new leader Ed Miliband gave a lecture with the theme of unity and change, elaborating the domestic and diplomatic policies and trying to establish an image of the new generation of the Labor Party. Miliband announced that the new generation of the Labor Party, led by him, would face failure humbly and seek for the majority's interest by listening to the people. This gesture of reform won a great deal of support from the people and improved the social foundation of the party.

Looking at the Presidential Election in 2012, the French Socialist Party has discussed around the strategy of economic and social development and the party's reforming issue and formulated new guidelines and policies. It held that neo-liberalism and financial capitalism should be criticized more severely and proposed to build socialism with left-wing characteristics. It also strived to build a new development model balancing economy, society and ecology, stressing social justice to improve people's livelihood, create jobs for the youth and protect the rights and interests of labors and inferior groups.

3. Strengthening Ties between the Party and the People and Increasing Its Political and Social Influence

To win the support of more voters, many countries' major parties have listed strengthening the ties between the party and the people as one of their responsibilities. The detailed measures include: First, strengthening the linking role of party members. Many countries' parties have attached importance to this role, asking party members to go to the grass-root areas and listen to people's wishes. CSSD makes full use of the Communication Day of Mps (Members of Parliament) with constituencies, letting MPs go back to their own constituencies and visit voters in order to know and collect their responses to and opinions of policies, big political decisions and hot issues. They will report these responses and opinions to the party's leading group and the MP Committee to form a uniform standing and new motions. The French Socialist Party asks the leaders of party affairs to venture out of their offices and into public places such as the streets, markets, bars and supermarkets to promote the party's policies and propositions; Second, using the internet as a new way of communication. After Cameron took office as Prime Minister, he sent each netizen registered on his personal web an email with his own signature and posted several blogs to state his concepts of governance and the party's policies and propositions. Other leaders of the Conservative Party also wrote essays to report on work, promoting things they have done for the people and their future work plan. These online interactions have played a role in strengthening the ties between parties' leaders and the public, which promotes the parties' policies and propositions at the same time.

4. Enlarging Inner-party Democracy and Promoting Scientific Decision-Making

In recent years, many countries' major parties were striving to expand the scope and ways for party members and people to participate in the party's decision-making and promote the democracy, scientification and institutionalization of decision-making within the party. The Social Democratic Party (SPD) of Germany, after losing the general election in 2009, decided to shift its model from the previous model characterized by small group decision making, to one that was open to all the party members and people outside the party.

The Democratic Party of Italy passed a guideline draft involving six themes like national revolution, labor, judiciary, college scientific research, green economy and European development at the Party Conference in 2010. It called on all party leaders to have a profound discussion and asked for advice from the public. At the same time, relevant forums were to be held and led by directors from the Party Secretary to attract famous people and specialists to give advice on working out the party's guidelines. The French Socialist Party also held discussions focusing on big issues, such as the model of economic and social development, social justice, party reform and diplomacy in 2010. It decided, in preparation for the Presidential Election in 2012, to start the primary election of candidates in 2011 for the first time. These targets cover all mid-left voters, including the youth, grass-root people and block residents. The Communist Party of Vietnam launched a pilot program of directly electing secretary of the Party Committee in 10 provinces and municipalities in 2010. People were pleased and excited to be able to directly elect the party leader, so this program passed successfully. The Bulgarian Socialist Party did not reject members with different opinions, but encouraged all members to discuss these opinions. These measures further involved party members in politics and increases democracy, which was conducive to attracting more people to join the party and winning more support both in and outside the party.

III. A Brief Conclusion

Since 2010, changes in the world political party politics indicated the following trend: First, a "Hung Parliament" frequently occurred. The general elections in developed countries such as Great Britain, Australia and the Netherlands was difficult, the ruling and the opposition party got similar number of votes, and no single party could gain the majority of votes in Parliament. This showed that western people hold diversified political opinions, and it became harder for a single party to seek a majority position in politics and a ruling coalition seemed to become the mainstream.

Second, the turnouts in Western countries were low. The abstention rate in national and local elections in Western Europe frequently hit high records. In the 2010 French Grand District Council Election, the abstention rate in the two rounds of voting reached as high as 53% and 48% respectively. In March 2010, in the local Italian elections, less than half of the voters cast their votes, 9% down compared with five years ago. This demonstrated a decreasing loyalty towards political parties in Western Europe. The reason why those voters had "political apathy syndrome" was because the guidelines, which differentiated the two parties, became similar, and there were not big differences between the two ideologies, and the political positions tended to become more obscure, as a result of which voters felt hard to choose and some therefore just gave up the right to vote.

Third, the multi-party system did not fit some developing countries. In the 1990s, influenced by the drastic changes in the USSR and Eastern Europe, as well as the Western democratization wave, many developing countries started to adopt the multiple-party system. However, reality showed that the multiple-party system did not run smoothly in some countries. Since its introduction, the western multiple-party system had constantly run into conflicts with the complicated situation in developing countries. Factors such as the problematic military forces and strongman politics of these countries and the intervention of great powers constantly threatened to impede the political party development of developing countries. Some ruling and opposition parties in some developing countries did not follow the rule of the political games, and the conflicts in elections caused conflicts, and even fighting on the street at times, and the struggle for power continued destabilizing the political environment. It was said that the reason why some African countries frequently had military coups was because the ground for strongman polities still existed and the tradition that military power controlled politics had not been eliminated. The Indian media commented that the difficulty in electing a new Nepal Prime Minister had something to do with India's intervention. India hoped that the moderate party, the Congress Party, in Nepal could come into power, rather than the leftist party, the Maoist. The political party development in developing countries indicated that the local characteristics carried by parties should be respected and party politics must be developed step by step. The multi-party system introduced from the West had conflicts with the traditional political culture, especially when some traditional political powers still had social influence. Since it was almost impossible to end the competition and political games among parties, political stability could not be restored.

Fourth, the debates over developing modes became more and more fierce. After the global financial crisis, the major political parties in some countries started to reflect on the traditional way of development, conduct policy adjustments and put forward new social and economic development strategies, in order to gain an upper hand in the future world competition on the concepts, mentality, systems and modes of economic development. The global financial crisis manifested that there was no perfect development mode that could be applied anywhere in the world, and only the mode that best fitted ones own country and the development stage and could be adjusted according to the change of time was the best.

Fifth, major parties in the world paid more attention to the construction of their own party, in order to keep up with the pace of the world with fast information and the flow of the media. In recent years, especially since the financial crisis, to overcome the challenges brought by globalization and information society, political parties started to reform the election system, increase political participation both inside the party and in society, and improve the effect of communication by using modern communication tools, in order to expand democracy inside the party and enhance the construction of the party. Although the situation varied from country to country, some innovative measure in foreign countries still can serve as important references for us.

Chapter 14

Reflections on the Financial Crisis by Western Left-Wing Scholars and Communists

Liu Zhiming

1. Reasons for the International Economic and Financial Crisis

Facing the international and economic crisis that swiftly aroused global turmoil and accelerated reform and adjustment of the world in 2008. In the western world, some of the left-wing scholars and communists thought back about this financial and economic crisis from different point of views. The major opinions are as follows:

1.1 Classify the Underlying Reason for the International Financial and Economic Crisis into "Financialization"

Although the international community always took the United States as example with which to analyze the reason for the global financial crisis as a "product for a long-term process." Sam Webb, Chairman for the Communist Party of the United States, believed that many people only realized the direct reason for the crisis; they "did not know financialization was the underlying reason that brought the financial system and economy of the United States to the edge of abyss." He pointed out: "financialization was a double-edged sword. It was the success of financialization that gave birth to new weak links in the economy of the United States and the world, which made the economy unsustainable for development." The Portuguese Communist Party also regarded the "recurring" financial crisis that "has become increasingly serious international infectious diseases" as the result for "continuous financilization of the world's capitalist system and the financial capital dominating the world."

1.2 Thought of the Underlying Reason for International and Economic Crisis as the Stagnation Trend of Capitalism

John Bellamy Foster, the chief editor for the world famous left-wing magazine

Monthly Review and professor of Sociology at Oregon University of the United States, thought the underlying reason for this crisis was: since the end of post-war prosperity in 1960s, production and investment in real economy kept in the situation of stagnation. Since then, capitalism started to financialize the economy to compensate the result for the stagnation, which made the financial bubbles' inflation gradually separate from with the real economy and led to the present financial crisis in the United States and the world. Coincidentally, Robert P. Brenner, famous left-wing scholar of the United States, also believed "the reason for the crisis rooted in the decline of the activity for the developed economic bodies since 1973, especially since 2000."

1.3 Emphasis on Neo-Liberal as the Root for International Financial and Economic Crisis

Avram Noam Chomsky, the famous left-wing scholar and professor at Massachusetts Institute of Technology (MIT), thought that, to a large extent, the food crisis in most of the countries in the southern hemisphere and the financial crisis in the northern hemisphere shared one root: "The shift of neo-liberalism since the 1970s, which ended the Breton Woods System established by the United States and Great Britain after the Second World War." David Kotz, Economics professor at the University of Massachusetts and well-known left-wing scholar, also thought: "This financial crisis was a logical result for the deluge of neo-liberalism all over the world since 1980." He regarded the capitalism of neo-liberalism as the root of the financial crisis. From his point of view, the financial crisis was more likely to occur when neo-liberalism "released the constraining over finance" and "the polarization between rich and poor was worsening".

1.4 Emphasis on the Explosion of the Economic Crisis as the Result of the "Basic Contradiction of Capitalism"

Many foreign Communist organizations insisted on this point of view. The Ukraine Communist Party thought: "The interior contradiction of the Capitalism… finally led to this absolutely logical result—an overall global economic crisis. This crisis proved again that the relations of production under the Capitalism did not have the capability of self-regulation." The Greek Communist Party pointed out that: "When the crisis is approaching, the irreconcilable contradiction between socialized production and occupation over the productive materials of the capitalists is more obvious." William K. Tabb, a famous left-wing scholar and professor at Queens College of New York University believed "the contradiction between overproduction and the needs of the society" resulted in this financial and economic crisis. He pointed out: "Residual value occupied by the capital could not find the way in production; therefore, it entered financial area where it was suck in the bubbles of speculation. These bubbles finally broke and brought chaos and pain in the whole economic area."

1.5 Thought of the Financial Crisis: "Inevitable Result for Decades of Globalization"

Sitaram Yechury, Committee of Indian Communist Party (Marxism) Political Bureau, concluded this point based on the "two important features of globalization." He thought, to seek for the reason for this crisis, people must pay great attention to the following two important features of globalization: "First of all, this procedure was accompanied with the economic inequality between rich countries and poor countries and the economic disparity between the rich and the poor within one country. 20% of the rich takes up 75% of the total income of the world. Second, globalization worsened the phenomenon of "economy and unemployment rate jointly grow." The only way for capitalism to keep its benefits was to encourage the poor to make efforts to gain loans. However, when the due date for the repayment arrived, bad debts were inevitably arriving at the same time. This is the most accurate explanation for the recent significant drop for the price of real estate resulted in sub-prime crisis in the United States and the bad debts for housing loan."

2. Strategies to Face the International Economic and Financial Crisis

In the western world, left-wing scholars and communists sharply criticized the strategies of governments that fundamentally "protected the interest of propertied class" and issued strategies, tactics and policies concentrating on social fairness and the improvement of public life.

2.1 Western Governments' Measures against Crisis only "Protected the Interests of Propertied Class"

After analyzing various constraining measures of western governments to fight against the financial crisis, the Portugal Communist Party expressed that the fundamental starting points of these plans were as the same as the neo-liberalism implemented by the right-wings, Social Democratic Party and major capitalists, financial speculators and major capital oligarchies. Nom Chomsky also criticized: "While billions of people are suffering from famine, to save banks is not the most important affair. Do not forget that in the richest countries, millions of people are trapped in hunger." On "the most important" measure, the reduction of the interest rate of the Federal Reserve Bank that was figured out by the United States to relieve the crisis and promote the reduction of the market interest rate, Makoto Itoh, academician at Japan Academy, professor emeritus of Tokyo University and famous Marxism economist, revealed that its nature was to maintain and protect the benefits of financial oligarchies and speculators. He commented: "With this kind of interest rate policy, it obviously attended to the interests of these financial organizations and their investors, those fell into deficit, because of the price decline of the securities related to sub-prime and the shortage of liquidity."

2.2 Criticism That Western Governments' Measures Did Not Touch the Root of the Economic Crisis

Slavoj Zizek, world famous left-wing scholar, professor of Philosophy Department of Ljubljana University in Slovenia, thought, in light of the present crisis, mainstream ideology did not declare global capitalism system to be the fault of the financial crisis, but to its deviation—loose management or corruption of major financial institutes. This was the prolongation of ideology of neo-liberalism, which could not defeat crisis. [135] Chris Harman, a theorist of Britain Socialist Labor Party and left-wing scholar, believed western governments' measures against the crisis were limited within choices between the free market economy and governmental intervention. Now, they shifted to "governmental intervention" to fight against the financial crisis. From his point of view, this did not "touch the root of the economic crisis". [136] Fuwa Tetsuzo-Pre-chairman of the Japanese Communist Party, criticized: "Measures of the capitalist countries are palliative drugs," because "the recent crisis is a combination of both finance and overproduction. However, the rescue measures of the developed countries attended only to the financial crisis, by using national finance to rescue, which could not solve the fundamental problem."

2.3 The Claim on Fundamental Reform of Capitalist System

Due to the fact that "people in power attempted to get rid of the crisis without any change of the existing class strength structure," David Harvey thought, if people would like to "change this structure," there was no doubt that the "fury of populist is in need," because it could arouse a similar political campaign of Latin America." He also expressed that he

135 Slavoj Žižek,"Use Your Illusions: Obama's Victory and the Financial Meltdown", London Review of Books, 14 November 2008.

136 http://www.cctb.net/llyj/llgc/zbzyyj/201004/t20100406_21212.htm.

wished "a consensus of these political campaigns"; that was to aim at "fundamental reform on capitalism system." Attilio Barron, a well-known left-wing scholar, sociologist and political scientist of Argentina, pointed out that to realize the fundamental reform on capitalist system must be on the basis of Leninism to "enhance public organization and awareness," to "rebuild people's social and political thoughts," "make the whole world believe that capitalist system could not eliminate the crisis from the root," and "make people aware that the only battle to gain positive results was to fight against capitalism." He also pointed that the plan should not "only aim at one policy or one phase of neo-liberalism, but also at the basic structure of capitalist society."

2.4 Emphasis That the Actual Way to Rescue the Crisis is to "Meet the Basic Request of the Social Underclass"

John Bellamy Foster pointed out that the real way to rescue the crisis was to meet the basic request of the social underclass, but not to consume the wealth of tax-payers to make "golden parachutes" for the minority at the top of society. The Britain Communist Party proposed in *Left-Wing Program* that it desired to try its best to meet the basic requests of the underclass in society to fight against the crisis. For instance, carry out public investment and ownership in housing, energy and transportation, implement deep strategic intervention in manufacture and improve retirement pension and welfare. The Portugal Communist Party also thought that to commence fundamental solution for the crisis, it was necessary to take measures to meet the basic requests of the underclass: at home, offer basic social insurance for workers and the people suffering from crisis; strengthen the purchasing power of them to increase salary and pensions; improve the distribution of national income as a key measure to stimulate consumption and productive capability; implement social ownership over major productive materials under democracy and the government control the financial system; enhance the function of the government in economic development, draw up policies to promote public investment and recover the social function of the government; the government must intervene and require banks to implement a lower interest rate; and reduce the financial burden for the companies by paying their debts especially the public funds.

2.5 Claim the Socialism is the Only Way to End the Financial Crisis

From the point of view of the Russian Communist Party, the financial and economic crisis of capitalism proved the necessity of winning the battle to achieve socialism. As Zyuganov said, "Capitalism inevitably goes to destructive crisis, social disaster and military conflicts. As long as the power and benefits of usurers and speculators are beyond those of the creators of material and spiritual values, there will not be harmony in society. All of these factors force us to enhance the battle to gain social fairness, rights and freedom of labors and the triumph of socialism. The time strongly proved the necessity and inevitability of this battle." [137]Professor David Kotz also pointed out that, because of its inherent contradictions, capitalism could not get rid of the long-term influence of cyclical economic crisis. Only Marxism scientifically illustrated the root of the recent crisis and also offered prescription. Kotz trusted that, under the influence of social reality, supporters of socialism would inevitably increase. For the progressive groups, they may find opportunities to reform the economic and political system of capitalism all over the world.

3. The International Economic and Financial Crisis' Impact on International Politics and Security

From the point of view of many western left-wing scholars and communists, the major influences of this financial and economic crisis on global politics and security are as follows:

3.1 International Balance of Power Shift and Multi-Polarization Becomes Clear

Western, especially American, west-wing scholars thought, the influence of this crisis was asymmetric. That was to say, the attack on the United States and western developed countries was more serious and the extent of its economic recession was deeper. In addition, the crisis revealed the solid limitation of western capitalist countries and growing decay; it accelerated the shift of regional power balance moving from west to east, the balance of emerging powers in the whole world and the procedure of the change from uni-polar to multi-polar. For example, Nom Chomsky thought "the global structure was changing and Asia played an important role in the change. China functioned as the core of the shift of global strengths. Although emerging powers with China as the major representative did not take up the core position in the global structure, they started to shift from labor- intensive to multi-national capital business."[138] William K. Tabb also believed: "A multi-polar world is offering opportunities to some countries. If the cooperation trend among China, India and

137 LIU Shuchun: *Communist Party of Russia Under the World Financial Crisis*, *Chinese Academy of Social Science Review*, February 3rd 2009.

138 Quoted from Views Of Scholars On Post-Crisis International Relations, People's Daily, Edition 23 of September 20th.

Russia is matured, the shift of strength balance will be realized from Washington. Therefore, we are probably entering a new time."

3.2 Globalization of Neo-Liberalism Reaches its End

Many western scholars noticed that, after the financial crisis, many countries increasingly intervened in the market procedure. Measures against the crisis of Keynesianism seemed to be on the way to "obey the historical trend." Policies inclining to the redistribution of social welfare acted like the new idol of the day and global trading, capital movement, migrants and protectionism for finance and trade were showing a rise. Therefore, most of them believed that although this crisis could not lead to the absolute collapse of capitalism, it certainly was a changing point for the globalization of the economy, which would end the globalization time of neo-liberalism since the 1980s. The freedom market model of America and Great Britain would lose some of its charm and influence. Due to the reality that "global political balance was waving backwards," Immanuel Wallerstein believed that neo-liberalism would be recorded as one cyclical wave in the world capitalist economic history. From his point of view, the real problem was not concerned with whether this period could end, but, like in the past, whether it could recover the comparative balance of the global system. However, the question remained: Is the damage too great? Are we now in the violent chaos of the global economy and the integrate world system?

3.3 Left-Wing Will Welcome its New Opportunity of Development

Through this international financial and economic crisis, western left-wing scholars and communists absolutely enhanced the idea that it was the chronic illness that capitalism could not conquer, and the prospect for the renaissance of socialism and Marxism turned up under the environment that lacked left-wing political movements. Joel Geier, editor of Socialist Workers' Party, thought, because of "this disaster of free market, we gained arguments to discuss the inevitable failure of capitalism and the institute change to the request of human beings." The financial crisis, without a doubt, means "left-wing which was marginalized for decades finally got its huge opportunity of development." Sam Weber, Chairman of Communist Party of the United States, thought, although in the past half of the century, left-wing forces, including the Communist Party in the United States, struggled arduously and made great contributions. Left-wing forces stayed in the "marginalized area" because of Mechanism, Cold War Ideology and the refusal on revolution. Left-wing force was not a policy maker in the U.S., which could neither influence the political procedure like in the 1930s, nor function like left-wing parties in other countries. Sam Weber said, "It was not a main role and could not control the direction of the politics of the United States." However, he believed that, facing this financial crisis, "history would not repeat. In the new political prospect, left-wing forces have opportunity to enter the main stream in politics of the U.S. from the marginalized area; therefore, they have the right to speak in the discussion about the future of the country and have opportunities to move and influence the thought and behaviors of millions of people."[139] In France, because of the threatening global economic crisis, the offensive power of its right-wing government and the dissatisfaction on social parties of reformists, the left-wing trend among the French people, was even more obvious, which made a "New Anti-Capitalism Party" based on the radical left-wing party, "Alliance of Revolution Communism," and other left-wing forces to be set up in the rural area of Paris in February 2009. Within several months, "New Anti-Capitalism" established 460 local committees around France with 9,000 members. This party issued the political goal was to "adjust the integrated structure of the whole society," and also claimed state ownership over major industries, closed the exchanges and made use of this crisis to set up one force that could protect revolution reform of sociality, fight against private ownership and rebuild a socialist future with more "democracy." Zhu Jiajin of the Communist Party of Malaysia thought, "This is a new start of left-wing forces of France in the brutal and revolution time, which aids the development of radical left-wing force around Europe, and even the world.

On the development situation of the left-wing in Latin America, one article on *Levantamiento* of Spain pointed out that "a solider of nationalism born in Venezuela, aboriginal president of Bolivia, pre-metallurgy worker of Brazil, women in power in Chili and Argentina, the pre pope of Paraguay who took office in the slippers and the economists in Ecuador who support Keynesianism, all of these composed the left-wing map in South America."[140] It also believed that, although the present "global capitalist crisis" occurred, a large amount of left-wing governments in South America offered the "soil of optimism."

3.4 Possible Arrival of New Waves of War and Reform

Left-wing scholar of the United States, Loren Goldner, believed that after the financial crisis, none of the countries could play the role of a "great" America and the fight between

139 http://www.cctb.net/llyj/lldt/zdyj/201001/t20100127_20080.htm.

140 *Left Wing in South America: A Piecing-together Map* , See LI Shenming: *World Is Reflecting, Views on International Financial Crisis and Neo-Liberalism*, Social Sciences Academic Press, July 2010, P142.

two possible futures would unfold: either one government of global capital, or a "stormy heaven" of new workers class. From his point of view, the most serious capitalist crisis since 1929 might prepare for the biggest workers' strike after 1919. The revolution might break through, as he said, "History offered us with a precious opportunity; if we could not seize it, there would not be another same opportunity in our whole life." He used the quote from Rosa Luxemburg, from 90 years ago, who said, "Revolution told us: 'I existed, I exist and I will exist.'" Samir Amin also believed that after the financial crisis, "New wars or revolutions will arrive. It is possible because the governments in power just want to come back to the situation before the finance collapse, but without any other idea."

4. A Brief Review of Western Left-Wing Scholars' Reflection towards the Financial Crisis

From the stand, point of view and method of Marxism, various views on the reflections about international financial crisis of western left-wing and communists can be concluded into the following points:

First, the deep reflections from different point of view on the financial crisis from western left-wing scholars and communists are the awareness that should be followed at the present time. It is of great meaning for us to understand the reason and the influence of the financial crisis and the nature of the measures of western nations against the crisis, to judge the domestic and international situations in the post-crisis era, to enhance and improve macro control with specific target and to develop the effects against the shock of international financial crisis. It is also of great help for us to accelerate the change of economic development model, insisting on the strategy of enlarging the domestic requests with stronger will, guarantee and improve people's life, establish the new world political and economic orders with more confidence, and actively participate in international cooperation to protect our own sovereignty, security and interests of development.

Second, although some of progressive western left-wings who recognized that "Marx's viewpoints have important guiding meanings for understanding and discussing the present financial crisis" started to move their sight to "the critics of Marx on capitalism" and attributed the fundamental reason for this international financial crisis to the point revealed by the father of Marxism on the fundamental contradict of capitalism. However, it must be pointed out that there are also left-wings, especially moderate ones, avoiding the basic contradict between capital and labor. They gave up the basic concepts of the Marxist class theory and the theory of surplus value on purpose and preferred to use the language of western capitalist as "humanitarian," "global currency," "market economy," "undeveloped," "the third world," "east and west," "north and south," and willingly regarded this crisis as the result of people's greediness with the same idea as the western right-wing capitalists. Therefore, although they reflected the financial crisis with criticism on capitalism, their class position was not Marxism or even anti-Marxism.

In addition, since modern capitalism started "the shift from national monopoly to international financial capital monopoly" from the 1970s, developed countries, especially the United States, demonstrated the fundamental features of the international financial monopoly period of the capitalism—"fast financialization of the economy," "virtualization and bubble of finance," "liberalization of the liquidity and operation of finance," "gradual hollow of the real economy," "poverty of working masses," and "general debt of economy and national operation." In view of the international financial monopoly period of capitalism, the contradiction between socialization of production and the private ownership over productive materials continuously developed. In the enterprises, especially financial enterprises, the contradiction between organization, plan and the worldwide anarchy beyond territory were very fierce. The contradiction between the unlimited production and the lack of purchasing power of a society with enough ability to pay, which resulted from the comparative poverty of the labor masses, was worsening. We believe that, to analyze the reason of financial and economic crisis, it is necessary to take "the basic view of Marxism on capitalist finance and the economic crisis" was " close" to the new reality of international financial monopoly period of capitalism. Therefore, we reasonably believe that to attribute the international financial crisis to the "inevitable result of the contradict intensification of the international financial monopoly capitalism" is the practical development or further deepening of the "basic view of Marxism on capitalist finance and economic crisis", which does not only insists on the principle, but also enriches the basic view of Marxism on capitalist finance and economic crisis with present practice.

Third, we could not say that the critics of western left-wing scholars on the western governments' measures against the crisis and their policies to improve social fairness and people's life absolutely had no impact on the policies of European and American countries, but they fundamentally helped to relieve the crisis for the capitalist system, or it could be said they served to the "reformed" capitalist institute and the world political and economic orders under it. Therefore, it could be said that many western left-wings and communists got rid of the "ideology net" of the neo-liberalism of capitalism, but they fell into other "ideology nets" of capitalists, especially that of democratic socialism. Under the background when financial crisis made the European economic development model suspected by people and when European Union members generally fell into economic depression, "welfare model" of left-wings seemed not practical for the present situation. Although Russian Communists claimed the necessity of socialism and some left-wing scholars issued the request and strategy of "anti-capitalism" and declared the "possibility of reform," they did not resort their strategy to the labor people, nor positively shaped the social strength described by Marxism or to gain the support from this social strength. Therefore, it could be concluded that their claims and policies would stay only in the "forum" or "academic conferences." In other words, they would "possibly" lose another historically excellent opportunity offer. As Osvaldo Martinez, Economic Affairs Committee of National People's Conference of Cuba and famous economist, pointed out, "The serious economic crisis of capitalist system could not lead to a planned political direction. From these crises, both the left-wing and the right-wing movements may turn up. All of these did not depend on the economic crisis, but relied on the various political powers under specific environment. It could be answered by the flexibility of each political power, their art of fighting, correct strategies and the leadership."[141]

Fourth, on the point of views from western left-wing scholars on the influence of the financial crisis, we should analyze them from two sides: they seized the historical trend of the polarization of world structure in the post-crisis period, the approaching adjustment of world capitalism and the precious opportunity for the left-wings; but the "limitation" of their influence on the financial crisis mentioned above should be pointed out. For instance, regarding how to understand the change of the international political structural adjustment, on one hand, we should admit the global polarization, the serious weakening of the hegemony of the United States because of its economy and the reality of its declining soft-power and global influence; and on the other hand, we should note that for the global political structure, the influence from the international financial crisis stayed in the period of "quantitative" but not "qualitative," which did not shake the base of the existing structure. At least, it did not bring a "leap" for the international political structure with one super power and several major powers. As Jürgen Storm, a researcher at the Institute of Security and Development Policy of Sweden, pointed out, in the security structure, as the most powerful military nation, the United States played a key role in regional and global security. In the productive structure, the United States took the domain position and in the financial structure, the U.S. dollar was one of the major storage and settlement currencies.

---

141 Quoted from SONG Xiaoping: *Present International Financial Crisis, Globalization and Development-Summary of the 11th Globalization and Development Conference*, *World Communism Research*, Issue 5 of 2009.

In the knowledge structure, the soft power of the United States could not be neglected and its creative power still ranked first among all nations. Therefore, the United States was badly hurt in this crisis, but its capability and will to maintain its hegemony never disappeared.

Furthermore, on how to understand the issue of neo-liberalism coming to its end, on the one hand, it is reasonable to believe that in the past 30 years, economic policy doctrine of neo-liberalism that was "flattered as a world outlook permeating around all aspects of life" or so-called "laissez-faire," "free market," western capitalist ideology has lost all its reputation in the world. However, we should also see that as the "most successful ideology" or "ideological hegemony," neo-liberalism that was tightly tied with capitalism and private ownership, especially with major capitalists and monopoly groups, could not be "buried in the mud." It was still rooted in a thick world political, economic and social source. In the future, once the economy starts to recover, it may emerge again. Maybe, as long as the major monopoly groups exist, especially the major financial capital, there will be a deluge of neo-liberalism theory in society.

In addition, on the influence of the financial crisis on left-wings, at one aspect, we should realize that left-wings face a huge opportunity of development with many years worth of reality to experience and test. Its objectivity cannot be neglected nor be regarded as a "pure" subjective. At the other aspect, we cannot deny that this financial crisis brought serious challenges to the left-wings, especially the new left-wing governments in Latin America was faced with the most serious challenges of the financial crisis. As the famous left-wing scholar James Petras pointed out, although new left-wing governments (or post-neo-liberalist governments) in Latin America took measures to fight against poverty and enlarge the social expenses, they have not changed the basic economic structure of neo-liberalism they inherited: the recovery of economy in recent years has highly relied on the export of primary agricultural and mineral commodities and the inflow of international money. Compared with the labor, the capital took the absolute advantage. Therefore, when the world economic crisis was approaching, the fragility of these governments turned up gradually. They may make use of Keynesianism to gain temporary stability, but after the failure of Keynesianism in the following years, they would be replaced by radical left-wing, communism or by extreme right-wing, Fascism. We should also see that western left-wings and communists were not ready to think deeply on how capitalism replaced the class organizations and its replacement practice and theories. They have not issued any aggressive idea of the realization of reform until recently. Due to this, the Chairman of the Communist Party of the United States, Sam Weber, thought, although after the post financial crisis investigation showed that socialism became more charming for Americans, "socialism could not be listed on the political agenda. The present strength comparison and the ideology of millions of Americans could not reach the level to accept socialism—this was the starting point for all serious statistic and strategic discussions." The situation faced with western communist parties and world left-wing parties was reminiscent of Mr. Deng Xiaoping's brilliant speech when he met Nicholas Ceausescu, Secretary General of Romanian Communist Party and President of Romania, on October 17, 1988: "The present situation differs greatly from the past. We took the way of the October Revolution, which may be difficult for other countries because the conditions are different. Communist Parties out of the ruling class are seeking for other, new ways, but have not gained a mature point of view or method. Generally, the communist parties out of the ruling class is shrinking as the same as their influence." Surely, we also believe that if the financial and economic crisis of capitalism recur, if the class contradiction deepen and intensify, if the socialist way of China continues to grow, if other socialist countries constantly create and write new articles of development, it can be foreseen that communist parties of western countries and the world left-wing parties will gradually be active in their own countries and the central stage of the world political structure and the world communist movements will walk out from the valley of the "drastic change of Soviet Union and East Europe."

Part VI International Relation Theories

Chapter 15

A Brief Review of International Studies in 2009~2010

Yuan Zhengqing

The following is based on research on international issues of selected major international academic journals from 2009 to 2010. Selected publications include *International Organization, International Security, International Studies Review, International Studies Quarterly, Foreign Policy Analysis, International Studies Perspective, and European Journal of International Relations.*[142] These publications are selected for the representation of the advancement of international issue studies. Essays in the above-mentioned publications cover a very wide range of topics. Due to the limited space, instead of covering everything, the following is a selection of some of the more relatively important topics from the author's point of view.

I. China and the U.S. in the World Pattern

What regional and international impact does a rising China bring? Robert Ross says in *China's Navy Nationalism: Sources Prospects and the U.S. Response* that recently, China's political situation and the development of a national defense demonstrate that China will adopt an ambitious marine policy—the marine delivery capability based on aircraft carries.[143] Nationalism, rather than security, drives forward the Chinese naval strength. The navy nationalist demands were shown as follows: Navy is the symbol of comprehensive national strength. By building a strong navy, China may put an end the disgrace of sea invasion suffered in modern times and to regain their "lost territory." In order to safeguard China's maritime sovereignty, to obtain prestige and respect and to realize China's

142 Names of the publications are *International organization, International Security, International Studies Review, International Studies Quarterly, Foreign Policy Analysis, International Studies Perspective, European Journal of International Relations.*

143 Robert Ross, "China 's Naval Nationalism: Sources Prospects and the U S Response," *International Security*, 34 (2), 2009, pp.46~81.

renaissance, China must expand its water area and strengthen the capacity of carriers, which are regarded as the symbols of great power. Chinese navy nationalism and the construction of aircraft carriers will have a clear strategic and political influence on Sino-U.S. relations. Although China's naval nationalism will not pose a challenge to U.S. maritime security and the U.S. does not need to increase military expenditure or significantly change the strategic naval deployment, it will still pose a challenge to Sino-U.S. cooperation. Challenges facing the United States Navy are to make a limited military response to Chinese navy nationalism while avoiding unnecessary and harmful tensions in bilateral relations. The American political dilemma will be how to combine appropriate strategic response to limited expansion in the Chinese navy with its diplomatic strategy, which is bound to deal with U.S. nationalism and Chinese navy nationalism, to ease political tensions and push forward an overall sustainable cooperation between the two countries. Naval competition between China and the U.S. may lead to politicization of the entire agenda and pose challenges in a wide range of bilateral cooperation on issues including the nuclear non-proliferation issue on the Korean peninsula, the Taiwan issue, bilateral economic issues and cooperation on human rights issues. Even during the naval race, they should also respond to domestic and each country's nationalism to maintain diplomatic cooperation. It is crucial that the United States make early and positive contacts with the Chinese navy to establish mutual confidence-building measures, including the implementation of joint naval exercises and bilateral agreements on maritime emergencies. Cooperation on the basis of strategic competition is not only feasible, but also in line with the broader interests of the United States.

Michael M. Glosny and Phillip C. Sauneders doubted the view of Robert Ross, questioning that the Chinese navy nationalism is not the reason for China's pursuit to development in naval forces. They believe it is the expansion of the interests caused by variability in China's security environment and integration into the world economy that is the real call for limited expansion of China's naval delivery.[144]

In addition to military forces, the academics are much more concerned about China's impact on state power. Daniel W. Drezne published an article entitled "Bad Debt," in which he analyzed and discussed on this topic.[145] Through assessment on a creditor country converting financial power into political power, the author believes that the accumulation

144 Michael A. Glosny and Phillip C. Sauneders, "Debating China's Naval Nationalism," *International Security,* 35(2), 2010, pp.161~175.

145 Daniel W. Drezner, Bad Debts, "Assessing China's Financial Influence in Great Power Politics," *International Security,* 34 (2), 2009, pp.7~45.

of capital can increase resistance to external pressure or the ability to exert pressure. However, when a capital-exporting country tries to use financial power to force other countries to change policies, they themselves shall encounter great difficulties in limitation of coercive capacity. Financial power may bring an effect on weak and small countries, but would cause hardly any effect on big powers. China's financial power has increased its deterrent capability, but no effect on its coercive power. China can use its financial ability to ignore the pleas of the United States, but it cannot force the U.S. to change its policies. Policy community has exaggerated China's financial influence on U.S. policy.

Regarding China's post-Cold War strategic intentions and objectives, Deborah Welch Larson and Alexei Shevchenk, using analytical framework of social identity theory discussed in the "Status Seeker: Chinese and Russian Response to U.S. Primacy," that China's grand strategy after the Cold War is to restore the prestige and glory in the past of China and desire the recognition of other big countries. The establishment of partnerships with some big powers, summit conferences, and the proposal of the concept of responsible power have, with no exception, reflected the desire for status. However, although China has acceded to many international organizations, it does not accept the liberalist core values of these organizations in terms of intervention for the protection of individual rights.[146]

The status of the United States is another area arousing concerns and intense debate of the international academic community. Five American publications in 2008 were involved in this topic from five different aspects. Christopher Layne made a profound comment on these works and related issues in "The Waning of U.S. Hegemony—Myth or Reality."[147]

U.S. National Intelligence Council published *Global Trends 2025: A Transformed World* to state the view that the U.S.-led unipolar world will be replaced by a multi-polar one within 20 years. Major reasons are the rising of new great powers, represented by China, India, and probably Russia, as well as economic, financial and domestic political constraints on U.S. capacity. U.S. military superpower status will be no longer as dominant as it was at the end of the Cold War. Its soft power is also declining because of its liberal development model of politics and economy being

146 Deborah Welch Larson and Alexei Shevchenk, "Status Seekers: Chinese and Russian Response to U.S. Primacy," *International Security*, 34 (4), 2010, pp.63~95.

147 Christopher Layne, "The Waning of U.S. Hegemony—Myth or Reality," *International Security*, 34(1), 2009, pp.147~172.

challenged. A multi-polar world will be fundamentally different from the superiority of the United States after the Cold War.[148]

Zach Maria in the "Post-American World" pointed out that China and India are two rising powers that will become the world's second and third largest economy. The U.S. remains the center of the international system. It will face the challenges to soft power rather than hard power. It can maintain a superior status in the international system by means of soft power rather than hard power.[149]

Singapore's former Foreign Minister Kishore Mahbubani wrote in *The New Asian Hemisphere: The Irresistible Shift of Global Power to the East* that the power of the international system has undergone profound changes, transmitting from the United States to East Asia, especially China and India. The West should welcome the rise of Asia, the soft power of which is more attractive than the U.S. The moment of restructuring international order has come.[150]

The Second World, written by Parag Khanna, painted a brand new picture of international politics. Globalization and the competition among the U.S., EU and China for the world's leading power and the support from "the second world" will become the components of international politics. Second world, on the boundary between the first world and third world, is the zone for geopolitical and global collision. It includes Russia, Ukraine, Southeast Asia, North Africa, the Middle East, the Balkans and Central Asia. The decline of the hard power and soft power the of U.S., the rise of Chinese power and its role as imperial power center in East Asia, the constant expansion of the EU in its geopolitical scope will lead to increasingly fierce competition among the three. The U.S must adapt to the non-U.S. world. Globalization used to be equal with Americanization, but now it is accelerating the decline of the United States.[151]

Stephen G. Brooks and William C. Wohlforth wrote, in *World out of Balance,* that the world for a long period of time (at least 20 years) will remain in a unipolar state without establishment of a coalition capable of balancing U.S. hegemony. The super power status enjoyed by the United States makes it particularly difficult for other countries, even for soft

---

148 National Intelligence Council, *Global Trends 2025: A Transformed World,* Washington, D.C.: U.S. Government Printing Office, November 2008.

149 Fareed Zakaria, *The Post-American World,* New York: W.W. Norton, 2008.

150 Kishore Mahbubani, *The New Asian Hemisphere: The Irresistible Shift of Global Power to the East*, New York: PublicAffairs, 2008.

151 Parag Khanna, *The Second World: Empires and Influence in the New Global Order*, New York: Random House, 2008.

power balancing. In this unipolar world, the United States can take advantage of hegemony to change the international system by reshaping the international mechanism, the legitimacy standards and, through globalization, without having to worry about other countries' ability to counter U.S. hegemony.[152]

Layn made unique comments on fundamental arguments of the five works from the perspective of "polar," American power and international relations theory. In his view, the unipolar stability theory raised by Brooks and Wohlforth is problematic, because they failed in looking at the distribution of power in a dynamic way, or noticing that hegemony nurtures the seed of its destruction. Technology diffusion, the advantage of latecomers, as well as the high cost of maintaining hegemony will eventually affect the hegemonic powers. The consequence of no constraint to American hegemony does not equally mean that there is no country trying to constrain the United States. The result of the system and the unit behavior are separate concepts. China and India, as the representative of emerging powers, most clearly reflects the trend towards a multipolar system, but this may not be sufficient proof that the international system is becoming multipolar. The emergence of great powers is the result of pressure from inside the structure and unit interactions. GDP cannot solely determine the prospect of a single country to constitute one aspect of the global system. For China, although in the past 30 years it has achieved double-digit GDP growth, its ability to maintain this momentum remains unclear. It remains unclear what impact the global financial crisis will bring on China and the U.S., but, more importantly, domestic issues faced with China may affect its future to become a big power. For the moment, China's development momentum will make it a potential military and economic big power in the international system. As for the U.S., through soft power and the international system, its ability to maintain its political status has encountered problems. The economic crisis put a negative effect on its soft power. International institutional arrangements created by the United States after World War II have also been shaken under the impact of the financial crisis. The emerging powers urgently require to seek reforms in the international system. At the G-20 summit, China and some other countries were requiring more shares in international financial institutions.

II. The Creation and Spread of International Norms

An international norm has always been the concern of the international academic

152 Stephen G. Brooks and William C. Wohlforth, *World Out of Balance: International Relations and the Challenge of American Primacy*, Princeton, N.J.: Princeton University Press, 2008.

community. Finnemore emphasized that the appearance of norms lie in the mass' attention being drawn to certain issues or created problems by norm-advocators who take the means of redefinition or explanation to make the issue eye-catching, and then become acceptable by major countries through advocators' persuasion.[153] Price lays emphasis on grafting a new norm into the existing framework to resonate with the original norms. Alexandra Gillies in the *Reputational Concerns and the Emergence of Oil Sector Transparency as an International Norm* provides a third explanation to the appearance of norm.[154] She believes that reputation is a factor to the appearance of international norms. The so-called reputation is the impression of one country held by other countries. Scholars of international relations used to connect reputation with compliance and with norm. This article, on the other hand, goes beyond this limitation to connect reputation with the appearance of norms, in which reputation is regarded to be the motivation to the emergence of norms. Giving an example in the case of transparency in petroleum sector, the author makes a comprehensive survey on the reason why, in recent years, oil companies discuss transparency in such a high-profile manner, while having encountered with great difficulty in making transparency in previous ten years through his track and personal interviews. One reason is that the oil sector operations in developing countries received great impact from advocacy organizations, which had paid close attention to the West's economic activity, and thus posed a huge challenge to the reputation of Western governments, international institutions and the company. Therefore the oil sector has to reduce risk on reputation by increasing transparency.

Brian Greenhill studied the impacts on human rights brought byinternational organizations bearing no human rights provisions. He selected data of 137 countries' violation of the right to health during 1982 to 2000, to test intergovernmental organizations' role in promoting human rights norms through data analysts of time series. The results show that international intergovernmental organization did have a positive impact on human rights, even if there are no clear human rights provisions on the agenda of these organizations. This conclusion is implied in its practical significance that researchers pay attention to human rights record of member states of intergovernmental organizations, instead of to human rights provisions, and in turn, can better encourage some countries to participate in those organizations without the relevant human rights provisions, but with

153 Matha Finnemore and Kathryn Sikkink, International Norm and Political Dynamic, International Organization, Autumn 1998, pp.887~917.

154 Alexandra Gillies, "Reputational Concerns and the Emergence of Oil Sector Transparency as an International Norm," *International Studies Quarterly,* 54 (1), 2010, pp.103~126.

human rights records of its member states higher than average level, which can affect these countries' human rights policy. In addition, to change state behavior and realize socialization of the nation by means of international intergovernmental organizations, policy makers should more seriously consider engagement rather than isolation.[155]

III. International Relations Theories: Thoughts from Scholars in China, Europe and the U.S.

From 2009 to 2010, research on international relations theory have achieved some new progress. Shiping Tang from Fudan University wrote in *Social Evolution of International Politics: From Mearsheimer to Jervis* a reflection of debate over offensive realism and defensive realism. He proposes a social evolution paradigm of endogenous evolution in the international political system.[156] He believes that international politics have been an evolution system. Grand theory of international politics in the past was merely a systematic theory, not a theory of evolution. The authors explained the international political system evolution from BC 1044 to the Second World War in 1945 from a macro point of view by examining the ancient Chinese system and the European system after the Holy Roman Empire period. He proposes that human society has developed from "a world of offensive realism" (that is, without expansion of territory, a country will not be annexed) to "a world of defensive realism" (that is, with no need or capability to expand territory, a country can obtain security). Offensive realism and defensive realism are two explanations of international politics at different times. One single theory is not enough to explain the changes in international political system. Different international political theories are from and suitable for different times of international politics and different eras of international politics and actually require different international political theories. International political system, as an evolutionary system, cannot be preceded through by non-evolutionary approach. Mearsheimer to Jervis made a mistake in their recognition of international political system as a non-evolution system. Therefore, the interpretation of international politics must be an evolutionary one as well. International politics must adopt a real

155 Brian Greenhill, "The Company You Keep: International Socialization and the Diffusion of Human Rights Norms," *International Studies Quarterly*, 54 (1), 2010, pp.127~145.

156 Shiping Tang, "Social Evolution of International Politics: From Mearsheimer to Jervis," *European Journal of International Relations*, 16 (1), 2010, pp.31~55; Tang S, "Fear in International Politics: Two Positions," *International Studies Review*, 10 (3), 2008, pp.451~471; Tang S, "From Offensive to Defensive Realism: A Social Evolutionary Interpretation of China's Security Strategy," in Ross R and Feng Z (eds), *China's Ascent: Power, Security, and the Future of International Politics*, Ithaca, NY: Cornell University Press, 2008, pp.141~162.

scientific theory of evolution, in other words, "to entitle Darwin the status he deserves."

Balancing of power is another important branch of international relation theories. Ever since the Cold War, the discussions on the topic basically centered around the explanation or confusion of big powers' behavioral response towards the U.S., which is why the other major powers did not come together to balance the U.S. who was taking global lead at that time. Jack Levy and William R. Thompson gave new interpretation to this in "Balancing on Land and at Sea."[157] Previous realism proposed four explanations to the unbalanced situation: First, Waltz said the balancing of the United States is only a matter of time, which is not in existence at present, but will appear in the near future; second, the charitable intention and inclusive policies of the United States reducing the other countries' perception on threat; third, Mearsheimer said offshore balancing will not help the establishment of a balanced alliance. Regional countries more tend to worry about the threat of hegemony in the region. These countries are actively seeking balance from outside the region; four, it is too risky and costy to adopt balancing strategy towards the U.S. In the author's view, these explanations have some truth, but are not completely satisfactory. There are two errors in such an interpretation. First, the balance of power theory is not universally applicable. The core assumptions on balancing strategy and non-enduring-hegemony in the multi-national system can apply only to the European system, but not to global ocean system. Maritime powers are more interested in expanding the market than in expanding territory, so that the last five centuries witnessed the difference of system model established in the European system and the global ocean system. To this end, the author proposed five propositions: 1) big powers generally do not balance the most powerful maritime power, even if the strength of this maritime power has significantly increased; 2) the more powerful the leading maritime power is, the less likely it will be balanced; 3) the more powerful the leading maritime power is, the less likely a coalition against it will be built; 4) the more powerful the leading maritime power is, the more likely one or two big powers is to build a coalition with it; 5) allying with the dominant maritime powers happens more often than allying against them. The article tested and analyzed on relevant historical data, with the conclusion to support these five propositions. Sea powers are different from land powers, constitute a different type of threat, and lead to different reactions. Dynamics to seize power and the specific behavior of the alliance system are not the same for the sea and the land system with fundamental logic

157 Jack S. Levy and William R. Thompson, "Balancing on Land and at Sea: Do States Ally against the Leading Global Power?" *International Security*, 35 (1), 2010, pp.7~43.

divergences. The original balance of power theory extracted from the land system, therefore, cannot be generalized into the global maritime system. This conclusion has great significance to the current debate. That big powers did not establish an alliance to balance power against the United States is not, as some scholars asserted, to be "confusing," but in line with what has happened in the global system for at least five centuries. The balance of power theory can help scholars understand the dynamic power to the interaction among big powers; however, it must be clear of the terms and conditions applicable to the theory. Unconditional assumption that a state would adopt the balance of power or balance of threat will lead to mistakes.

Amir Lupovici proposed a new research agenda on deterrence theory.[158] The author first summarizes the basic contents in first three waves of deterrence theory: the first wave was produced after World War II, focusing on the strategic connotation and value of nuclear weapon. The concept of deterrence, which was neither systematic nor rich, had little impact on policy. The second wave came in the late 1950s. The introduction of game theory to the study of deterrence successfully converted cognitive concept into habit of thinking so as to enable scholars to better understand actors' strategy. However, it also led to a lot of criticism because of the lack of evidence to support and confirm this idea. The third wave is also facing the same problem that the second wave faces, but research has gone deep into effects from error awareness, domestic and bureaucratic politics. This three-wave study has a strong impact on international relations theory, especially on the development of realism and security studies, as well as on policies to massive retaliation, the first blow, and flexible reactions etc. At the start of the Cold War, nuclear weapons production and the dominance of realism paradigm triggered early researches on the theory of deterrence, then the end of the Cold War, the emergence of "new threat" interpretation and development of interpretivist perspective promoted the fourth wave of deterrence theory studies. "Steering of interpretation perspective" appears in the fourth wave of deterrence theory. It focuses on the study of inter-subjectivity scenes, which mainly consists of four themes: Firstly, deterrence can be learned. Classical rationalism also known as the so-called theory of deterrence, regarding deterrence as self-evident, the behavior of which is limitedly impacted by learning, mainly determined by the power of players. The learning theory emphasizes that deterrence itself depends on the learning process; Second, socialization influences the deterrence approach. Countries need to not only learn the

158 Amir Lupovici, "The Emerging Fourth Wave of Deterrence Theory," *International Studies Quarterly*, 54 (3), 2010, pp.703~732.

general strategic concept, but also know that these ideas can be put into action in their strategic relationship. Learning and socialization can help to explain how and why the United States and the Soviet Union adopted deterrence strategy in a gradual manner and how to ensure stability of nuclear deterrence by means of the institutionalization of arms control; Third, deterrence is a social construct. Like any other strategy, deterrence depends on concepts, knowledge, and interpretation of concepts and knowledge. It can be understood as a self-fulfilling prophecy or myth. Some specifications, such as transparency and the nuclear taboo, will also affect the credibility of deterrence; Fourth, deterrence is a discourse. Discourse is not just a natural language, but also gives meaning to the objective. Discourse not only reflects reality, but also constructs reality. Deterrence is not just words to communicate, but also rules and habits that can shape awareness of self and others in the international political arena. New wave of research on deterrence strategy is a supplement to previous rationalist research perspective. Classic rationalist deterrence study can benefit from emphasizing learning, socialization, social construction and interpretivist framework of discourse, while interpretivist approach needs to be enriched by solid evidence. A combination of these two will be the trend for development in the future.

IV. New Progress on Non-Conventional Security Issues

After the Cold War, the concept of security is constantly changing and the content of security is also extended. Non-traditional security has become an important topic. In recent years, a variety of international epidemic diseases such as SARS and H5N1, caused discussion on security issues. Gregory D. Koblentz proposes a basic framework in *Biosecurity Reconsidered: Calibrating Biological Threats and Responses* of the basic concepts of biological security, its content, cause, classification of biological threats and strategy to deal with biological threats.[159]

In the author's view, the concept of bio-security is closely related to the understanding of security. In the past, diseases had a significant impact on international security, but were not seen as a security hazard. Until the 21st century, health issue was included in security range by state governments and international organizations. Such a change is related to the following three understandings: first, the redefinition of security includes environmental degradation, climate change, organized crime, terrorism, etc.; second, recognition that these

159 Gregory D. Koblentz, "Biosecurity Reconsidered: Calibrating Biological Threats and Responses," *International Security*, 34 (4), 2010, pp. 96~132.

threats do not come from individual countries, but from transnational or non-state participants; third, focuses on individual and group security, rather than state security. The concept of human security has played a key role in the changing process. Health is part of human security. The development of technology, especially breakthroughs in genetic research, the emergence of new diseases, globalization and the change in nature of conflict, make biological threats an international topic for discussion. For the definition of bio-security, academic and policy makers have different understandings, which are dominated by an integrated concept. This security is for the careless, inappropriate or malicious use of potentially dangerous biological agents or biological technology. This broad definition sets difficulties for the establishment of a unified analytical framework. The author does not use the so-called biological threat spectrum, which was adopted in the previous studies. Instead, he employs an analytical framework of bio-security for the assessment of bio-security risks, providing a new way of thinking to reduce security threats.

Terrorism remains an important topic on the international politics field. Scholars give three main explanations to Islamic suicide terrorism: first, the interpretation at the level of international system. As the international system and domestic systems are different, in the international community, there is a state of anarchy. The nature of the international system creates difficulties for international governance. A number of failed states become hotbeds of domestic conflicts, providing a breeding soil for terrorism; Second, the United States make use of their status as a post-Cold War super-power for military intervention, such as the invasion of Iraq and deployment of military forces in some areas. Maintaining a military presence in Saudi Arabia and promoting the so-called democratic reforms in the Middle East aroused tension in the above-mentioned regions, and intensified the internal contradictions within the Arabian world. The Middle East and North Africa have become high-risk areas of terrorist attacks; Third, the Islamic fundamentalist belief claims to be in accordance with the Koran and Hadith to return to the beginning of the pure Islam. Terrorist suicide attacks are committed for jihad for the safeguard of the purity of Islam, and thereafter will be registered in heaven in the afterlife. These explanations are reasonable, but not sufficient. Bradley A. Thayer and Valerie M. Hudson, from a scientific point of view of life, made the fourth interpretation of suicide terrorism in "Sex and the Shaheed: Insights from the Life Sciences on Islamic Suicide Terrorism."[160] They believe

---

160 Bradley A. Thayer and Valerie M. Hudson, "Sex and the Shaheed: Insights from the Life Sciences on Islamic Suicide Terrorism," *International Security*, 34 (4), 2010, pp. 37~62.

that the Islamic society holds a long standing existence of gender inequality. The prevalence of polygamy and postponed marriage-age as a result of the poor condition of the marriage market has made a profound impact to the emergence of suicide terrorism. Their perspective, as a supplement, does not contradict with the previous explanations. From this point of view, to deal with terrorism, there is another school of thought, such as to raise the status of women in the Muslim world, to reduce the cost of dowry and marriage expenses, to establish a free and democratic government in the Middle East, and to respect individual rights and freedom.

V. The Challenges and Results of the Sino-American Nuclear Strategy

After the Cold War, especially in recent years, the trend of proliferation of nuclear weapons, changes in nuclear power, and Obama's goal of a nuclear-free world once again activated the interests of the academic world in nuclear strategy, reflect on nuclear strategy and policy options.

"International Security" published two articles in 2010 with "nuclear doctrine and strategy: challenges and consequences" as the theme to discuss on the United States and China's nuclear strategy and policy. Michael S. Gerson profoundly reconsiders the U.S. nuclear policy in "No First Use: The Next Step for U.S. Nuclear Policy."[161] The U.S. nuclear strategy contains an important part of the threat to use nuclear weapons first. This policy is based on the following four considerations: First, when faced with conventional dominant rivals, threatening the first use of nuclear weapons can provide a useful asymmetric deterrence; Second, the first to use nuclear weapons can deter threats and respond to biological or chemical weapons attack; Third, a pre-emptive nuclear strike can destroy the opponent before the opponent's use of nuclear weapons; Fourth, it can destroy strong and deeply-buried targets. The author believes that such a reason is not credible, but dangerous. First, there is no real need for military emergency to use nuclear weapons first. On the contrary, after the Cold War, the U.S. military has shown that the conventional forces can be quite credible. Second, the first use of nuclear weapons to the United States bears potentially high political costs. The United States has been working to prevent the spread of nuclear weapons worldwide. The first use of nuclear weapons will not coordinate

161 Michael S. Gerson, "No First Use: The Next Step for U.S. Nuclear Policy," *International Security*, 35 (2), 2010, pp. 7~47.

with nuclear non-proliferation promotion mechanism, and will weaken its credibility. Third, nuclear taboo after World War II has a binding effect on a range of military operations against the United States. The first use of nuclear weapons will also lead the crisis into the direction of further instability. If the U.S. may pledge of giving of the first use of nuclear weapons, it will gain some benefits, at least on the political and military level. First, opponents of the United States will reduce the fear of nuclear attack, which can reduce the possibility of the use of nuclear weapons from intentional, accidental and casual excuses. Second, U.S. nuclear policy can maintain its coherence and feasibility. It will increase the credibility of nuclear deterrence to retain nuclear weapons for retaliation purposes. Third, the U.S. can maintain its advantage in conventional forces in a better way.Fourth, it will help ease criticism on the U.S. missile defense and nuclear storage initiatives. Fifth, it can inspire changes in nuclear policy of other countries. Sixth, it will further promote nuclear non-proliferation mechanism, thus changing the other countries' hypocritical awareness of the U.S. nuclear policy to enable the United States take the initiative politically and morally. Although there might be obstacles in order to not be the first to use nuclear weapons in the government and military level, the author still believes that an oath to not be the first to use nuclear weapons should be the next choice of the United States.

In "China's Search for Assured Retaliation: The Evolution of Chinese Nuclear Strategy and Force Structure," M. Taylor Fravel and Evan S. Medeiros explained why the Chinese are willing to maintain a small amount of nuclear warheads for over four decades, being vulnerable to the first a nuclear strike. This question is confusing to structural realists, according to whose logic, China should develop more and diversified nuclear forces and a more elaborate nuclear strategy. In fact, China only gradually establishes a modest scale of nuclear forces to assure its second nuclear strike capability for retaliation. For this anomaly, the authors proposed two explanations. First, China's top leaders and military strategists believe that the role of nuclear weapons should be a deterrence to aggression to prevent coercion by other nuclear countries. It reflects China' international status as a great power. More importantly, a small amount of nuclear retaliation can achieve the purpose of nuclear retaliation. Nuclear weapons on the battlefield are actually useless. Second, China is short of nuclear strategy experts. Nuclear strategy research has been paid little attention. Although significant progress has been made in China's economic strength and reserve of talents in the past 20 years, and the pace of military modernization is being accelerated as well, China still maintains a nuclear retaliation strategy rather than the minimum nuclear deterrence strategy. This reflects that China's nuclear strategy is a prudent one.

Based on a limited scan through annual works on international studies, the international academic progress can be found in some areas. The voice of Chinese mainland scholars being heard in international relations theory is a pleasing outcome. In terms of research methods, case studies, process tracing, statistical model analysis, and in-depth interviews have been widely adopted. Economics, sociology, and psychology have been linked more closely with international relations. The potential for one discipline may gain development in interdisciplinary studies. Relations among major powers and non-traditional security issues remain the major concerns. Relation between international economic relations and international politics under the influence of the financial crisis has gained re-understanding. These issues are worthy of academic attention and analysis from the public.

Chapter 16

Clarification of Some Terms in International Relations Theory: Building the Discourse on Socialism with Chinese Characteristics

Li Shenming

According to the Marxist theory, language is not a part of the superstructure. Language and superstructure are not necessarily linked. Language is not created by a particular class, but is the creation of entire human society in millions of years' working and living exchanges. Language as a communication tool, like any other productive tool, that equally serves all types of social patterns, social systems, different classes and social groups. In addition, superstructure can only have an indirect connection with production through the intermediary of economic base, while language and human production activities are directly linked. Colorful production activities constantly produce changing languages. Some new vocabulary develops in production and life. Some old words gradually disappear, or are given new meanings.

The phrase "discourse power" is derived from the French sociologist Michel Foucault's theory on relations between discourse and social power. In December 1970, Foucault put forward the well-known proposition—"discourse is a power, by which people empower themselves." He believed that discourse was not just symbolic thinking or a communication tool, but a means to fight. Thus, ideology-free discourse is given the functions of rights and interests. Discourse power, in essence, is a political and economic right, reflecting the political and economic status of a person in community or a state in the world.

For this reason, culture and language are different. Language has nationality distinction, but there is no class distinction itself. Language is always an internal communication tool among the various ethnic groups and nations. In whatever social form, culture also has nationality distinction, but in class society, culture also bears class distinction. As an important part of culture, language cannot be separated from human thinking. Therefore, the language as a communication tool that bears no class distinction in form, but in class society it expresses some of the specific ideological content with class nature. Therefore, in terms of language in international communications, attention should not only be paid to the connotation of a word, but also the denotation of it, that is the actual concern it bears, to discover the powers, rights and interests behind the word.

Since the geographical discovery, the United States and Europe launched over 500 years' expansion, aggression, killing and conquest, completed its primitive accumulation, and continued to exploit the rest of the world. Since then, Western developed countries, especially the United States, gradually monopolized the international financial world. They created a money-printing machine to issue currency whenever they needed in order to maintain the orientation of public opinions by making use of news media. Western discourse often leads the trend of global discourse, to induce the non-Western civilizations into the so-called discourse framework of "freedom and democracy." The West gradually monopolizes the discourse power in international relations. This process was once weakened by the birth of the Soviet Union and development of New China, but with the Soviet transformation, especially the disintegration of Soviet Union, the U.S.-led Western discourse has been further strengthened. In the majority of development countries, "soft power" put forward by Joseph Nye has been achieved to a certain extent, beneficial to the Western and without a profit for the non-Western world. It also consolidated the irrational international political and economic and cultural order set up by the West, which was backed by capital and force. In 2008, the outbreak of the international financial crisis shook and broke the superstition to Western theory and caused reflection on Western discourse. Chinese scholars must not be hostile to all concepts in Western discourse system. As it becomes necessary, we need to boldly learn for our own use. However, we must pay attention to the fundamental differences that may exist in the nature of denotation. In international exchanges, we must construct the independent discourse system of socialism with Chinese characteristics, and make our own contribution to safeguarding our country's political, economic and cultural rights, and establishing a fair and reasonable new order of international relations.

The following is an analysis on several words popular in today's international relations.

I. "International Society"

After violent crimes occured in Tibet on March 14, 2008 and in Urumqi on July 5, 2009, a small number of Western countries strongly condemned the Chinese government in the name of "international community," while more than a hundred developing countries expressed strong support to the position taken by the Chinese government. Recently, the Nobel Committee awarded the Nobel Peace Prize to Liu Xiaobo, who claimed China needed three hundred years of colonial status. Western countries said it won the praise from the "international community," while the majority of developing countries have dismissed it. What is the real "international community"? It seems a clear answer can be directly received from the American linguist Noam Chomsky. On June 9, 2010, the UN Security Council adopted a resolution on Iran to implement the fourth round of sanctions since 2006. On May 3, 2010, when Chomsky was interviewed by Germany's *Friday* magazine on the topic of "the risk of the Iranian revolution," he was asked about his view on the international community imposing sanctions on Iran. Chomsky replied that "international community" was a strange phrase. Most of the world belongs to the Non-Aligned Group, and strongly supports Iran to enrich uranium for peaceful purposes. But they do not belong to the so-called "international community." Only those countries subject to U.S. orders belong to the "international community."[162] Another example: on September 23, 2010, when Iranian President Mahmoud Ahmadinejad accepted an interview from the Larry King Live Show of the U.S. Cable News Network (CNN) and asked, "Do you not understand the fears about nuclear -- nuclear weaponry in your country? With all the hostility in the region, don't you understand the fears over your having nuclear weapons? Ahmadinejad immediately replied with "Who is the world? Who represent the world? The United States? Its friends? No, the world is a very big place. And what U.S. officials are wrong about is that they see themselves as the world but they are not."[163] The "world" talked about by Ahmadinejad and Larry King contains equal meaning with "international community" from Chomsky after his explanation to the denotation of the word. "International community" is on behalf of hegemonies and power politics, therefore, a distinction should made before using the phrase "international community."

II. "Terrorism"

According to statistics, the official use of the word "terrorism" has existed for 200 years. There are thousands of works and documents, definitions and meetings on the term "terrorism." Still, there is not a generally accepted definition for "terrorism." the Eighth Meeting on United Nations Crime Prevention and Treatment formulated "Measures against

---

162 P7 of Social Science on May 27th, 2010.

163 http://www.tudou.com/programs/view/G533ks4XZ5E/.

International Terrorism," in which pointed out that "the international community has been unable to reach a general agreement on the meaning of international terrorism and effective measures against it since the first research started in 1972." In essence, different countries and different political groups will not form a universal view on "terrorism." W *Declaration on Measures to Eliminate International Terrorism* adopted by the 49th session of the UN General Assembly in 1994 pointed out: "Terrorism is a crime intended or calculated to cause terror for political purposes in population or a group of population." The only problem with this definition is that it is too narrow, unable to rise to the national level. In fact, hegemony and power politics, in essence, are magnified terrorism. They pose more dangers to peace and the development of human society and the world, and thus requiring of firm opposition.

III. "Meeting International Standards"

International rules, including political, economic, cultural, military, and diplomatic and other areas of concepts, laws, regulations, treaties, agreements and conventions, are formulated under certain historical conditions, through international exchanges and recognized by the sovereign state. These international rules are embodied in the contemporary international transactions, international laws (constitutions), international treaties and international news, international cultural exchange and academic researches. It appeared in the last century when China was making efforts to join the World Trade Organization, and is gradually applied to political, economic, cultural, military, technological and diplomatic fields, and then developed into a concept. It seems that the ultimate "convergence" is the ultimate expression of this concept. China should follow the signed international treaties and conventions, and there is no doubt for convergence. However, there should not be easy mention of "meeting international standards" if China did not sign the treaty or convention.A generalization of "international standards" should be avoided, The convergence into Western economic and political and law system regardless of China's basic economic system and political system and the relevant law with Chinese characteristics should also be avoided. It is connected to Chinese nation's fundamental lifeline.

IV. "Integrating into the Economic Globalization"

Chinese Communist Party and Chinese government have been mentioning "active participation in economic globalization." But many articles, often mentioned it as "integration into economic globalization." Comrade Jiang Zemin pointed out that the current economic globalization is dominated by Western powers. International division of labor led by Western powers is very unreasonable. Economic globalization is a two-edged sword. China should actively participate in economic globalization. We should unswervingly pursue a win-win strategy of opening up to the world, learn from all countries and culture and civilization of every ethnic group and allow our own culture and civilization to spread for the development and progress of the world. At the same time, we must not fully integrate into the economic globalization led by Western powers. We must always uphold the policy "pursuit of an independent foreign policy of peaceful development" put forward at the 17th Party's Congress and unwaveringly adhere to the basic economic and political system with Chinese characteristics, and maintain national security, stability and development.

V. "National Interest Above All Else"

In a socialist country, the interests of the country enjoy absolute superiority over thecollective and personal interests. When necessary, the collective and individual is encouraged to sacrifice their own interests or even lives for the country's fundamental interests. But it should be prevented that special interest groups in the name of "national interest above all" illegally and improperly deprive individual lawful rights and interests. In a capitalist nation, there is no such saying to the working class and working people. To the bourgeoisie, the phrase is "working class has no homeland." In international relations theory, there is no general saying like "national interest above all." UN Charter clearly states in Article II of the first chapter: "All member states enjoy equal sovereign. Therefore member states have equal right to safeguard their national interests. Because of the differences in member states' size and strength, reorganization of "national interest above all" will make small and weak countries become the victims." This is tantamount to an admission of legitimacy of hegemony and power politics and an acknowledgement of the law of the jungle ("The weaks are the prey of the strong"). If this theory holds true, thre would have been no problem with the U.S. bypassing the UN to invade Iraq and have Saddam Hussein hanged in 2003 and Japanese attempting to embezzle China's Diaoyu Islands would be well reasoned. Correct theories should not be contradictory or have double standards. In essence, it should not be mentioned as the interests of a certain country are beyond that of others.. The essence of this theory is a crafty expression for hegemonies and power politics. It is a theoretical base for the defender of hegemonies and power politics who are narrow-mindedly protecting interests of their own country. The theory is also employed asan excuse for intervention into other countries' domestic affairs and sowing discord among developing countries. In international relations theory, we should justly claim the "UN Charter" and "five principles of peaceful coexistence" superior to interests of any individual country, and resolutely oppose some developed countries damaging the legitimate rights and interests of other countries for their own This is the only way to maintain world peace.

VI. "Global Governance"

Global issues have to commit to global governance. Through effective global governance, results can be obtained with the least cost. Some believe that governance should be mainly within the framework of the United Nations. Global issues should not be governed by a small number of countries or a few persons. Otherwise, it is inconsistent with the spirit of the "democratization of international relations" raised by the Chinese Communist Party. In addition, common governance of global issues must be accompanied with the appropriate transferring of sovereignty. However, the transference must be equalized with no destruction in reciprocal interests. It also should be noted that no country should impose hegemony and power politics in the name of "global governance" to violate other state's sovereignty and territorial integrity, interfere in the internal affairs of other countries, propaganda their so-called "universal value," or use their "soft power" and "hard power" to subvert the basic economic and political system other countries. The world is composed of a number of countries. In essence, it should be "multi-governance on one globe" instead of "common governance of one globe." Disguised implementation of hegemony and power politics under the pretext of "global governance" should be prevented.

This book is the result of a co-publication agreement between Social Sciences Academic Press (China) and Paths International Limited (UK). This book is translated into English from the original 《全球政治与安全报告（2011）》with the financial support from Innovation Project of CASS.

Title: Annual Report on International Politics and Security 2012 (English Edition)
Chief Editors: Li Shenming, Zhang Yuyan, Li Shaojun
ISBN: 978-1-84464-154-3

Lightning Source UK Ltd.
Milton Keynes UK
UKOW012028040512

R1252600001B/R12526PG191993UKX1B/1/P

9 781844 641543